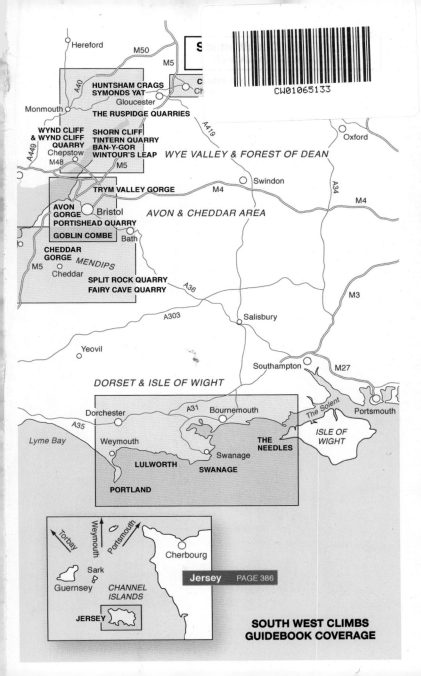

SOUTH WEST CLIMBS
GUIDEBOOK COVERAGE

Hereford

M50

M5

CW01065133

HUNTSHAM CRAGS
SYMONDS YAT

Gloucester

Monmouth

THE RUSPIDGE QUARRIES

A419

Oxford

WYND CLIFF
& WYND CLIFF
QUARRY

SHORN CLIFF
TINTERN QUARRY
BAN-Y-GOR
WINTOUR'S LEAP

WYE VALLEY & FOREST OF DEAN

Chepstow

M48

M5

Swindon

M4

A34

M4

TRYM VALLEY GORGE

AVON & CHEDDAR AREA

AVON
GORGE

Bristol

M3

PORTISHEAD QUARRY

GOBLIN COMBE

Bath

CHEDDAR
GORGE

MENDIPS

M5

Cheddar

SPLIT ROCK QUARRY
FAIRY CAVE QUARRY

A36

A303

Salisbury

Yeovil

Southampton

M27

DORSET & ISLE OF WIGHT

Dorchester

A31

Bournemouth

The Solent

Portsmouth

A35

Lyme Bay

Weymouth

THE
NEEDLES

*ISLE OF
WIGHT*

Swanage

LULWORTH

SWANAGE

PORTLAND

Torbay

Weymouth

Portsmouth

Cherbourg

Jersey PAGE 386

Sark

Guernsey

*CHANNEL
ISLANDS*

JERSEY

**SOUTH WEST CLIMBS
GUIDEBOOK COVERAGE**

Castle Rock

A scenic, 6 to 9 metre-high block right at the top of Castle Hill that hosts many short climbs in the lower grades. The south face is clean and mostly solid – the sunniest cliff on Exmoor. Towards the right-hand end of the south face is a large stack of blocks at the cliff base; above is a roof line split by the striking *Hand-Crack*.

Eros

ICARUS TOWER
36

P

To Coast Path

THE DEVIL'S CHEESEWRING
29 30 31

32 Flake Crack S 4a 8m
FA Unknown

Starting immediately left of the stack of
blocks, follow the interesting flake crack as it
trends left from the roof.

⭐ 33 Hand-Crack S 4a 8m
FA Unknown

Superb; an exercise in hand jamming, and
with as much gear to throw in as you would
like. Take the vertical crack that splits the roof.

⭐ 34 Crack of Noon VS 5a 8m
FA S Cardy, C Dawson 1983

34

The Castle's dominant line which is eminently open to audience participation. Jam strenuously
up the overhanging crack in the east wall onto flakes. Avoid escaping onto ledges on the right
and continue up a little groove to the top.

Southern Buttress

A narrow, roof-capped buttress low on Castle Hill, in the centre of its south slope.

⭐ 35 Seagulls on Steroids VS 4c 8m
FA A Evans, F West 1992

Very pleasant, and reasonably protected. Start at the lowest point of the buttress, just left of a big
overhang under an arête. Follow flake cracks slightly right onto the arête, and continue with a
delicate move onto a sloping shelf under the sharp roof at the cliff-top. Step left and pull through
the roof.

36 *Icarus* (HS)
Rob Stanfield MARK DAVIES

Icarus Tower

To approach *Icarus* first walk down from the car park to a col (seaward of the roundabout) between the rocky ridge and Castle Hill. Take the coast path (North Walk) north-eastwards from the col onto the seaward side of the rocky ridge. After 250 metres you pass under a fairly tall buttress high up on the ridge which contains the green groove-line of **Eros** (S 4a) – concrete remains of a seat next to the path here. Seventy-five metres further on, the path begins to rise and overhead is the Icarus Tower, an unmistakable tapering pillar with stepped roofs.

36 Icarus HS 4b 30m
FA J Fowler, C Gibson 1976

Obscure, though something of a local classic – it certainly has the exposure to qualify. An ivy patch near the base of the route comes and goes, but you can usually climb through it readily enough. Five metres up and right of the lowest point of the buttress is a groove under an arête. Climb the groove and move right onto a triangular ledge. Climb the arête up to the left into a niche under a roof near the top (peg out right). Move left around a bulge and traverse a ledge to gain the top. (A worthwhile variation climbs rightwards out of the niche at a steep and airy HVS 5a.)

The Yellow Stone

OS Ref SS 706 500

This is arguably the finest of the sea-cliffs in the vicinity of Valley of Rocks. It is a north-west-facing buttress of compact and mostly solid slates that is undercut by two caves, the larger and right-hand of which is known as Dog Hole.

Access to all routes is by abseil. Take a 60-metre static rope minimum for routes starting from the left-hand platform; access to *Locked and Loaded* requires a second abseil rope. The base of the cliff is extremely tidal making on-foot access from the beach of Wringcliff Bay to the west rarely possible. However, all the routes commence from platforms 6 to 8 metres above foreshore level. Only the right-hand of these (serving *Locked and Loaded*) is tidal (access is limited to one to two hours either side of high tide). The routes should be avoided in rough seas.

From the col above the roundabout, follow the coast path (North Walk) north-eastwards for 50 metres to an overlook point on a pedestal block left of the path. This provides a good vantage point of the descent to the Yellow Stone sea cliff, the top of which can just be seen. Walk approximately 250 metres further along the path. Here there are small steep buttresses on the

Archer's Lost Route

Mindlight

37

38

39

40

hillside above, and down to the right is the top of a huge chasm (The West Inlet). Make your way down the rocky hillside keeping left (facing out) of the chasm until beneath a prominent pinnacle-like outcrop (a good place to stash the gear). Continue directly down from the outcrop to some rocks where an abseil can be set up. The abseil runs down a corner, **Archer's Lost Route** (S 4a), to a non-tidal platform on the left (east) edge of the buttress.

To the right of the corner abseil line, in the upper half of the crag, is a hanging yellow slab.

⭐37 Yogi E4 5c/6a 40m
FA M J Crocker, J Harwood 1997

The photogenic, sharp left-hand arête of the hanging yellow slab; crisp and exhilarating. Only the crux is hard (but protected). Start at the foot of the corner. Climb the corner for 4 metres; then scramble up its right arête to a deep break where the arête steepens. Swing right and boldly ascend the flat wall to a bulge under the top arête – good wire slot. Feel over for crimps, and balance onto the slab. Move left onto the arête and follow it without any real difficulty to ledges above the corner (optional belay). Climb easily to stake belays.

⭐38 Seagull Salad E1 5a/b 45m
FA T Cheek 1994 or I Parnell, J Cheshire 1994

An elegant climb up the centre of the hanging yellow slab. Start from the platform, under the slab. Climb to an undercut, leftward-slanting ramp and follow it into a narrow corner. Move up the corner, step right onto a rib, and pull up to a small overhang beneath the slab (peg). Shuffle awkwardly left, and get established on the slab. Follow the thin crack in the centre of the slab for 6 metres and then traverse left along narrow ledges to the arête (optional belay). Climb easily to stake belays.

⭐39 Book of Birds E3 6a 45m
FA T Cheek (some aid), I Parnell, J Cheshire 1994; Direct Finish M J Crocker, T Cheek 1997

A magnificent route up the black corner above the left-hand of the two caves. Start from the platform and scramble to a bulge under the corner. Strenuously enter the corner and follow it, sidestepping three bulges to their right. At the break above the corner, traverse left to exit as for *Seagull Salad* or do the **Direct Finish** (E4 6a): tackle a wild bulge direct, pulling out using a triangular flake overhang on the right.

Locked and Loaded climbs through the roofs above the right-hand cave (Dog Hole). It starts from the (tidal) arm-like platform between the two caves, which is reached by abseil from rock outcrops. Above the eastern edge of the platform are two cracks. The left-hand one is tackled by **Mindlight** (E5 6a,6a), the second pitch of which traverses right after a flared slot in the roofs to finish up the prominent crack.

⭐40 Locked and Loaded E6 40m
FA M J Crocker, J Harwood 1999

A high-powered route that features an awesome pitch 2. Start under the right-hand crack.
  1 15m 6a Climb up into a groove under a roof 7 metres up. Work out over the roof, using the finger crack, so gaining the deeper crack above. Follow the easy V-groove to a good stance.
  2 25m 6c Step up to roofs that undercut a triangular niche with a flake above. Extend for holds in the niche (two pegs) and, somehow, grab the flake that soars from it. Follow the flake to a bulge, traverse right 2 metres, and take another flake to a solid exit up a rib on the right.

There are three routes on the right wall of the cave that start from a (tidal) projecting ledge reached by abseil. The best of these is the groove of **Dubcat** (E3 5c).

40 *Locked and Loaded* (E6)
Martin Crocker   CARL RYAN

Wringcliff Bay

OS Ref SS 699 497

Of the many awe-inspiring hidden lines on the Exmoor Coast, the routes here are some of the most accessible. Lee Cliff lies immediately west of Wringcliff Bay, which is the bay west of the conical craggy hill of the Castle.

Approach   A footpath runs down from a point 200 metres west of the roundabout under the Castle to the bay. The routes are reached by a short walk westwards along the beach, low to mid tide.

The multi-pitch climbs here exit onto the private grounds of Lee Abbey, a spiritual retreat. A conditional climbing access agreement has been reached with Lee Abbey, which must be adhered to by visiting climbers.

Conditions of Access for Climbing on Lee Cliff, Lee Abbey Estate

1 The cliff forms part of an SSSI and no damage to its flora, fauna, or geology should be caused.

2 The cliff is a nesting-site for auks and birds of prey. Climbing must not take place between 1 April and 30 June.

3 Climbers must be in possession of valid civil liability insurance with cover up to £10 million. (This can be obtained through membership of the BMC or Mountaineering Council of Scotland.)

4 All climbers must, before climbing, report to Lee Abbey reception where they should sign the visitors' book. If leaving a vehicle in Lee Abbey's car park they must also supply their vehicle's registration number.

5 Climbers must follow the way off from the cliff-top described in detail below. This is the only permitted way off, which minimizes impact on the site including any disturbance to residents and visitors. On no account should anyone attempt to traverse from the way off eastwards towards the Valley of Rocks or climb over fences other than the single fence identified.

6 Climbers are welcome to park their cars at Lee Abbey car park when climbing on Lee Cliff, subject to spaces available. The approved way off the cliff-top takes you back to this car park.

7 Anyone climbing on Lee Abbey land does so entirely at their own risk, in line with the Participation Statement of the British Mountaineering Council.

The Route to Take from the Cliff Top to the Lee Abbey Car Park   From the tops of the climbs at the cliff edge, walk diagonally up leftwards to the far left end of a fence. There is a stout post here to use to mount the fence without damaging it (a small set of wooden steps may be in place in future). Follow the fence-line which rises gently leftwards until the fence kinks and descends leftwards in the direction of Valley of Rocks. Do not turn left and traverse leftwards across fields here, but continue walking in the same line for 100 metres, along a path and then track, to a gated opening in another fence (gate often open). A fence-line now rises steeply up rightwards (in a south-west direction): follow it for 200 metres to a kissing gate on the left (a metal-roofed cowshed is visible ahead). Go through the kissing gate and head across a small field, through a gate, and cross another small field (right of some tennis courts) to a kissing gate next to the entry road to the Lee Abbey car parking area.

41 Flight of the Gull HVS 4c 30m

FA M J Crocker (roped solo) 2012

A fine route up the seaward arête of the ridge bounding the left side of the face. Protection is abundant by Lynton Slates standards, and the rock is solid apart from the top 6 metres. Climb the grooved arête; then work up and right around a bulge into a crack and white crystalline vein. Step up left onto a ledge on the arête, and follow easy cracks carefully up leftwards to the crest of the ridge. To descend: stay roped and climb down the left-hand (facing out) arm of the ridge, or abseil from sacrificed kit.

★★ 42 The Chimney Sweep E5 87m R

FA D Turnbull, J Tidmus 1997 (1 pt aid pitch 3 for cleaning)

Described as 'the best unclimbed line in the South West' before it was onsighted with shale-climbing bravado. The climb aims for the widening crack and chimney high in the centre left of the cliff and will feel as it looks: a serious and committing venture. Take a hammer and a few pegs for the second belay. Start under a nose of rock 6 metres up, right of the diagonal fault in the shallow cave.

CASTLE HILL

THE YELLOW STONE

1 25m 5b From a break, gain the top of the nose from the right. Trend fairly easily leftwards up flat ledges for 6 metres. Above is a bulging crack; climb up to it (microwires vital) and make exhilarating moves to ledges above. Belay on good cams and nuts at the right-hand end of a long ledge.

2 12m 5a Traverse left along the ledge, and take a mighty flake crack into a triangular niche: peg belays.

3 25m 5c Climb up large but shaly holds to a crack (jammed first ascent cam above). Fix good gear in the crack and make a descending traverse rightwards to the foot of the main crackline. Pull over a bulge into the offwidth, and continue over a second bulge into a narrow chimney. Squeeze the chimney and exit very carefully over blocks to belay in a gully.

4 25m Scramble up the gully, passing behind a pinnacle, to tree belays at the cliff edge.

★★ 43 Terry E5 70m R

FA M J Crocker, I Parsons 2012

A magnificent line up the pink grooves in the centre of the face. No single pitch is quite E5, and the gear is mostly reasonable. Apart from the last (marker) peg, the pegs are marine grade stainless steel – so they will not fall to pieces when you clip them.

EYRIE

LEE CLIFF

1 25m 5b *The Chimney Sweep* pitch 1.

2 15m 5c Climb into the corner above the stance. Bridge up the corner before shuffling right to a deep crack in the right wall. Move up to a loose shale bulge, and pull carefully up right over this to a large flat ledge; thread and cam belays.

3 10m 6a Climb into the pink groove above (two pegs). Take the groove for 2 metres; then swing right onto its leaning right wall. A good but weak flake should be handled tenderly before making crux moves up a crack to a good stance above. Cam belays.

4 20m 5c/6a Climb the corner for 3 metres to a shaly ledge. Finger-traverse left onto the exposed face (peg) and make bold, technical moves into the pink groove above (peg). Follow the groove over a small roof onto easier ground. Take cracks and flakes above until the rock runs out (marker peg) and a few untaxing pulls up a mattress of flowers and ivy must be made to arrive at a sycamore tree belay at the cliff edge.

both photos: **43** *Terry* **(E5)**
Martin Crocker DON SARGEANT

⭐ 44 Under the Weather on a Lee Shore E2 70m R

FA I Parsons, M J Crocker 2012

While not the finest route on the cliff, the amenable grade and enjoyable climbing could see it become its most popular. It follows the narrow corners high in the right-hand side of the cliff. It is quite a good introduction to the longer routes on the Exmoor coast, and still adventurous. Start under a prominent dark roof 12 metres up, and about 6 metres right of *The Chimney Sweep*.

1 30m 5b Climb up to a V-groove under the roof (stainless steel peg). Either climb the groove and move left or take the wall on the left before moving awkwardly back right to a standing position above the roof. Climb a crack and groove, duck left, and move back right into a short, square-cut corner (peg). Climb the corner to nut and cam belays on a rubbly ledge.

2 15m 5a Climb an easy if soft band of shale and move up gingerly over giant jammed flakes onto a grassy ledge. Take the corner-crack above to another ledge and belay on nuts and cams on the right.

3 25m 5c Move back left into the corner-crack and climb it strenuously to a little overhang. Step round left and pull up into an eyrie (remnants of hawk's nest). Now follow the difficult narrow corner in a great position to a small yew tree. Some handfuls of veg and a short final corner lead to the top. Tree belays.

Baggy Point

This is the prominent headland on the north side of Croyde Bay, one of the South West's finest surfing beaches. It is probably the most popular climbing venue in North Devon thanks to the firm gritty rock, the southerly aspect of the cliffs, and the light-hearted, exhilarating nature of the climbing. Slab climbing is Baggy's principal attraction, and the main slabs are laced with routes of a common character. Almost all are worth doing so the selection is a little arbitrary, favouring those with most individuality.

Baggy Point lies in the Bristol Channel, which has the second largest tidal flow in the world. The tide surges in at terrific speed and has caught many an unwary second.

14 *Ben* (HS)
Hazel Jones DON SARGEANT

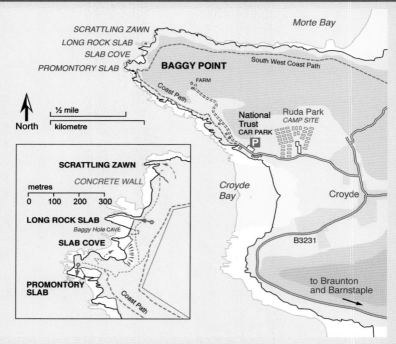

Seasonal Restrictions   Long Rock Slab is subject to restriction from 15 March until 30 June inclusive. Climbs affected are marked R in the usual manner.

Approach   A road runs out to the point from Croyde and, just before it becomes an access road to private houses there is a National Trust car park on the right. From here, a good track runs out along the point to the cliffs, giving a gentle uphill walk of about a mile. The track ends at a slight saddle near the tip of the point, from which all the cliffs described can be seen. Directly below on the south side is The Promontory; Slab Cove is immediately north with the slender slab of *Pink Void* clearly visible; and Long Rock Slab is the sheer-looking cliff which bounds Slab Cove to the north. Scrattling Zawn is the most distant of the cliffs.

Scrattling Zawn

OS Ref SS 421 410

This is the prominent set of cliffs at the northern end of the headland. Viewed from a distance, they are dominated by the large corner of *Scrattling Crack*, a great old classic route in its own right as well as being the traditional culmination to the sea-level traverse of the point (an interesting and fairly serious expedition best undertaken at low tide).

The blind corner to the right (facing the cliff) of *Scrattling Crack* can be used to descend (Diff standard if dry), or there are large stakes on the cliff-top for a 45-metre abseil.

1   Scrattling Crack   VD   37m
FA T Longstaff 1898

A route with great atmosphere and impressive rock architecture. There is virtually no protection for the leader but the deep crack gives a sense of security. Climb the slab-angled corner-crack. Boots are the recommended footwear as they are the ideal width for jamming (and also the best footgear for traversing the point).

In the back wall of Scrattling Zawn are two imposing cracklines. The wide left-hand crack gives **Egg** (HVS 4c) which skirts right around the final overhangs, and the right-hand is **Satisfaction** (E1 5a).

Long Rock Slab

OS Ref SS 420 408

Long Rock provides much of the best climbing at Baggy, being both steeper and cleaner than Promontory Slab and with more positive lines.

At low tide the cliff may be reached by crossing the boulder beach of Slab Cove. Alternatively, descend the steep grass above the slab (there is a stake in place for a fixed rope), and abseil 40 metres from good natural anchors to the higher end of the large sloping ledge at the foot of the slab. Rising above the lower, left-hand end of this ledge (which is more affected by tides) is the obvious groove taken by *Doors of Perception*, while at the right-hand end of the ledge is the obvious straight corner of *Urizen*. The cracked face just to the right of *Urizen* gives the classic *Shangri-La*, which is the best escape route if the sea threatens.

2   Doors of Perception   E1 5b   37m   R
FA B Wintringham, J Browne 1970

A very enjoyable climb going directly up the prominent groove towards the left side of the promontory. Start beneath the groove at low to half tide. Climb easily to the first overlap; then more sustained climbing up the groove above leads to a roof. Move left and up to a ledge (peg), and follow the groove past another peg to the top.

3   Twinkletoes   VS 5a   40m   R
FA B Wintringham, M Wintringham, A D Baker, D Johnston 1969

Start just right of *Doors of Perception* and climb up to the right to a short blank corner. Go up the corner, and then either move right to a crack leading to a slanting overlap, or move left to the arête, step up, and traverse right and move up to the overlap. Continue right into the inverted-V and then up a right-slanting ramp to the top.

4   No Sweat/Inferno   E4 6a   43m   R
FA P Bull, N Tetley (l pt aid) 1985; FFA C Nicholson 1986

A sustained and elegant combination. Start midway between *Doors of Perception* and *Undercracker*. Climb straight up, following a line of weakness, until a horizontal break is reached at 27 metres. Move left here. Thin climbing just right of the arête gains a good finger slot. Climb up and rightwards to reach two short diagonal cracks (peg), move right, and then go straight up to a good break. Scramble leftwards to finish.

⊙5 Undercracker E1 5b 43m R

FA P Littlejohn, P W Thexton 1974

A fine sustained pitch, mainly following the leftward-slanting overlap which is the first real feature to the left of *Urizen*. Start about 15 metres left of *Urizen*, at a tiny groove capped by a small block overhang. Climb the groove; then traverse left along the crystalline crack to a steep ramp leading to the start of the main overlap. Follow this to meet another overlap rising from the left. Move over the bulge and climb directly to the top via a thin crack.

★6 Slip It In Quick E3 5c 43m R

FA S Bell, D Carroll 1979

A modern favourite. Start at a thin crack about 3 metres right of the start of *Undercracker*. Climb the crack, and bear right up the open slab above to some good holds below the arched overlap. Move left, then up and rightwards to a horizontal break. Climb the left side of the arched overlap to reach some large pockets on the left. Continue straight up the thin cracks above until moves left gain a short final crack and the top.

★7 Terrapin E3 5b 46m R

FA P Littlejohn, D Garner, P Buttrick 1976

Good varied climbing on a natural, if indirect, line. Fairly bold. Start about 8 metres left of *Urizen*. Climb the slab to a narrow ledge above an overlap. Continue, bearing left to a horizontal break. Move left, up, and back right along the next break to beneath a shallow arching corner. Climb up on the right using thin flakes to reach a horizontal crack (peg); then step left and climb past a pocket to an obvious traverse line which is followed rightwards to a narrow ledge. Finish via the thin face crack.

SCRATTLING ZAWN

★8 Lost Horizon VS 5a 40m R

FA B Wintringham, M Wintringham, 1970

Just left of the corner of *Urizen* is a perfect crackline running the full height of the cliff – a rare feature in the UK. Abundant protection and sustained interest make this route a 'must' for the grade. Follow the crack, simple as that.

★★ **9 Urizen** VS 4c 40m R
FA A C Willmott, M J Spring, D Godfrey 1969

The clean, striking corner line is another 'must' for the grade, having bombproof protection and sustained (if repetitive) climbing. Ascend the corner, generally facing left but occasionally using footholds on the right.

★★★ **10 Shangri-La** HS 4a 40m R
FA B Wintringham, M Wintringham, A D Baker, D Johnston 1970

One of the finest easy routes in Devon and justly popular. A pitch best accompanied by thunderous seas. Start at the foot of *Urizen*. Climb the right arête of *Urizen* for 3 metres; then bear right into the main crackline. Follow this, generally on excellent holds and jams, to block belays at the top.

10 *Shangri-La* (HS)
Tammy Pay   DON SARGEANT

The continuous crackline some 6 metres right of *Shangri-La* gives **Wee Beastie** (VS 4c) requiring a low-tide start from the zawn bed. Further right is the huge sea cave of Baggy Hole, which lends a lot of atmosphere to the next climb.

⭐**11   The Great Beast**   E1   48m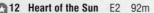

FA A D Baker, D Edwards 1970

An interesting and worthwhile route with a distinctly bigger feel than other routes on Long Rock. The rock demands care higher up. Start at lowish tide directly beneath the edge of the enormous roof of Baggy Hole.

1 21m 5b Follow a series of steps up to the right to reach a thin crack. Climb the crack, passing a small overlap on the right, to a stance.

2 27m 5a Move up to the big corner and climb it (peg at the first overlap) to an awkward finish.

Slab Cove

OS Ref SS 420 407

The foot of the *Pink Void* slab is approachable at all times, except high spring tides, by descending the small path which leads down into the south side of the cove from above the Promontory.

⭐⭐**12   Heart of the Sun**   E2   92m

FA A C Willmott, M J Spring (aid) 1969; A Strapcans, C King 1977

One of the great slab routes of the South West, mostly following the thin crack running up the centre of the *Pink Void* slab. A line of thin cracks runs

12 *Heart of the Sun* (E2)
Sue Hazel PETE SAUNDERS

up rightwards to the base of the long groove taken by *Pink Void*, Start beneath this, at a small overhang near the left side of the base of the slab.

1 46m 5b Follow the thin crack up the steepening slab until, after a bulging section, easier climbing leads up and rightwards to the vertical crack in the centre of the main slab. Follow the crack with increasing difficulty to peg and nut belays in a horizontal break.

2 46m 5b Follow the thin crack diagonally rightwards to an overlap. Cross this, and then either move left to join *Pink Void* or (harder and more serious) ascend the friable corner to reach a thin crack leading leftwards to the finish of *Pink Void*.

⭐ **13 Pink Void** VS 104m
FA A C Willmott, M J Spring 1969

Although not the regional classic it once was before a series of rockfalls destroyed the first pitch, this remains a worthwhile climb, providing a long and technically straightforward expedition up an impressive cliff. It basically follows the long groove running up the left side of the tall slab in the centre of the cliff. Start just right of the loose corner bounding the slab on the right.

1 40m 4b Climb cracked slabs for some 12 metres before moving left over blocks to reach a break leading leftwards across the main slab into the groove line. Follow the groove to a stance and peg belays.

2 30m 4b Continue up the groove for 9 metres; then step right and climb the slab for a few moves before regaining the groove. Continue until the groove peters out, and then move right and climb to better holds. A stance is taken up to the left, at some good cracks.

3 34m 4a Climb diagonally right to reach a rib, which is followed on good holds until an exit left avoids the very loose final wall. A serious pitch.

Promontory Slab

OS Ref SS 419 406

A boulder beach beneath the slab is exposed for about two hours either side of low tide, and is most easily reached by descending the well-defined ridge just to the left (west) of the main slab. In descent the standard is Diff at most but a stake exists for a fixed rope if required (advisable in the wet). The subsidiary slab to the left of the ridge (taken by the first three routes) is best reached by descending through the cleft beneath the precarious boulder bridge halfway down the descent ridge.

14 Ben S 4a 40m
FA B Wintringham, M Wintringham 1970

A central line on the subsidiary slab gives a most enjoyable introduction to climbing at Baggy. Start at a rightward-slanting line 5 metres from the left edge of the slab. Follow the cracks easily for 10 metres or so; then more interesting climbing on excellent rock leads to a horizontal break near the top. Step up to the continuation of the line and climb to a solid finish.

15 Marion HS 4b 40m
FA B Wintringham, M Wintringham 1970

About 5 metres right of *Ben* is a parallel line of thin, slanting cracks. This gives another worthwhile pitch in a similar style to *Ben* but just a touch harder.

16 Sheet Whitening VS 55m
FA G Gibson, P Wilson (VL) 1979

This rises from right to left across the subsidiary slab giving the most substantial route and arguably the best climbing. Start at the foot of the descent cleft.

1 18m 5a Climb a thin crack to the first quartzy break. Traverse left to another thin crack and climb this to a horizontal break which is followed leftwards to the crack of *Marion*. Belay slightly lower.

2 37m 5a Traverse horizontally left into the crack of *Ben* and continue to a large undercut flake. Move left to finish up the arête.

17 *Kinkyboots* (VS)   Mark Davies   ADY SHORT

17 Kinkyboots VS 61m
FA D Johnston, B Wintringham 1969

This climb boasts a memorable first pitch, which is the key to accessing the Promontory Slab at high tide. Unfortunately, the second pitch is not as good. Between the descent ridge and the main slab is a narrow slanting zawn: start at some small ledges 8 metres below the top of this.

1 18m 4c Reach some good holds on the far side of the zawn and swing spectacularly across the gulch. Move over the first small overlap (peg); then continue rightwards round the large overlap to gain the slab. Traverse right for 6 metres to a stance and peg belays.

2 43m 4b Reverse the traverse; then climb straight up, keeping left on the most open line, to a large detached flake. Continue up the cleanest line above to the top.

★ ★ ★ **18 Midnight Cowboy** HVS 72m

FA B Wintringham, M Wintringham 1969

The epitome of Baggy Point slab climbing. It follows the stepped overlap which rises rightwards across the slab. Start at a boulder 5 metres from the left edge of the slab, or at high tide, reach the first stance via the first pitch of *Kinkyboots*.

1 18m 4c Climb the slab to some thin cracks and continue to a stance at the obvious red bulge beneath the overlap.

2 27m 5a/b Step over the overlap and move up, trending right. A tricky move down to the right gains a good hold beneath the overlap. Traverse right to a small flake; then step up to the overlap and follow it for 9 metres until it merges into a shallow corner. Climb for 5 metres to a foothold stance with good nut belays.

3 27m 4b Climb straight up to the top on the cleanest line. Poor stake near the edge, or belay from the other side of the neck of land.

★ **19 Long Rock Eliminate** HVS 61m

FA D Johnston, A D Baker 1971

A good delicate first pitch. Start 3 metres right of *Midnight Cowboy* (lowish tide), beneath a prominent inverted-V overlap.

1 18m 5a Climb to the overlap; then go straight up the thin cracks above until it is possible to step left to the stance of *Midnight Cowboy*.

2 43m 4c Climb through the overlap and continue up to the next overlap. Move up the shallow scoop above to a small ledge, and then follow the right-hand of two cracks to reach vegetated ledges and the top.

★★ **20 Gladiator** E1 60m

FA A Brazier, J Colwell (pitch 1), G Gibson, J Walker (pitch 2) 1979

An eliminate line offering the most sustained and technical climbing on the slab. Start at a prominent, pointed boulder below a small diagonal ramp.

1 30m 5b Follow a very thin crack diagonally rightwards to some small ledges. Climb directly up the slab above to an overlap which is almost level with the stance of *Midnight Cowboy*. Traverse left to the stance and belay.

2 30m 5b Step left and climb the slab, bearing left at first, then rightwards to an overlap. Climb through the overlap on the right, and continue directly to the top.

The large rightward-facing corner on the right-hand side of the slab is taken by **Slip Sliding Away** (E1 5b), a good pitch leading to a choice of finishes.

Lundy

Lundy is a rugged, windswept island in the Bristol Channel, twelve miles from the nearest mainland at Hartland Point. It is the most remote of the South West's climbing areas, and arguably the finest. The granite cliffs of the precipitous west coast are on a bigger scale than those in Cornwall, frequently attaining 100 metres in height, and the rock is less faulted than on the Cornish crags, presenting many huge sheer walls and slabs more akin to Yosemite than anywhere else in Britain.

The remoteness of Lundy means that its inclusion in a whistle-stop tour of the South West requires good planning. Generally it is the object of a special trip. The island has seen increased popularity in recent years so early booking is strongly advised. The island is served by a ferry service from the port of Ilfracombe in North Devon and by a helicopter service. Also, a small boat can be chartered from Clovelly (the shortest approach by sea). Details of these and general information about the island including the various types of accommodation available, can be obtained from the present managers

– The Landmark Trust, Shottesbrooke, Maidenhead, Berkshire SL6 3SW (tel 01628 825925) www.landmarktrust.org.uk.

There are far fewer boats running in the winter months, and there is thus a higher chance of getting stranded on the island in bad weather. This factor and the nesting restrictions have led to a favoured 'Lundy season' among climbers, running from August until early October.

Seasonal Restrictions R

Lundy is famous for its bird life and climbing is severely restricted during the nesting season, 1 April to 31 July. The restricted cliffs are in the majority and vary somewhat from year to year. Because of this, the R siymbol is not used against individual routes, and climbers should make enquiries with the Agent or resident bird Warden before visiting within this period. Of the areas described in this book, the following are very likely to be open: Focal Buttress, Landing Craft Bay, Devil's Slide, and the Constable. In certain years other cliffs may be open too – **but be certain to check first**. Climbers should not be put off by the restrictions as there is usually more than enough for a week's climbing at all grades, especially for the first-time visitor.

The climbing areas and the climbs are described from south to north (**right to left** facing the cliffs of the west coast) as climbers would normally approach them from the village. Three prominent stone walls cross the island and these are invaluable for locating the crags: These are (from south to north) the Quarter Wall, the Halfway Wall, and the Threequarter Wall.

THE CONSTABLE

North Light

North

kilometre

Gannet's Bay

ARCH ZAWN

Torrey Canyon

St John's Stone

THE DIAMOND

DEVIL'S SLIDE

St James's Stone

THREEQUARTER BUTTRESS

PARTHENOS

Threequarter Wall

GRAND FALLS ZAWN

BEAUFORT BUTTRESS

Jenny's Cove

Halfway Wall

EGYPTIAN SLABS

DEVIL'S CHIMNEY CLIFF

DEEP ZAWN

Needle Rock

Dead Cow Point

FLYING BUTTRESS

Quarter Wall

Battery Point

ST PATRICK'S BUTTRESS

LANDING CRAFT BAY

FIRST BUTTRESS NORTH

FIRST BUTTRESS SOUTH

The Old Light

WOLFMAN JACK WALL

Marisco Tavern

Pilots' Quay

Montagu Steps

The Devil's Limekiln

FOCAL BUTTRESS

Great Shutter Rock

Southern Lundy

Focal Buttress

OS Ref SS 1338 4343

Near the southern tip of the island is the vast bowl of the Devil's Limekiln, an important climbing venue until a landslip in 2008 filled much of the chasm. Focal Buttress is the large, handsome buttress at the western side of the Limekiln, directly opposite Great Shutter Rock. The foot of the crag is approached by a narrow path running down its southern edge to the broad ridge linking Great Shutter Rock to the mainland. A slope of massive boulders is then descended, keeping close to the cliff which rears up in a smooth vertical wall of golden granite. The wall culminates in the great arête of *Golden Gate*, and then swings around to the entrance of the Limekiln.

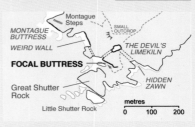

1   Ulysses Factor   HVS   103m

FA P H Biven, I F Howell 1970

Despite a smattering of loose rock this is a great expedition with a lot of fine climbing in impressive situations. Start about 30 metres up the boulder slope, to the right of the long narrow ledge giving the first stance.

1 9m 5a A serious pitch for both leader and second. Traverse left along the obvious line of holds to reach the ledge.

2 37m 4c Move up steeply from the right-hand end of the ledge and continue to a traverse-line leading back left to a crack. Follow the crack into the prominent groove and climb this until a move left can be made to ledges.

3 15m Climb a jagged crack in the wall on the right and continue over broken ground to a block belay below the next wall.

4 15m 4b Move down to the right for 3 metres; then climb steeply up the yellow wall, trending right, to ledges beneath the final tower.

5 27m 4c Move right and climb the shallow depression that runs up the face of the tower. Bear left to finish on solid holds.

The next two routes start on the arête, which is virtually devoid of holds for the first 5 metres. It has been overcome in various ways over the years, including aiding with *RURP*s, using combined tactics to place a microwire for aid, shinning up a large plank, etc. There may be a length of knotted rope hanging down from a good thread, but be prepared to improvise!

2   Golden Gate   E4   97m

FA P Littlejohn, F E R Cannings (1 pt aid) 1977

A route of the highest calibre which, after a fantastic pitch up the arête, seeks out further good climbing on the narrow face set directly above the entrance to the Limekiln.

1 46m 6a Gain the thread; then move right round the arête and climb steeply for 5 metres to better holds leading to a ledge. Follow the arête, using the thin crack, to another ledge, and continue up the true arête to reach the easier-angled rib above. Continue to good nut belays in a cracked slab beneath an overhang.

Olympica

2 30m **5b** Make a rising traverse left into a corner and climb for 5 metres until level with a tall pointed block. Move on to the left wall, continue diagonally left, and just before the edge of the wall is reached climb directly to a stance.

3 21m **5b** Climb an easy ramp for 5 metres and enter the overhanging groove which overlooks it. Move up awkwardly to reach easier ground and belays well back.

The big wall to the right of *Golden Gate* is taken by the fantastic **Olympica** (E5 6a). The initial crux wall is problematic due to the shifting of huge boulders at the base of the cliff, but the line can also be reached via a rising traverse starting a little lower than the traverse of *Ulysses Factor*.

⭐⭐⭐ 3 The Great Divide E3 103m
FA F E R Cannings, A Strapcans (2 pts aid) 1977; FFA P Littlejohn 1977

The superb crackline snaking up left from the arête of the cliff. A phenomenal jamming pitch – obviously strenuous but perfectly protected with cams and large nuts.

1 43m **5b** Gain the thread; then launch leftwards into the crack and follow it to belays on the slab above.

2 30m **4b** Climb the slab into the corner on the left and follow this to a large ledge below the final wall.

3 30m **4c** Step left off the pointed block and climb the wall to a crack leading rightwards to easy slabs.

Wolfman Jack Wall

OS Ref SS 1289 4442

Some 200 metres north of the Old Light is an obvious promontory connected by a narrow earthy rib to the mainland. This is Sunset Promontory. A narrow buttress immediately south of this is Alpine Buttress, and Wolfman Jack Wall is the next feature to the south again. Its top can be quickly accessed by descending the slope fairly directly from a point about 130 metres north of the Old Light. The routes are non tidal and best approached by abseiling down the right-hand side of the wall (good nut anchors on a small platform) to a point about 15 metres up the grassy ramp which bounds the wall on the right.

The Old Light
DAN LANE

★
★
★
4   Venus Flytrap   E2   55m

FA S Keeling, G Gibson, D Beetlestone 1980

An easier offshoot of *Wolfman Jack*, every bit as
good as the parent climb.

1 15m 5b *Wolfman Jack* pitch 1.
2 40m 5c Step up, traverse right to a
shattered flake, and then move up and
rightwards again to a good ledge. Climb the
wall above the right-hand end of the ledge to the long overlap, and follow this up left to a
broken finger of rock. Pull over onto the wall, reach holds above the next overlap, and move
right to a crack leading to the top.

★
★
★
5   Wolfman Jack   E3   45m

FA P W Thexton, K J Wilson (4 pts aid) 1974; FFA R Edwards 1979

The central crackline of the wall gives a magnificent varied route with good protection (take a
couple of very large nuts or cams). Start on some good ledges below a little arête in the foot of
the face, about 15 metres up the grassy ramp.

1 15m 5b Climb up and step left onto the arête. Move left and up to a break in the overhang
at the foot of the central crack and follow the crack to a good stance on the left.
2 30m 5c Step back right and continue following the crack, past a ledge, to where it splits.
Take the right-hand branch to the overhang, where teasing moves gain good finishing holds
above the square-cut groove.

Landing Craft Bay

A very popular area with easy access, few tidal problems, and a good selection of routes throughout the grades. Some 250 metres north of the Old Light a stream runs down a shallow valley. Descend just north of the stream to the top of a rocky ridge, from which the crags can be seen running northwards. Directly below, forming the base of the ridge, is First Buttress South. All routes are approached by descending the ridge until it is possible to cut back right along some turfy ledges to a steep path leading to the boulder beach (care required – fixed rope or abseil recommended).

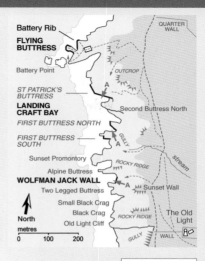

First Buttress South   OS Ref SS 127 4458

...of the descent path is reached by scrambling over or around a promontory from the foot of the path.

6   The Indy 500   E1   45m

FA G Gibson and party 1984

A tremendous route – steep, well protected (take plenty of gear!), and on positive holds throughout. It takes the best of the cracklines in the southern flank of the buttress. Start just right of the large wet corner which bounds the main bulk of the buttress on the right.

1 18m Climb the slabby right wall of the corner for 9 metres; then cross it and ascend the left wall to belay where the obvious crack branches off left.

2 27m 5b Move up and tackle a steep section of the crack to a slight easing in angle. Higher up, the crack steepens again but good holds and jams always appear.

First Buttress North   OS Ref SS 1292 4462

Easy of access, non tidal, and very popular, this is the buttress immediately north of the descent. Its right side is a smooth wall split by the obvious cracks of *Road Runner* and *Ice*. Its left side, beyond a sharp arête, is all blocky and bulging and contains the chimney-groove line of *Centaur*.

7   Ice   E2 5c   27m

FA G Gibson, A Kassyk 1980

Safe, technical climbing up the superb thin crack to the right of the flake crack of *Road Runner*. Climb to the crack and follow it to a blanker section near the top. Difficult climbing gains a slab leading to the belays/abseil point in the recess.

8   Road Runner   VS 4c   27m

FA G J Gilbert, P Littlejohn, R D Moulton 1972

A delightful pitch taking the striking flake towards the left side of the smooth, southerly face of the buttress. Start on the jumble of blocks beneath the crack. Climb up to the crack and follow it

to the large recess beneath the steep headwall. Multiple belays and abseil point. Most parties abseil from this stance – to continue to the top is several grades harder.

9 Centaur HVS 48m

FA C J Lawrence, A D Caswell (l pt aid) 1972; FFA P Littlejohn 1972

A route of character weaving through some impressive rock. Friendly, with good resting places and a short safe crux. Start by scrambling up easy rock on the north side of the buttress to belay where it steepens.

1 18m 4a Climb rightwards over slabs to a stance beneath the deep V-chimney.

2 30m 5b Climb the chimney to a roof, and then move right to a ledge. Continue to the bigger overhang and turn this on the right to a small ledge around the arête. Climb the groove above; then follow a ramp, easily at first, until tricky moves gain a wide flake crack and a final rib.

13 *Rampart* (E3)
Renny Croft DON SARGEANT

St Patrick's Buttress OS Ref SS 1283 4478

This is the most northerly of the crags in Landing Craft Bay and by far the most extensive, consisting of several facets. The first encountered is a steep grey wall split by the

rightward-slanting crack of *Destiny*. To the left of this, some striking ramps and flying arêtes give *Rampart* and *Slip Tide*; then, beyond the obvious corners of *Shamrock*, the cliff swings around and becomes more affected by the tide.

★ **10 Destiny** E2 64m
★
★ FA P Littlejohn, C A G Morton 1972

A superb crack pitch requiring a variety of jamming techniques. High in the grade but with perfect rock and protection. Start beneath the left end of the right-slanting crack which splits the south face of the buttress, at a groove in the lower wall.

   1 34m 4c Climb the groove, and then easy ground leading to the crack, which is followed for 12 metres to a stance where it narrows.

   2 30m 5c Follow the crack, which eventually leads to a sloping ledge. Move right and climb a corner to finish.

★ **11 Meninirons** E1 56m
★ FA G Gibson, D Beetlestone 1981

Intricate face climbing leads to an exciting finish through the left side of the large overlap which caps the *Destiny* wall. Start 10 metres left of *Destiny* at a shallow groove.

   1 16m 4b Climb the groove; then move right to belay on good ledges.

   2 40m 5b Move up left onto a pedestal and follow a vague, thin crack until it fades. Step left and climb direct on small positive holds to the left end of the overlap (peg). Pull through on large hollow holds, moving first right, then left to finish.

★ **12 Slip Tide** E2 46m
★ FA G Gibson, M Brown 1982

A prominent feature of the cliff is a big tapering ramp (taken by *Rampart*). The slab poised above this gives an exposed and fairly bold pitch on which small wires are useful. Start beneath the rib immediately right of *Rampart*,

   1 9m 4b Climb the rib to a stance.

2 37m 5b Gain the ledge on the left, step up left again, and break right through the steep retaining wall to reach a thin crack above. Follow the lip of the roof up leftwards for 4 metres, and then climb past an overlap to the upper slab, which leads to the top.

13 Rampart E3 39m

FA P Littlejohn, A McFarlane (l pt aid) 1972; FFA D Beetlestone, G Gibson 1980

A powerful line with exciting climbing up the obvious, narrowing ramp. Start at a wide crack 5 metres right of a large corner (*Shamrock*).

  1 9m 4b Climb the crack to a belay.

  2 30m 6a Move left and follow the ramp with increasing interest until it ends at an overhang. Make an exposed move right to reach good holds in a crack and follow this to easy ground.

15 *Double Diamond* (HVS)
Steve Kirman   KIRMAN col

14 Shamrock VS 45m

FA T Thompson, R D Moulton (pitch 1) 1972; P Littlejohn, K Darbyshire (pitch 3) 1972

Classic and very popular; quite steep but with good holds and protection throughout. It takes the lower part of the huge corner in the angle of the buttress, and then a subsidiary corner to its left. Start on the big ledge beneath the corner.

   1 18m 4c After a strenuous start, the corner is followed to a spacious ledge and belays on the left.

   2 9m 4a Climb the jagged crack above, and then move left to belay beneath another, slightly leaning corner.

   3 18m 4c Follow the corner until exposed moves gain easier ground above. Continue with care up to block belays.

Flying Buttress

OS Ref SS 1271 4489

This colossal leaning block of granite forming a giant natural arch is another of Lundy's outstanding coastal features. It lies directly beneath the Old Battery, a gun emplacement reached by a walled path beginning about 200 metres south of the Quarter Wall. From the Battery, scramble seawards along the promontory until the broken seaward face of Flying Buttress can be descended to sea-level ledges, which are exposed at all states of the tide (see page 80).

Diamond Solitaire climbs the large slab on the south side and can be reached until mid tide at least. *Battery Rib* requires lowish tide to cross the channel between Flying Buttress and the landward cliff.

15 Double Diamond HVS 5b 43m

FA First recorded in 1984 but climbed frequently over the years as variations on *Diamond Solitaire*.

A higher quality and more sustained version of *Diamond Solitaire*, taking the shallow vertical crack which runs all the way up the centre of the slab. Belay in the recess below the slab. Move up into the cleft; then pull rightwards over the overhang to a thin crack right of the corner of *Diamond Solitaire*. Follow the crack until it is possible to step into another crack on the right which leads up the centre of the slab to the steeper headwall. Climb the headwall directly on good holds.

The right arête of the slab gives a superb bold pitch, **The Cullinan** (E5 6a), gained by a rising traverse above the initial overhang of *Double Diamond*.

16 Diamond Solitaire VS 48m

FA B Martindale, J F McBratney 1965

The classic ascent of the impressive slab on the southern flank of Flying Buttress. Excellent rock and fine positions. Start in the recess below the slab.

The Old Battery

To start of routes 15 & 16

17

1 24m 4c Move up and break out of the deep cleft to gain the corner which bounds the slab on the left. Follow the corner to belay on the halfway shoulder.

2 24m 4b Traverse right for 3 metres; then climb directly up the slab on excellent holds.

The stunning thin crackline in the leaning, north wall of Flying Buttress provides one of the best hard routes in the South West, **The Flying Dutchman** (E7 6c). It can be climbed as two pitches or as one mega-pitch, and pitch 1 is also a challenging deep water solo at high tide (S2 F7b+). The next route is on the mainland cliff north of the arch and is accessible around low tide.

17 Battery Rib VD 34m
FA B Martindale, J F McBratney 1965

A fine and popular little climb, steep and juggy, taking the prominent rib which bounds the landward cliff to the north, Start in a recess just left of the foot of the rib. Move up the recess until it is possible to traverse right to gain the rib. Climb the rib using huge holds on its left wall to a ledge about 20 metres up; then follow the less distinct rib above to the top.

Jenny's Cove

Devil's Chimney Cliff

OS Ref SS 1320 4568

This big brooding cliff is tucked into the southern corner of Jenny's Cove, behind the fine granite spire of the Devil's Chimney. Both crags are approached by descending the grass and boulder slope on their west side, passing beneath another impressive tower, the Devil's Tower, joined to the parent cliff (the obvious crack in the west face of this gives an excellent sustained jamming pitch – **Hob's Lane** (E2 5b).

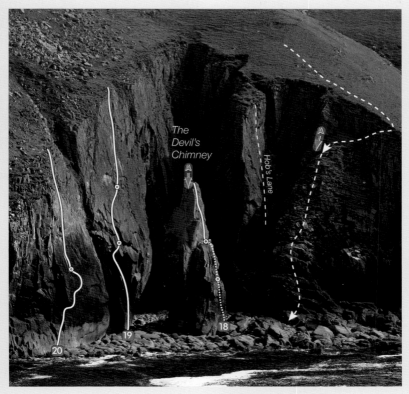

A prominent feature of the main cliff is a leftward-slanting gully or depression towards the right-hand side. Left of the depression the lower half of the cliff is guarded by large overhangs, through which *The Promised Land* finds its way. Further left, the undercut lower wall gives way to the huge white slab taken by *The Fifth Appendage*.

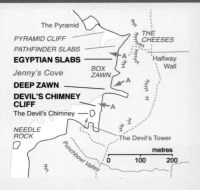

EGYPTIAN SLABS

18 The Devil's Chimney HVS 43m
FA R Shaw, J Logan 1961

The ascent of Lundy's most notable summit is a classic expedition requiring careful judgment of tides so that retreat is not cut off.
Technically harder following a rock fall but well protected. Start beneath a shallow groove at the south-west corner of the pinnacle.

1 11m 5b Climb the groove to a comfortable platform.

2 12m 4a Take the right-hand of the twin cracks above, and then move left to a boulder-strewn ledge.

3 20m 4c Follow the thin crack in the centre of the steep slab above to reach an overhang. Climb the overhang and the wall above, trending left to the arête which leads to the summit. Descend by abseil.

19 The Promised Land E3 85m
FA P Littlejohn, K Darbyshire 1974

One of the island's major undertakings – a brilliant, varied route tackling some very impressive terrain. A section of the first pitch is likely to be wet but this is no real problem as the holds are very positive. Start 30 metres left of the gully/depression on the main cliff, at a line of holds beneath a corner 8 metres up.

1 30m 5c Move up for 3 metres, and then climb the black slab on the left into grooves, which are followed to the big roof. Traverse left on good incuts for 6 metres, past a wet section, until below the left side of a huge block wedged into the roof. Pull up to gain a chimneying position beside the block; then traverse right and swing around to a small stance above the roof.

2 15m 6a Climb the groove above until everything blanks out, when a thin move right gains good holds trending rightwards to a stance.

3 40m 5b Climb the crack above to reach a big spike on the right; then climb diagonally right to a jug-rimmed ledge. Continue up the groove above to a cluster of spikes after about 6 metres, and then traverse right to another groove which leads to the top.

JENNY'S COVE

DEEP ZAWN

The Devil's Chimney

DEVIL'S CHIMNEY CLIFF

← 21 22 23

★
★ **20   The Fifth Appendage**   E1   55m
★ FA A McFarlane, I Duckworth 1973

Open, delicate climbing in an impressive setting. Start around low tide on weed-covered ledges 25 metres left of the right-hand edge of the white slab.

    1 21m 5b Scramble across to a rightward-facing groove, and climb this until a delicate traverse right leads to some small ledges. Move right again for a couple of metres, and then trend left to a small stance.

    2 34m 5a Climb the slab above, going directly over the first overhang, and turning the second on the right. Move up and left to a good flake; then follow the crack on the right to finish.

Deep Zawn

OS Ref SS 1324 4574

Perhaps the most atmospheric of all the major Lundy cliffs, this huge echoing zawn provides some of the best and hardest routes on the island. Despite their intimidating surroundings, the climbs described are easy of access, non tidal, on perfect granite, and following superb natural lines.

The zawn is easily located by descending the slope 100 metres south of the Halfway Wall. The north side provides the best climbing but on first acquaintance it is worth viewing the routes from the top of the south side. Near the arête of the wall is the snaking crack of *The Serpent*, right of which is a smooth face split by the fingertip crack of *Supernova*. Twin cracks leading to a large, stepped corner mark the line of *Quatermass*, while the long groove dominating the right-hand part of the face gives the compelling line of *Antiworlds*.

The climbs are approached by descending the ridge on the north side of the zawn. A fixed rope is recommended and most parties will abseil the final 24 metres (though with good route finding it is possible to climb down at V Diff standard). A ledge system above high-tide level leads into the zawn, giving access to all the climbs described.

21 Antiworlds   E5   75m

FA P Littlejohn, R D Moulton (4 pts aid) 1972; FFA M Carr, B Molyneux 1989

The slanting groove system in the right half of the wall gives a route of unique stature. Sustained climbing with excellent rock and protection. Start at the far right end of the ledge system (peg belay).

1 34m 6a Gain the thin crack on the right, and climb steeply to some ledges at the foot of the big groove. Move up a thin crack on the right for 5 metres and then climb the groove itself to where a smooth fin of rock divides it. Difficult climbing past this gains better holds on the right leading to a stance and peg belay.

2 21m 6a Climb the corner above until it begins to bulge, and harder climbing gains good holds at its top. Continue up left for a short way to a good stance.

3 20m 6a Move back down and right to beneath thin parallel cracks. Follow these to a narrow horizontal slot; then gain the thin crack above and follow it on improving holds to the top.

22 Quatermass   E2   60m

FA K Darbyshire, H Clarke (1 pt aid) 1973; FFA R Evans 1974; P Harrison S Wilkie pitch 3 1986

The most popular route in Deep Zawn, having consistently good climbing and tremendous atmosphere. It centres on the conspicuous twin cracks at half height and begins where the crackline extends to the foot of the face.

1 24m 5b Climb leftwards to a scoop, step up left, and then climb the thin crack on the right to a small incut ledge. Move up to an overhang (peg), continue straight up for 8 metres, and then bear right along ledges to the halfway ledge beneath the parallel cracks.

2 12m 5a Climb steeply up the twin cracks to another good ledge.

3 24m 5c Above is a large, stepped corner (the original finish – 4b). Climb a short way up the corner to a thin crack which branches off rightwards. Follow the crack to the top.

23 The Serpent   E1   48m

FA P Littlejohn, C A G Morton (VL) 1973

A gentle introduction to Deep Zawn, featuring steep but well-protected climbing. Start beneath the seaward arête of the wall.

1 21m 4b Climb the groove just left of the arête for 15 metres. Move right and up ledges on the rib to belay at a pointed block.

2 27m 5b Move up right to a ledge. Gain the crack and follow it all the way to the top, a narrow section after about 10 metres providing the crux.

The awesome thin crack splitting the smooth face right of *The Serpent* is taken by **Supernova** (E5 6b), a very demanding route which sees few clean ascents.

Egyptian Slabs

OS Ref SS 1325 4586

These are the extensive slabs in the northern corner of Jenny's Cove. Their left side attains a height of 90 metres where a substantial route – **Pathfinder** (E2 5b) – takes the most obvious line. The routes described are further right, on the much lower Immaculate Slab – a smooth, yellow-streaked slab characterised by a long diagonal overhang above its left side. The slab is left

of the prominent narrow slab running up to a lichen-covered tower which is the lowest of the Cheeses (the curious set of buttresses on the slope above). Approach by abseiling to large sea-level ledges below broken rock just to the right of the yellow-streaked slab.

24 Immaculate Misconception   E3 5c   30m
FA G Gibson, M Ward 1984

Excellent bold climbing up the centre of the streaked slab. Start 3 metres right of the left end of the narrow ledge below the slab. Climb some thin cracks just left of a small groove to gain the slab. Bear slightly left to a black streak and follow this on small incuts up the centre of the slab to a good hold where it steepens. Move left and finish more easily.

25 Immaculate Slab   HVS 5a   34m
FA P W Thexton, K J Wilson 1974

Perfect granite and superb climbing up the left side of the slab. Start on the left end of the thin ledge below the slab. Move up and follow the shallow groove which leads up to the slab below the overhang. Climb up to the right, below the retaining wall, to a final steep section which is tackled from a large foothold on the right. Belay, and then scramble to the top.

Beaufort Buttress

OS Ref SS 1304 4629

This is the handsome promontory forming the extreme northern tip of Jenny's Cove. A little Mecca for climbs in the easier grades, its attractions include straightforward access, a sunny aspect, and lovely golden granite.

To reach the buttress strike west off the coast path about 500 metres north of Halfway Wall (approximately 300 metres south of Threequarter Wall if you walk too far!) and descend grassy slopes to the headland. Descent to the cliff base is via rock slabs on the north side, gaining a platform beneath the cliff which is only sea-washed at high tide – giving plenty of time to climb a number of routes in one visit. Even at high tide the main pitches may be accessed by traversing in along a ledge 9 metres up. The routes are described from **left to right**.

26 Streaky VS 31m
FA S A Lewis, A Stewart 1979

A great little route taking the grey-streaked corner at the far left side of the main face. Start at the left end of the platform beneath a short groove.

   1 9m 4b Climb the groove and belay below the corner.
   2 22m 5a Climb the corner, with continuous interest and plenty of protection.

27 Capstan's Arête VS 31m
FA R Edwards, B Cooper 1985

The left arête of the main face is pleasant with positive holds. Start right of *Streaky* at a shallow, stepped corner line.

   1 9m Climb the corner to belay at the left end of the ledge.
   2 22m 4b Gain the arête and follow it to the top.

28 Hurricane HS 31m
FA C J Lawrance, J Brown, A D Caswell, I Marriot 1971

Nice open climbing up the light-coloured face to the right of *Capstan's Arête*.

   1 9m Climb the stepped corner as for *Capstan's Arête*.
   2 22m 4a Move right onto the face and climb directly on small holds to a small ledge. Easier climbing leads to the crest of the buttress.

29 Force Eight S 32m
FA W Tolfree, G Raymont 1969

The centre of the front face of the buttress is split by a prominent crackline. Start directly below this at a short corner in the initial wall.

   1 9m Climb the corner and belay below the crackline.
   2 23m Climb twin cracks to the small overhang. Pull over into the left-hand crack and follow this (the right-hand crack is HS).

30 Stuka VS 32m
FA G Raymont, W Tolfree 1969; *Stuka Direct*: P Harrison, T Sawbridge 1997

High on the right of the main face is a prominent right-facing corner, giving the plum route of the buttress. Start 2 metres right of *Force Eight*.

   1 9m Climb a crack and short wall to the ledge.
   2 23m 4b Climb the twin cracks of *Force Eight*; then traverse right to gain the corner, which is followed to the top. **Stuka Direct** (VS 4c) climbs directly up the face into the corner – even better!

NB: Top pitches shown only

The right-hand arête of the face is taken by **Admiral's Arête** (E1 5a), while just further around is another worthwhile route:

⭐ **31 Fifty Pumps** VS 37m
FA P Scraton, A Stewart 1979

Start 5 metres right of *Stuka* beneath a slabby corner.

  1 15m Climb the corner and its continuation; then bear right to belay in a large recess.
  2 22m 4c Excellent jamming up the left-hand of the two slanting cracks above (the right-hand crack is HVS 5b).

Devil's Slide Area

Grand Falls Zawn & The Parthenos

OS Ref SS 1320 4641 & SS 1317 4649

These adjacent cliffs are well viewed from the top of Beaufort Buttress. Looking north from here, the Parthenos is the very steep concave wall, brownish in colour, set immediately behind the offshore island of St Mark's Stone. Grand Falls Zawn is just to its right, past an earthy rib, the tall slab of *American Beauty* forming its back wall.

To approach *American Beauty*, descend the slope approximately 150 metres south of Threequarter Wall and set up a 90-metre abseil with joined ropes (or a single static rope) from good block belays. This takes one straight down the slab (ascenders useful for the changeover at the knot, which can be done on a ledge) to a non-tidal ledge system about 12 metres above the zawn-bed. The first crackline right of the left-bounding corner of the slab marks the start of **American Shrapnel** (E2 5c).

32 American Beauty   HVS   91m
FA P Littlejohn, D Garner 1975

The original and cleanest line on the slab. Excellent climbing and a must at the grade. Take care to avoid rope drag on pitch 2. Start at the next crack to the right of *American Shrapnel*.

1 27m 4c Follow the thin cracks, and continue in the same line to a boulder-strewn ledge.
2 46m 5a Climb the thin cracks above, past a narrow ledge, until harder climbing gains a good hold just left of a tongue of turf. Follow the thin parallel cracks above to the roof and move right to a scoop at its narrowest point. Pull through to a good hold and traverse left, keeping low on clean rock, until more good holds lead to a stance at the foot of a steep corner.
3 18m 4c Climb the corner; then bear left over vegetated slabs to the top.

The approach for routes on the Parthenos is to abseil straight down the crag (towards its right-hand side) from thread belays near the cliff edge. The objective is a narrow ledge below the obvious rightward-sloping ramp which bounds the steep part of the face on the right. This ramp gives an easy escape route and a pleasant climb in its own right, **Zephuros** (VS 4c).

33 Cithaeron   E4 6a   43m
FA G Gibson, M Ward 1984

A wild, strenuous route weaving its way through very impressive rock. Start from the narrow ledge reached by abseil, below the obvious 'beckoning' flake crack. Move up and follow the flake crack to its end. Pull up through the bulge to a black fang of rock and pass this on the right to a black scoop. Exit left to a black block (peg) and climb through the bulge above into the steep and spectacular finishing groove.

Threequarter Buttress   OS Ref SS 1313 4659

Directly below Threequarter Wall is a huge open zawn, Big Zawn, home to **The Ocean** (E1), one of Lundy's longest routes. Immediately north of Big Zawn and just below plateau level is Black Bottom Buttress which has a useful selection of non-tidal routes. Beneath Black Bottom Buttress and at sea level is a clean juggy wall of delightful rock. Descend the grass slope beneath Black Bottom Buttress to reach a crested spur that defines the summit of Threequarter Buttress.

34 Quadratus Lumborum   S   41m
FA C J Lawrance, J Brown, S Perry, A D Caswell 1971

A wandering line but with some very enjoyable climbing. From the crested spur, scramble (or abseil) down the slabby south side of the buttress to a large tidal platform beneath a short, cracked slab.

1 12m Climb the thin crack in the slab, and move left at 8 metres to the arête. Follow the arête to a stance on a narrow ledge overlooking the buttress.
2 29m Follow the obvious leftward traverse-line across the buttress before gradually ascending to the foot of a steep wall. Zigzag up the wall to a good ledge and finish easily.

35 *Non Expectis Jugsimisius* (VS)
Alex Thompson   DAN LANE

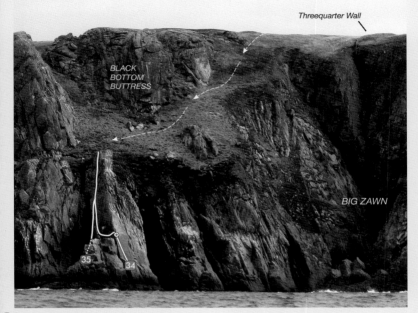

Threequarter Wall

BLACK
BOTTOM
BUTTRESS

BIG ZAWN

35   34

35   Non Expectis Jugsimisius   VS 4c   38m

FA D Kerr, C Gilbert 1985

A true gem tucked away in the north side of the buttress. Non tidal. It is committing for the grade, but a positive approach on the crux will pay dividends. Scramble down from the north side of the crested spur to ledges overlooking a recessed slab. A short abseil leads down to the lower of two huge jammed boulders beneath the recessed slab. Step awkwardly down to where a blind swing right around the arête gains good holds at the base of a thin crackline. Follow the crack and its easier continuation to the top of the buttress.

The Devil's Slide

OS Ref SS 1314 4688

A short distance north of Threequarter Wall is the unmistakable 120-metre sweep of the Devil's Slide, Lundy's most famous cliff. Its lower half, below an obvious break, can be climbed anywhere at V Diff standard, while the upper half of the Slide provides several sustained slab pitches in magnificent positions, all of which are worthwhile and quickly accessible from the halfway break (which can be reached easily by traversing in from the descent rib).

At the foot of the Slide is a huge smooth block which is only sea-washed at high tide. To reach this, scramble down the grassy gully on the south side of the Slide; then move left (facing out) and descend an easy rib. At high tide the climbs can be started from a horizontal fault which crosses the Slide 8 metres up.

View south from the Fortress
HANS GROENENDIJK

THE DIAMOND

FLUTED FACE

THE DEVIL'S SLIDE

St James's Stone

FORGOTTEN PINNACLE

Squire's View Zawn

36 The Devil's Slide HS 121m

FA K M Lawder, J Logan, R Shaw 1961

A great classic of the South West. If the best line is taken the climbing is consistently fine, with difficulties culminating in the exposed final traverse. Start from the large block at the base.

1 21m Climb easily up the right side of the slab to belay at a break.

2 30m Continue up the slab to the midway fault and move right to a flake belay in the gully.

3 40m 4a Traverse back; then climb the slab via a white scoop to the left of the right-bounding rib (or more easily up the rib itself) to belay when ledges are met (peg usually in place, nuts higher up).

4 30m 4a Climb the right side of the slab until level with the start of the steeper headwall. Traverse left along the obvious line until delicate moves gain the finish over blocks to the left.

37 Satan's Slip E1 98m

FA L P Fatti, D G Ward 1970

The quintessential slab climb, taking the centre of the Slide. Bold but reasonably well protected with small wires. Start at the base.

1 46m Saunter up the centre to the midway break and belay on the right.

2 43m 5a Move left into the centre of the slab and follow a line of faint vertical cracks just right of some black streaks. At 30 metres an overlap is reached; bear right above this, and then easily back left to belay at the flakes of *Albion*.

3 9m Finish easily leftwards. Those wanting a more challenging finish can climb the groove and crack in the headwall (E1 5b).

38 Albion VS 107m

FA P H Biven, V N Stevenson, C Fishwick 1963

Lundy's middle-grade classic taking the black-streaked corner formed by the left retaining wall of the Slide – a magnificent line. Start on the large block below the Slide.

1 37m Climb the left side of the slab and traverse left to a little stance on the rib.

2 24m Move back onto the slab and climb direct to a small stance with flake belays under the impressive retaining wall.

3 37m 4c Follow the curving corner until easier ground leads to block belays below the headwall of the Slide.

4 9m Finish easily leftwards.

Fear of Faust (E1)
Andy Turner DAN LANE

Devotees of climbing on the Slide should not miss **Fear of Faust** (E1 5a), an excellent slab pitch taking a line between *Satan's Slip* and *The Devil's Slide*, starting where the former belays at the halfway break. Other good routes hereabouts include **Shark** (E1 5a), which takes the elegant rib overlooking the upper part of the Slide, and **Devil's Spine** (VS 4b) the long slabby rib some 15 metres north of the Slide.

The Diamond
OS Ref SS 1317 4700

Offering some of the best granite face climbing in Britain, this magnificent wedge of high-angle slab dominates Squire's View Zawn (the first cove north of the Devil's Slide). Its base is non tidal and the best climbing conditions are usually in the afternoon, when it gets the sun. Approach by abseiling down the slanting dyke which bounds the lower half of the slab on the left. There are good thread anchors above the dyke and a 60-metre rope is useful to get right to the bottom, although it is easy to descend the last part by climbing.

39 A Widespread Ocean of Fear   E5   88m
FA G Gibson, D Beetlestone 1981
Superb in every sense and taking the classic 'natural' line of the Diamond – a shallow flake/overlap just right of centre. Reasonable at the grade. Start at the foot of the basalt dyke.
   1 24m 5c Move up and right across the black wall to gain the slab at a large scar. Move up to a good wire and continue up the slab, following a line of reasonable holds, to belay at the main diagonal break (small wires and cams) below the 'flake' line.
   2 37m 6a Climb to the first bulge and pass this rightwards to the continuation groove. Sustained moves gain better holds beneath an arched overlap. Pull past this (peg) and continue on the obvious line to a final large overlap, which is passed on better holds to a small stance above. Various small and medium wire belays.
   3 27m 5a Climb the cracks above to a niche; then traverse right and finish up easy ribs.

40 Watching the Ocean E6 82m
FA G Gibson, M Ward 1985. As described: P Littlejohn, N White 1989

The central line of the Diamond gives a bold and extremely sustained piece of slab climbing of impeccable quality throughout. Take plenty of small wires. Belay using the abseil rope on some small ledges a few feet up from the bottom of the turf tongue which extends down the dyke.

1 18m 6a/b Step onto a small shelf on the edge of the slab. Difficult moves right gain better holds beneath a faint crack running up to the left. Follow the crack to reach a line of flakes leading to belays (pegs and cams) in the obvious horizontal break.

2 40m 6b Climb the staggered groove above to a small roof. Pull over onto the slab and follow the twin hairline cracks (runners in the left one) until a series of scoops in the right-hand crack are used to gain a good slot. Continue, bearing slightly left into a shallow corner, which is followed up rightwards past an overhang to a stance at the end of the difficulties.

3 24m 4c Traverse right on large rugosities to a rib, which leads to the top.

41 Diamond Life E4 6a 43m
FA S Boydon, P Harrison 1985

The continuous crackline towards the left side of the Diamond is probably its most popular route. Protection is good after bold climbing to gain the crack. Start at a thread belay 21 metres down the dyke followed by the abseil approach. Move back up the dyke for 6 metres to a peg; then step right onto the face and climb to reach a diagonal break. Continue to a second break (two poor pegs) and follow the thin crack above until holds on the left are used to make a difficult step back right into the crack, which is climbed to the top.

Northern Lundy

Arch Zawn

OS Ref SS 1293 4738

This is the large open zawn (or cove) with a stream running into it, roughly 450 metres north of the Devil's Slide. It is characterized by a fine natural arch on its south side while the climbs are on the steep, south-facing wall forming the north side of the cove. Descend via the grass slopes on the south side of the cove (south of the arch) until easy rock leads down to sea-level platforms from where it is possible to traverse to the boulder beach, which is exposed until about half tide. Alternatively approach by abseiling in down the north side of the zawn.

42 Headline E1 43m
FA F E R Cannings, J Kingston (VL) 1973

A great little climb weaving through some impressive terrain at a reasonable standard. Start at lowish tide from the left-hand of the two blocks/pillars which abut the base of the wall.

1 23m 5b Climb directly to a bulge. Difficult moves gain holds on the right, and a rightward traverse leads to a break in the overhang. Pull through, and traverse right again for 5 metres to an exposed stance.

2 20m 4c Climb the open groove above the right side of the stance to an overhang. Move up left into another groove and climb the wide crack to the top.

42 *Headline* (E1)
Claire Reading & Paul Innes
SIMON CARDY

43 Stop Press   E2   46m
FA F E R Cannings, J Kingston (VL) 1973

This fine route takes the left side of the main (seaward) face, then a crack in the exposed buttress above. Start as for *Headline*, on the left-hand block.

1 26m 5c Step down to good holds and climb to a traverse-line leading left to a large niche. Climb the diagonal crack on the right to a block; then step left and up the overhanging arête to a smooth slab beneath the overhang. Move left with difficulty into a crack, and then climb through the overhang to a stance in a large recess.

2 20m 5a Climb direct, and then follow a rising traverse-line to a crack on the right which leads to the top.

The Constable

OS Ref SS 1326 4802

At the far north of the island is a handsome granite spire known as the Constable. It gave the second recorded rock climb on the island and remains a popular objective, whether for its original route or one of the more recent additions. To approach, take the main track from the village to the North Light. When this ends (just short of the lighthouse), the Constable is now directly below, set high above the north coast.

⭐ 44 The Original Route   HS 4b   15m
FA J Logan, R Shaw 1961

The right-hand of three cracklines in the south face. Start at a big detached block. Gain the crack from the left, climb it to the summit crest, then onwards to the summit.

The central crack is **Eveninawl** (VS 4c), while the left-hand is the brutal **Thug** (E1 5b).

⭐ 45 Caught in the Act   E1 5b   22m
FA M Snell, P Harrison 1990

The best and most substantial route on the Constable – both delicate and strenuous. Lower down and left of the north-west arête is a brown-streaked groove. Ascend the groove and continue to reach a prominent flake, which is followed to the top.

The North Light
SIMON CARDY

Inland Devon and Cornwall

The friendly, accessible crags of inland Devon provide a delightful contrast to the South West's more imposing sea-cliff climbing venues. Here one can relax and enjoy the technicalities of the climbing, whether on the perfect Devonian Limestone of Chudleigh Rocks or the firm, rugged granite of the Dartmoor Tors. In good weather the moors are a magical place to climb, with or without a rope (the bouldering being brilliant), while the sheltered, wooded settings of The Dewerstone and Chudleigh can give excellent climbing days in less settled conditions.

27 *Outward Bound* (HVS)
climber unknown   SEAN KELLY

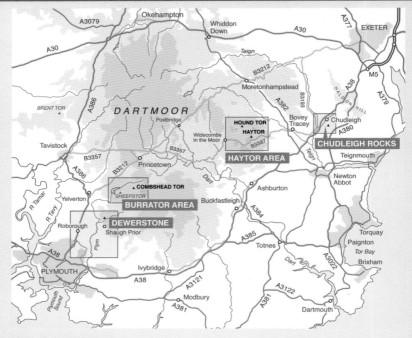

Chudleigh Rocks

OS Ref SX 865 788

This crag of solid, natural limestone has always been one of the most popular climbing venues in Devon. There is excellent climbing at all grades, though the hardest routes tend to be somewhat escapable. The extensive South Face can offer pleasant, sheltered climbing conditions even in the depths of winter, and also has certain sections which remain dry during rain. Although less popular, the quarried North Face provides good climbing in exotic surroundings and is pleasantly cool in the summer months.

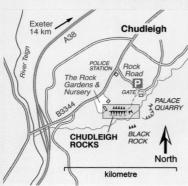

Approach Chudleigh is about nine miles south-west of Exeter, on the south side of the A38 dual carriageway. To reach the cliffs, turn down the road beside the police station (Rock Road) and proceed for 200 metres to limited parking places on the right before the lane forks. Valuables should not be left in the car. From here a path leads westwards to the crag.

2 *Combined Ops* (E2)   Henry Castle   CASTLE col.

Follow the main (level) path for 200 metres to a neck of land where the cliffs begin. A left-hand branch leads down to the South Face; descend a steep bank on the right for the North Face.

South Face

The cliff begins at a barred cave entrance, above which is an overhang split by an obvious line, **Chudleigh Overhang** (VS 4c). To the left of this, the testing line of **Dripdry** (E4 6b) is marked by two large threads. There is good all-weather bouldering around the cave entrance. Left of the cave is a buttress of excellent grey rock with a sheer front face.

The South Face routes are described from **right to left**.

Slybools McCall

⭐ **1   Logic**   E1   27m

FA F E R Cannings, P Badcock, A Thompson 1965

An elegant climb taking the right edge of the buttress, then a groove in the wall above. Start just left of the arête.

1 15m 5a/b Climb a slight groove for 5 metres, step right onto the arête, and continue to a large ledge and belays.

2 12m 4c Above left is a large block; move up on to it and then step right to a groove, which is climbed to a slabby exit on the left.

2 Combined Ops E2 30m

FA P H Biven, B M Biven (VL), C Fishwick, J Braven 1962

A fine sustained pitch taking the left edge of the buttress.

1 18m 5b Make a rising traverse to reach the arête and follow it to a whitish scoop. Step right and make a difficult move to reach obvious undercuts, after which better holds lead to easier ground and peg belays.

2 12m 4a Climb diagonally rightwards over blocks and pull through a double bulge to reach easier ground.

Immediately right of *Combined Ops* is **Slyboots McCall** (E4 6b), a fine testpiece going straight up the wall past two pegs.

3 Combat E3 33m

FA P Littlejohn, S Jones 1971

A steep and difficult route starting just around the corner from *Combined Ops*, at some thin cracks about 2 metres left of the arête.

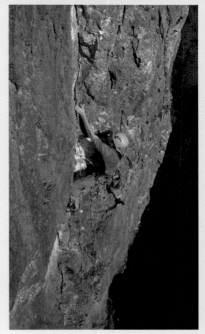

12 *Inkerman Groove* (VS)
Tony Hopkins   PETE SAUNDERS

1 21m 5c Climb to a projecting flake, which is hand-traversed rightwards to join *Combined Ops*. Move up into the scoop, and then break left up a slanting crack into a smooth niche. Pull out with difficulty and continue straight up steeply to a stance.

2 12m 4a *Combined Ops* pitch 2.

The next big feature is the great corner of *Sarcophagus*. The crack in its right wall gives a very good jamming pitch **Oesophagus** (HVS 5a) which finishes out right to the stance of *Combined Ops*.

4 Sarcophagus VS 33m

FA T W Patey 1960

A unique classic, very polished yet still most rewarding. Virtually always dry. Start beneath the large corner.

1 9m 4a Climb cracks in the corner by bridging to a cave stance. Belay back to the right.

2 15m 4b Climb the chimney to the large overhang. Traverse left for 3 metres along a smooth, exposed slab; then move up onto the nose on the right. Stance and peg belays above.

3 9m Climb the corner above the stance and exit to the right with ease.

⭐5   Greenmantle   D   33m

FA J Brooks, R Cochran 1964

A pleasant ramble which has launched many a
climbing career. Some 25 metres to the left of
Sarcophagus is another barred cave below a
gully. Start just right of this.

   1 24m Climb a crack for 5 metres; then
traverse right to a 'staircase' leading to a vegetated ledge. Continue to a higher ledge and belay.

   2 9m Climb the groove on the left, awkward at first, to the top.

6   Tar Baby   S   27m

FA S Dawson, P Butler 1966

A popular pitch featuring a teasing mantelshelf. Starting as for *Greenmantle*, climb the crack, and
then move up to gain a ledge at the base of the corner above. Take the corner to the top.

A little further on, the ground rises to an inset wall some 12 metres high, beyond which the main part
of the South Face begins at a much larger, blind cave known as Cow Cave.

⭐7   Salome   VD   15m

FA Unknown *c.*1960s

The obvious leftward-sloping break on the inset wall. Good steep climbing at the top, which can
be climbed using a crack on the right. The wall to the left gives the frequently top-roped **Seventh
Veil** (VS 5a).

The obvious chimney and roof crack above Cow Cave is **Lute** (HVS 5a), another fine line which
stays dry in bad weather. Just right of the cave entrance are the disjointed grooves of **Smoke Gets
in Your Eyes** (E2 6a), a safe, technical pitch.

⭐8   Reek   HS   19m

FA E Rayson, B Waistell 1961

A great little route starting beneath the short wall to the left of Cow Cave.

1 11m 4b Climb onto the ledge. Move up left to stand on the bulge and then climb a groove left of the prominent nose to a stance.

2 8m Climb the easy slab above for a short way; then step right and go up a short wall to the top.

⭐**9   Barn Owl Crack/Ashtree Buttress**   VD   37m

FA T W Patey, R Grant, S Bemrose 1960

Start beneath the large crack which is the first real break to the left of Cow Cave.

1 14m Climb to the large vegetated ledge beneath the crack. Follow the crack with interest for about 8 metres, and then make a short traverse right to a good stance.

2 8m Climb for 3 metres; then step left across the crack and follow the line of steps running up left to the terrace. Belay; then scramble up and right to a buttress with an ash tree growing from it.

3 15m Climb to the tree, pass it on the right, and continue directly to the top on good holds.

The next feature left of *Barn Owl Crack* is the short steep corner of **The Slot** (HVS 5a). The cliff then increases in height and presents a fine open wall of clean limestone, delineated on its left by an easier, stepped face taken by *Wogs*, which is a good reference point for all the routes in this area. The left side of the wall is dominated by *Inkerman Groove*, while the following two routes occupy the central section.

10   Machete Wall   E2 5c   30m
FA E Rayson and party 1961

An excellent wall climb, steep and intimidating. Start just left of a recess, and 6 metres right of the initial ledgy wall of *Wogs*. Climb easily for 5 metres; then mantelshelf onto a small ledge and continue, bearing slightly right, to a niche (high peg). Climb steeply up and make a fingery move (peg) to reach holds on the steep wall above. Climb diagonally left and up onto a slab, which is crossed to a large pointed block on the right. Standing on this, step left into a groove and follow it for 3 metres before climbing the wall on the right to the top.

11   Mortality Crisis   E4 6a   37m
FA N White, G Szuca 1985

Fine sustained climbing up the smoother wall between *Machete Wall* and *Inkerman Groove*. Start as for *Machete Wall*. Climb easily to the top of a pedestal, step up left (peg), and climb the wall above to the start of a shallow, leftward-leaning groove. Climb the groove to its end (peg); then move up and left past another peg to the edge of *Inkerman Groove*. Step up, move right to the obvious undercuts, and climb the steep wall above to the top.

12   Inkerman Groove   VS 4c   34m
FA E Rayson, N Hannaby 1960

One of the best pitches of its grade in the South West, giving fairly steep and technically interesting climbing on positive holds. It takes the long groove to the left of *Machete Wall*. Follow *Wogs* to a point halfway up its second pitch; then make a balancy rightward traverse to the base of the long groove. Climb the groove for 9 metres to a small ledge; then move right and up to a larger ledge. Climb the short wall above to the top.

13   Black Death   E4 6a   30m
FA D Rainford, E Phillips (aid) 1966; K Buckley, P Dawson (l pt aid) 1980; FFA P Littlejohn 1982

A brilliant route taking the narrow vertical wall between *Inkerman Groove* and *Wogs*. Follow *Wogs* to the stance and continue straight up to gain the traverse of *Inkerman Groove*. Starting on the left, climb the wall above to a slight niche (peg), and then move up and right again to a bulge. Pull straight through to good holds leading to the top.

A tougher and more sustained finish to *Black Death* is **White Life** (E5 6b), which breaks left from the niche, then climbs the smooth wall past three pegs.

14   Wogs   VD   37m
FA I B Prowse and party 1923

A classic of the cliff with fine positions and great character (now high in the grade due to polish). It goes up the obvious fault left of the smoother wall of rock taken by *Machete Wall* and *Inkerman Groove*. Start beneath the ledgy initial wall.
   1 9m The wall may be climbed in several ways, and leads to a good stance and belays.
   2 17m Climb for a couple of metres and pull up left onto a narrow ledge. Traverse left to the main fault and follow the long crack to a stance on top of the pillar.

3 11m Climb up into the recess, step left, and go up easier rock to a tree. Or finish more interestingly by stepping right above the recess and moving out to an exposed nose, above which easier rock leads to a stone wall on the cliff edge.

The 40-metre sweep of the Western Tower dominates the left end of Chudleigh's South Face. It is taken centrally by *The Spider*, while the following route climbs the corner fault which defines it on the right.

15 Scar HS 33m
FA N Hannaby, T W Patey 1960

A good climb following a great natural weakness. To the left of *Wogs* the ground falls 3 metres. Start at the bottom of this dip, to the right of two caves 3 metres up in the rock.

1 18m 4b Climb straight up past the right-hand cave, step left, and go up a slab to a large terrace beneath a corner with a tree stump in it.

2 15m 4b Climb to the tree stump on gritty rock. Climb the gently overhanging wall above to a tree belay. Scramble up a path to the top.

16 Never on Sunday HS 36m
FA D Bassett, A Allen 1961

Delightful climbing in a fine position on the second pitch makes up for a rather undistinguished start. Start beneath the two caves 3 metres up.

1 18m 4a Climb to the right-hand cave and move awkwardly out of this onto slabs. Climb to the terrace below the tree stump in the corner of *Scar*.

2 18m 4b Just right of the corner of *Scar*, climb a gritty corner for 3 metres, and then traverse right, rising slightly, to gain a small ledge round the arête. Follow the arête to a tree, from which a larger tree belay is easily reached.

14 *Wogs* (VD) Steve Whitfield HENRY CASTLE

17 The Spider E1 40m
FA F E R Cannings, P H Biven 1964

A regional classic having delectable climbing on the final wall. Protection is good on the crux but rather lacking on the first pitch. Start 5 metres left of the twin caves 3 metres up.

1 14m 5a Climb to a ledge at 2½ metres; then continue bearing left, up a steepish wall, to a ledge. From the left end of the ledge, move up to gain a large foothold on the slab above. Climb the slab, stepping left at the top to a stance and peg belays.

2 26m 5b Climb rightwards to the vegetated ledge; then continue up and around the left side of the large perched block above to a small ledge on top of it. Move straight up through the bulge and gain small holds on the steep slab above. Climb diagonally right to good finishing holds above and to the right of a small tree. Continue directly to the top.

★
★ **18 Great Western** VS 42m
★ FA N Hannaby, E Rayson 1961

A route of great character and quality, though rather polished and very tricky if wet. Near the western end of the cliff is a shallow corner just before the face becomes very fluted. Start here.

    1 12m 4b Climb the groove to the second ledge. Traverse left using a line of good handholds and mantelshelf onto a ledge. Peg and nut belays.

    2 6m 4c Delicate climbing up the narrow slab on the right leads to a large ledge and peg belays.

    3 9m 5a Climb the wall above to the overhang (peg); then move up with difficulty into the groove on the left and climb this direct to a good stance and peg belay.

    4 15m Climb the rib to the top, keeping right for the best positions.

17 *The Spider* (E1)
Jack Bradbrook MARK DAVIES

North Face

A neglected spot but well worth a visit, especially when the sun hits the face in the late afternoon. The most substantial routes are on the Garden Wall, which lies at the western end of the North Face beyond several clean but shorter walls (which are frequently used for top-roping and instructing).

The cliff forms the boundary of the private garden of Rock House, now a garden centre and leisure facility known as The Rock. It is necessary to ask there for permission to climb (preferably by telephone a day or two beforehand: 01626 852134) and the owners require people to have BMC insurance. Don't forget to sign the Visitors' Book, which is a fascinating historical chronicle of Devon climbing. Both past and present owners have always had a very positive attitude towards climbers, and this should not be jeopardised by any sort of antisocial behaviour. There is an excellent cafe attached to the garden centre.

The whole of the Garden Wall has been quarried and consequently has fewer features than the South Face. The climbs however are open and reasonably quick to dry, characterised by interesting moves requiring thoughtful footwork. Descent is simple at the far eastern end of the cliff.

19 Plexus   VS   30m
FA P H Biven, D Horley 1964

A fine route taking a positive line and having fairly steep climbing on incut holds. Near the left end of the wall are two obvious cracks about 5 metres apart. Start below the left-hand crack.
  1 15m 4a Follow the crack for 5 metres; then climb directly up the wall to the right (peg) to reach a sloping ledge beneath an overhanging wall.
  2 15m 4b Climb the short crack above; then traverse left beneath a large block to a small ledge (peg). Continue straight up to a bulge and make steep moves over this before ledges lead easily to the top.

20 Nexus   HS   27m
FA P H Biven, D Horley 1964

The classic of the face, having a strong natural line and interesting climbing throughout. Start at the right-hand of the prominent cracks 5 metres apart. Climb the cracks to a huge flake on the left. Move up onto the flake, and climb the steep wall to a small ledge. Make an exposed step up to the left to reach good holds leading to the top.

21 Nimrod   E1 5b 27m
FA F E R Cannings, B Housley 1965

Another gem of Chudleigh's North Face – sustained and delicate. Some 6 metres to the right of *Nexus* a steep slab runs up for a few metres to the left. Start below this. From a large ledge at 2 metres, climb the delicate slab (peg) to good holds. Move right, then up to the start of a thin, slanting crack. Follow the crack to its end, and take the ramp on the right (with the aid of a high borehole) to a peg. Continue up steep rock, on good holds, to the top.

Dartmoor

The cliffs of Dartmoor are composed of coarse, firm granite. Those described here offer the best and longest climbs in sharply contrasting surroundings. The Dewerstone lies in a fairly sheltered, wooded valley and is a reasonable venue in poor weather, while Low Man and Haytor are set on open moorland and are at their best on calm, sunny days. At such times, however, Haytor must usually be shared with large numbers of tourists. The tors are reminiscent of Almscliff in Yorkshire, both in their aspect and in the aggressiveness of the climbing.

Because of their length, steepness, and strong natural lines, Dewerstone classics such as *Central Groove* and *Climbers' Club Direct* can be compared with the best routes of similar grades on Cornish granite. Climbs on the stark north-west face of Low Man are also among Devon's best.

25 *Don't Stop Now* (E2)
climber unknown SEAN KELLY

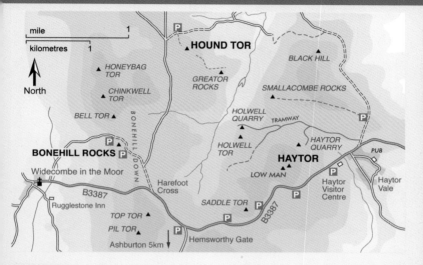

Haytor

OS Ref SX 757 771

Haytor is the very prominent rock mass just off the Bovey Tracey to Widecombe road, a few minutes walk from the large roadside car parks. It is clearly visible from the south and east, and is itself an excellent viewpoint.

Haytor abounds in good short climbs and boulder problems. The west face is the friendliest and most popular as it gets plenty of sun and offers routes of all grades. The east face has some pleasant slab climbing at D and VD standard, but the longest and finest routes are on the north face.

22 Canis HS 4b 30m

FA A J J Moulam 1952

An interesting, varied climb with little protection in the upper part. Start at some cracks just right of the north-east corner of the tor. Climb onto a rock tooth and follow cracks on the right before bearing left to a ledge on the rib. Move up to a bulge and over it on small holds to a delicate slab leading to easy ground.

23 Vandal and Ann HVS 26m

FA T W Patey and party 1959; G J Sutton, A Sutton 1955

Two fine delicate pitches, at one time quite serious but nowadays well protected with cams. The lower part of the north face consists of a huge flake split by a central chimney. The route begins by climbing the steep slab to the left of this chimney, starting below an iron spike.

    1 14m 5b Climb directly up the slab past the spike, avoiding the temptation to move left near the top. Belay beneath the rounded continuation groove.

    2 12m 5a Move awkwardly into the groove and climb it to a delicate exit, which gains the easy slabs.

115

The next route going right to the top of the tor is **North Face Chimney** (HS 4b), a challenging climb for the grade, and this is bounded on the right by an impressive steep wall:

24 Rough Diamond   E4 6a   18m

FA P Littlejohn, P O'Sullivan 1979

A sustained and technical pitch taking the deepest of the vertical cracklines in the wall. Start at a thin crack below and left of the main crack. Move up and right to the obvious sideholds. A difficult move gains the crack which is climbed to where it ends. Move up to a rounded crack above and climb this to exit on the right.

Leftwards and up the wall from the start of *Rough Diamond* is **Rough Justice** (E5 6a), a difficult and poorly protected pitch, while the thinner crack immediately right of *Rough Diamond* is **Glass Bead Game** (E5 6a), another sustained and bold piece of climbing.

The west face begins at a buttress which bulges in its upper half. In the steep lower wall of the buttress is a conspicuous slot known as the Letterbox. **Letterbox Wall** (VS 5a) climbs into this, then goes leftwards up the wall above. The steepest part of the buttress gives two more substantial climbs.

25 Don't Stop Now   E2 5c   15m

FA P Dawson 1980

Climb the vanishing crack right of the Letterbox. Then continue straight up the bulging wall above to the top.

26 Hangover   E2 5c   18m

FA J F Barry 1961

A good steep route, but harder and more serious since the loss of a couple of flakes near the top. Start at the short deep crack running up the right side of *Letterbox Wall* to the halfway break. Climb the crack and traverse left along the break for 3 metres or so until flakes lead onto the bulging wall. Make a long reach to better holds and the top.

To the right of this buttress is a wall covered in flake holds. It can be climbed almost anywhere but the easiest line is **Zig Zag** (D) which starts up the obvious rightward-sloping rake, and the best route is **Bulging Wall** (VD/S, depending on line), which wanders up the right-hand part of the wall. The various cracks and intervening buttresses further right give interesting pitches up to HVS which can be soloed, led, or top-roped according to taste.

Low Man

OS Ref SX 756 771

Low Man is 100 metres west of Haytor and from there looks insignificant, but its north-west face is the highest rock wall on the tors. As the face is approached from Haytor, the first obvious feature, above a pedestal, is **Honeymoon Corner** (S 4a), right of which is the large juggy overhang of *Outward Bound*. *Raven Gully* is the obvious break bounding the left side of the large, sheer mass of the main face.

27 Outward Bound/Raven Direct Finish   HVS   30m
FA T W Patey 1960

A combination giving two fine contrasting pitches, the first being bold and strenuous, the second delicate and exposed. Start beneath the overhang right of *Honeymoon Corner*.

1 21m 4c Climb to the roof, swing out right, and pull over on widely-spaced flakes onto a ledge. Climb the centre of the slabby face above to the stance of *Raven Gully*.

2 9m 4c From the right-hand side of the stance, climb the wall until beneath some bulges. Traverse right and step up delicately to gain easier slabs which lead to the top.

★
★ **28 Raven Gully** S 32m

FA W A Higgins, R G Higgins 1949

The original classic of the Dartmoor tors; a route of quality and character. A triangular slab is inset into the base of the gully: start at the right-hand end of this.

1 21m Climb the edge of the slab to a small ledge beneath a steep groove. Either continue up the groove or climb the slab on the left to a ledge. Continue up the chimney/groove above to a sloping terrace.

2 11m Go up the easy chimney, or climb the slab forming the outside of the block.

★★★ **29 Interrogation** E3 46m
FA F E R Cannings, P Badcock (5 pts aid) 1964; P Littlejohn (1 pt aid) 1971; FFA M Fowler 1980

A superb route giving sustained and technical climbing up the highest part of the face. Start 2 metres right of *Raven Gully*, below a faint line of weakness in the steep wall.

1 23m 6a Climb onto a rounded flake (peg) and continue straight up the wall to the obvious horizontal fault. Step left (peg) and make a hard move to enter a shallow groove. Climb the groove until it curves sharply lef; move left to gain some projecting footholds, and traverse to the stance of *Raven Gully*.

2 23m 5b/c Traverse back right and move up onto the obvious narrow ledge. Move delicately right; then climb to easier slabs leading to the top.

★★★ **30 Aviation** E1 39m
FA D Bassett, H Cornish 1961

The 'modern' classic of the tors, taking the easiest natural line up this impressive face. Start 6 metres right of *Raven Gully*, at a pedestal.

1 12m 5b From the top of the pedestal, transfer into the crack on the right and climb to a resting place in the groove. Move up a little, and then traverse delicately right, below the bulge, to a stance on the large flake. Climbing directly through the roof up to this flake is **Igneous Pig** (E3 5c).

2 27m 5a Climb the crack on the right and continue to a curious, rounded groove which leads to the easier upper slabs.

★★ **31 Rhinoceros** E3 42m
FA Pitch 1: J Collins 1968. Complete: P Littlejohn, S. Whimster 1971

A counter-diagonal to *Aviation* giving strenuous climbing on the first pitch and more open, delicate climbing on the second. Start 9 metres right of *Aviation*, at a pod-shaped crack.

1 12m 5c Climb to the bulge and pull over it with difficulty to an undercut edge which leads leftwards to a ledge. Climb directly to the belay of *Aviation*.

2 30m 5c Traverse left for 3 metres and pull into a leftward-slanting groove. Climb the groove, move right along a horizontal break to clear the bulge, and pull through onto the slab above. Climb the slab to easy-angled rock and the top.

The vicious, overhanging crack to the right of *Rhinoceros* is **Blood Lust** (E4 6b), and the next route begins where the overhangs end and some cracks slant up leftwards to a ledge.

● **32 Levitation** VS 4b 27m
FA A Powling, P Littlejohn 1967

A pleasant climb up the slabbier, right-hand part of the main face. Climb up left to the large ledge (optional belay). Move up and left to a flake, follow some discontinuous flakes straight over the bulges above, and bear left to easy ground.

30 *Aviation* **(E1)**
Jack Bradbrook   MARK DAVIES

Dartmoor Bouldering

Dartmoor is littered with tors and outcrops giving good bouldering and short pitches. The following two areas have been singled out mainly because of their proximity to Haytor.

Hound Tor (OS Ref SX 742 790)   Three miles north of Haytor and clearly visible from it, Hound Tor offers countless short climbs and boulder problems, mainly in the 'classic' grade of British 5c. It can be reached by driving towards Widecombe and taking right forks where possible to reach the National Trust car park beneath the tor (map page 115).

Hound Tor (*Top Hat*)
Jack Bradbrook   MARK DAVIES

Hound Tor   Bonehill Rocks   Combshead Tor   Cuckoo Rock   Burrator car park

Bonehill Rocks (OS Ref SX 731 775)   On the way from Haytor to Hound Tor there is even better roadside bouldering at Bonehill Rocks, reached by turning left up a narrow road after the first right fork (map page 115). Undoubtedly the most popular bouldering venue on the moor owing to its roadside location and high concentration of problems, which here range from easy grades to V11/12 (quite hard!), with some really classic problems in the British 6a to 6b grades.

Combshead Tor (OS Ref SX 586 689) and **Cuckoo Rock** (OS Ref SX 583 688)   This remote bouldering area is home to some of the finest problems in the region. They are mostly quite high so a mat and partner are recommended. A twenty-minute walk in seems to deter some visitors, but don't be put off as the bouldering is well worth it. Approach from the car parking area at the north-east end of Burrator Reservoir (OS Ref SX 568 694); there is a track most of the way.

Bonehill West   DON SARGEANT

nr Cuckoo Rock (*Hanging Flakes*)   Chris Carr   BRIAN HANNON

Bonehill Rocks (*Twin Cracks*)   Andrea Hayslop   BRIAN HANNON

The Dewerstone

OS Ref SX 536 637

Dartmoor's premier crag offering classic routes throughout the middle grades and a number of very worthwhile easy routes which are perfect for beginners.

Approach From Shaugh Bridge, eight miles north-east of Plymouth. There is parking near the bridge. Cross the Plym by a wooden footbridge and follow a path up through the woods above the river. After a quarter of a mile short crags appear on the slopes to the left, but the first rock of any size is the broken but distinct *Pinnacle Buttress*. A short distance to the right is the more continuous buttress taken by *Colonel's Arête*, and between the two is *Mucky Gully*.

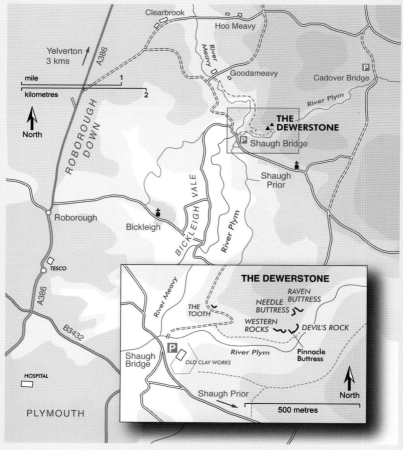

⭐ 33 Pinnacle Buttress   D   36m
FA R G Higgins, K M Higgins 1949

High in the grade on one move, but mainly on good holds and becoming open and exposed higher up. The broken buttress may be followed all the way but the start described gives more continuous interest. Start at the foot of *Mucky Gully*.

1 18m Climb *Mucky Gully* for about 12 metres until it is possible to move onto the left wall. Climb to an obvious ledge on the edge of the buttress.

2 9m Move back right around the corner and climb the wall to a large ledge beneath the pinnacle.

3 9m Make an exposed step out to the right on sloping footholds above an overhang; then move up the arête of the pinnacle and climb to its summit. From here, a bold leap can be made across to the main rock, or descend a little until the gap can be straddled. Belay on the cliff-top, not on top of the pinnacle where belays are poor.

⭐ 34 Mucky Gully   D   36m
FA Unknown, probably 1949

A very good and safe climb for beginners, much cleaner than the name suggests. Often climbed as one pitch. Start at the foot of the gully.

1 15m Climb the right wall of the gully to a stance and nut belays.

2 21m Follow the gully itself to the large chockstones. Climb onto the chockstones; then the face on the right is ascended to the top.

⭐ 35 Colonel's Arête   VD   38m
FA J L Moulton 1948

A very worthwhile route with continuous interest. Start to the left of the buttress proper, at a rightward-facing corner formed by a large, detached block to the right of *Mucky Gully*.

1 15m Climb the wide corner crack and continue direct to gain the edge of the buttress. Move up to a large ledge and belay here using the tree a little higher and the crack on the left.

2 14m Climb up to the right, past the tree, to a steep crack about 2 metres right of the arête. Climb the crack to a good jug on the right and continue up the arête, over a rocking stone, to belay beneath the final block.

3 9m Climb the outside of the block behind the tree to its summit; then cross the gap to the top.

Right of *Colonel's Arête* the cliff becomes more broken before forming the steep, sheer face of Devil's Rock, which rises to a height of 50 metres. The very obvious 30-metre-high corner of *Central Groove* splits the left side of the face.

⭐ 36 Leviathan   VS   51m
FA T W Patey 1957

The prominent, roof-capped groove in the buttress left of *Central Groove* gives an outstandingly good pitch.

1 24m 4c Climb easily to the base of the groove and follow it to the overhang. Move right around the arête and climb the wall to a ledge and tree belay.

2 27m 4b Move up and rightwards across broken rock to join the top pitch of *Central Groove*, which is followed to the top.

38 *Fruitflancase* **(E1)**
Tony Hopkins PETE SAUNDERS

37 Central Groove   HS   54m

FA J Simpson and party 1949

A magnificent route; one of the best of its grade in the South West. The big corner is continuously steep but with excellent holds and protection (medium to large nuts and cams). Start beneath the wall which leads up into the corner.

1 30m 4b Climb the wall; then follow the groove in its entirety until level with a small ledge and large block on the right arête. Move across to these and take an exposed stance with thread and nut belays.

2 24m 4b Climb easily to a ramp running up rightwards and follow it to beneath an obvious square-cut corner. Climb the corner to the top.

38 Fruitflancase E1 51m
FA A McFarlane, D Ball 1969

Excellent steep jamming up the face crack round the corner from *Central Groove*. Start as for *Central Groove*.

1 30m 5a Climb to gain the narrowing black ramp which leads up rightwards to the overhang. Climb to the overhang; then move up into the first crack on the right – the second crack is **Gideon** (E1 5b/c). Follow the crack without deviation to a good stance.

2 21m 4c Climb the crack in the wall directly above to easier ground, and finish up the short corner with a slab on its right.

39 Climbers' Club Direct HVS 51m
FA R A Hodgkin, A D M Cox 1936

A superb and impressive route taking a powerful central line up the main face of Devil's Rock. The climbing is strenuous and exposed, but technically reasonable and well protected. Start about 6 metres right of *Central Groove*, beneath a wide crack which runs through an overhang.

1 24m 5a Climb up to and over the roof strenuously and continue to a resting place. Move up and follow the crack; then step right onto a flake. Climb to the niche, and bridge up the groove above until large holds are reached on the left side of the overhang. Stance and chockstone belays above.

2 27m 5a Climb the V-chimney above to the overhang. Pull straight over this and climb the cracks above to a line of bulges. Move up left, then back right into the steep continuation crack, which leads to the top.

The very worthwhile **Climbers' Club Ordinary** (VS 4b) works an easier route around the same general line as the *Direct*, traversing in from the right above the initial crack, avoiding the overhang by moves on the right, and traversing left before the final crack to finish at the top corner of *Leviathan*.

40 Route B S 45m
FA K M Lawder, R G Higgins 1949

Uninspired at first but builds to a very special top pitch which is excitingly airy. Start to the right of the earthy gully beside Devil's Rock, beneath the centre of a large block.

1 18m Climb up and over a bulge to ledges above the block. Continue to another ledge and tree belay.

2 9m Move up and enter a shallow chimney from the right. Climb this to another tree on the right.

3 18m Climb up to the left, and move around to the edge of the main face, where the exposure hits. Climb a short groove, moving right at the overhanging nose; then bear left and climb just right of the arête to finish.

To the right of Devil's Rock (and further up the hillside) are the Upper Buttresses. Needle Buttress is the clean, narrow pillar topped by a needle of rock, while Raven Buttress is further right and is distinguished by the succession of overhangs on its front face.

★ 41 Needle Arête   VD   36m
FA J Simpson (solo) 1949

A clean, open climb following the crest of Needle Buttress. Start at the lowest point of the buttress, at a short layback crack in a subsidiary wall below the buttress.

    1 9m Climb the crack to a ledge.
    2 18m Climb slabby rock until the angle steepens and a groove just left of the arête is followed. Swing right round the corner using a prominent spike and move right to a small stance with tree and nut belays.
    3 9m Step up, move back left around the arête, and follow a groove more easily to the summit of the Needle.

★ 42 Cyclops   HVS   30m
FA F E R Cannings, B Shackleton (VL) 1964

A fine route taking the buttress to the right of *Needle Arête*. Begin above and right of *Needle Arête*, at a rib to the right of a tree.

    1 21m 4c Climb the slabby rib and traverse right to a block. Step left from the top of the block, and then climb directly via a rounded crack to a tree belay.
    2 9m 5a Climb the rounded crack above and move right to a good foothold. Steep climbing up and rightwards gains a groove, which leads more easily to the top.

Across on Raven Buttress the first climb is:

★ 43 Fly on the Wall   HS   30m
FA T W Patey 1958

A good little route with high technical interest. A steep wall, taken by **Valhalla Wall** (HVS 5a), forms the left side of Raven Buttress. The route takes an obvious curving line up the left side of this wall. Start below a small tree in a corner.

43 *Fly on the Wall* (HS)
Jez Brown
DON SARGEANT

1 15m 4b Climb past the tree into the groove and move up with difficulty to reach a slab. Climb the slab to a tree belay beside a flake.

2 15m 4a From the flake move left and climb a ramp to the overhang. Move diagonally right beneath the overhang to the rib and follow slabs to the top.

44 Spider's Web HVS 42m
FA T W Patey, B G Page, P C Henry 1959

This delicate and intricate route weaves through the overhangs on the front face of the buttress. Start at a small tree below the centre of the buttress.

1 18m 5a Climb the slab to the first overhang and traverse right to enter a smooth groove. Climb the groove for 3 metres, break left on to the slab, and continue left and up to a stance and peg belay.

2 24m 5a Climb up behind the belay and move delicately right onto a slab. Move over the right-hand side of the overlap and up the slab above to the next overhang. Traverse to the left edge of the overhang; then continue up to easier final slabs.

45 Raven Face VD 15m
FA R G Higgins 1949

A popular little route on the Upper Raven Buttress, starting from a saddle which is reached by scrambling up to the left of *Fly on the Wall* to reach a line of flakes and ledges leading rightwards to the notch. Start from the highest point of the saddle. Climb a series of slabs and bulges to a crack beneath the left end of the prominent overhang. Traverse right across the slab beneath the overhang and finish up an easy, open chimney.

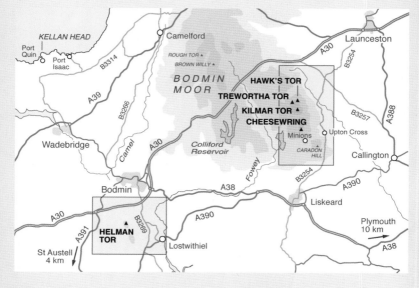

Cheesewring Quarry

OS Ref SX 258 724

High on the southern slopes of Bodmin Moor, and overlooking the old tin-mining hamlet of Minions is the 30-metre-high granite Cheesewring Quarry. Featuring easy access from either the A30 or the A38, it provides a convenient and accessible stopping-off point, as well as a venerable climbing site in its own right. The huge TV aerial of Caradon Hill a few kilometres to the south provides a long-range marker.

In recent years, local climbers turned their attention to rejuvenating this site and regearing many of the climbs. That work, coupled with a strong historical pedigree and a spread of clean routes of contrasts, has enabled Cheesewring Quarry to rank with the best of the South West's inland cliffs. It provides a mix of traditional climbs from the 1960s and well-bolted sport climbs, some of which started life as aid routes. While bursting with character, the traditional climbs can prove fairly serious since natural protection in the compact granite is limited and often spaced. The climbs described here are amongst the better protected.

Cheesewring Quarry is a south-facing suntrap, but it's no easy business gripping its smooth granite slopers and crimps when the summer's sun is full on! In winter, or after prolonged rainfall, the central part of the main face in particular can seep profusely and is best avoided. Only the truly courageous (or reckless) will try to climb here in wet conditions.

Approach Park in a large car park in Minions where a road branches north-east to Henwood. The car park is 100 metres from a tall stone building and chimney (an old engine house in which tin ore was ground). The Cheesewring, a squat tower of granite blocks balancing close to the quarry's edge, is signposted from the car park. Follow the track from a locked gate beside a cottage in a north-easterly direction. On nearing the quarry, skirt round a fenced-off area of collapsed mine shafts and return to the track which leads into the quarry – a kilometre's walk.

The quarry is dominated by an expansive 30-metre-high main face, with smaller walls either side. The right-facing groove system in the left-hand side of the face is the line of *Simanon Direct*. In the centre of the main face is an impending black bay (home for *Psychokiller*), with the tall arêtes of *Dead Exit* and *Reñe* either side. The right-hand side of the main face is set back in the form of a bay, which is one of the most popular parts of the quarry since it offers a choice of easier climbs which are clean and generally adequately protected.

50 *Eyefull Tower* (E2)
Shane Ohly BARNY CARVER

Left of the main face, and in the eastern side of the quarry, is a sheer leaning wall bristling with bolts. The wall provides a refuge from the sun and a number of sport testpieces, and one top quality nut-protected route up a striking corner-line immediately to its right.

46 Double Agent F7a 12m
FA A Grieve 1993

Recognized as the finest route on the wall though it was not its first. Start in the centre of the wall, about 3 metres left of the corner. Climb steeply and slightly rightwards to a thin break. Move right and continue on increasingly small holds to an abseil station on the left.

The abseil station is shared by **Agent Provocateur** (F7b), a counter-line to *Double Agent* which starts to its right before climbing the headwall to its left.

47 Trouble with Lichen E3 6a 12m
FA M Dunning, T Mason 1975 (aided as *Summer Soldier*);
FFA A Grieve 1985

Brilliant. The smooth corner; intense and sustained. Microwires essential.

46 *Double Agent* (F7a) Dave Talbot HENRY CASTLE

To the right is an overhanging arête with two bolt-lines; that on the right is the much fallen-off **Tag** (F7b). Right again is the stepped arête of **Direct Route** (VS 4a) a virtually unprotected climb. At the extreme left end of the main face, starting halfway up the boulder slope, is a narrow corner:

141

The Cheesewring

Descent
gully

⭐ **48 The Purple Revrac** HS 4b 15m

FA P H Stanier, J Burley (AL) 1969

A reliable and amiable introduction to the quarry. Reach the base of the corner via the short walls and a groove, and climb it to the top.

The bare wall to the right is home to a cluster of routes in the sports mould.

⭐ **49 Simanon Direct** HVS 35m
⭐
FA W A Carver, R J Grose 1967

A classic climb of character that requires a very steady leader and expert double rope-work. It takes the groove 20 metres from the left-hand end of the face, unmistakable thanks to a 2-metre length of rusty chain hanging from it (not climber-placed!).

1 25m 4c Climb the groove to the chain and make hard moves alongside it to its anchor (uncomfortable stance possible). Move up the corner, and traverse right along a ledge for 4 metres. Enter a little groove awkwardly (welcome good wire), and traverse boldly back left before pulling up to a large ledge.

2 10m 4a Swing up and right, and hand-traverse a jug-rail leftwards to pull round to startled tourists under the Cheesewring.

★ 50 Eyefull Tower E2 30m
FA W A Carver, R J Grose, P H Stanier (2 pts aid) 1967; FFA N Hancock 1986

A great route with reasonable protection; as good a line as you'll find in any quarry. Much harder with any dampness on pitch 2. Start at a short, left-facing corner underneath a tall white arête (*Dead Exit*).

1 12m 5a Climb the corner to its top and, using the hand-width crack on the right, swing left onto a recessed ledge containing an iron spike (which can be backed up with nuts/cams in a borehole).

2 18m 6a Follow the groove past another iron spike, move left onto a rib, and step back right under a small overhang (good wires available). Pull round the overhang, and then take the slabby black ramp to the top, passing a bolt and a threadable borehole.

The smooth black corner left of *Eyefull Tower* is taken by one of the quarry's premier natural lines: **Bored of the Wrings** (E5 6a), a very delicate and nervy route that joins its neighbour at the overhang. Right of the arête of **Dead Exit** (E4 5c) is the groove of **High Noon** (E3 5c) that moves left to a bolt belay on the arête before finishing over an overhang – now less appealing given that a vital peg and a key hold have dropped off.

The next two routes take the back of the impending black bay in the centre of the face, starting from ledges 6 metres up.

★ 51 Real Live Wire F7b 20m
FA A Grieve 1993

A real battle. Climb a slim groove, using flake holds on the left, and step left across a diminutive slab. From a resting place above, fling yourself up a slick black ramp, clipping the bolts whenever you get chance. Abseil station.

★ 52 Pyschokiller F7c 20m
FA S Mayers 1988

Possibly Cornwall's best hard sport route. Superb, especially now it has been rebolted with stainless steel staples. Work up the smooth grey face and enter a hanging triangular niche. Powerful moves straight above lead to an abseil station.

Immediately right is **Wring the Changes** (F7b+), which was rebolted in 2013. The right-hand arête of the bay is climbed by **Reñe** (E4 6a), a serious lead, though with absorbing moves between its two bolts.

The steep wall to the right, which contains sport and trad routes, is prone to moss growth, though the following route, its best, stays clean.

★ 53 Warrior F6c 18m
FA L Benstead, S Chadwick (aid) 1970; FFA A Grieve 1988

A fast-paced route. Start at a borehole right of the arête of *Reñe*. Climb a short thin crack and gain a small ledge on the left. Take the slight groove to an abseil station.

The right-hand side of the face forms a large bay, with a grooved arête high on the left – this is the line of the following climb. Its first pitch as far as the huge scoop known as The Fortress is **Traitor's Gate** (VS 4a), a very poorly protected pitch, which can be finished up either corner behind.

52 *Psychokiller* (F7c)   Tom Rainbow   KEN PALMER

54   Khyber Wall   E2 5c   30m
FA L Benstead, D Morrod (aid) 1970; FFA A Grieve 1986

The spectacular grooved arête; safer than it once was since a couple of crucial old pegs have been replaced by bolts, and wires go in too. Start in the open corner between the mossy wall of *Warrior* and the right-hand bay.

   1 18m 4a Climb a flake crack, and then hop leftwards up grassy ledges before a short brown groove and hollow flake lead to the right-hand edge of the Fortress, and block belays under the grooved arête.
   2 12m 5c Stretch to clip a bolt in the groove and, using good holds on the left wall, improvise up to an overhang (passing a second bolt). A crack on the left aids a strenuous move straight up the tip of the arête (peg) to a mantel exit.

The remaining four climbs are located in the bay in the right-hand side of the main face.

55   Juliet's Balcony   HVS   28m
FA W A Carver, S Bramble 1967

A delightful climb, having an exciting, thought-provoking crux. It takes the clean orange slab in the bay. Start at the left-hand end of a sloping pink rock-ledge in the left-hand side of the bay.

   1 10m 4b Take an interesting line left of a break to a ledge under the slab.
   2 18m 5a Starting in the centre of the slab, follow the line of small steps and breaks diagonally rightwards to reach the top right-hand corner of the slab (peg runner out left). Gain the 'balcony' up to the right and finish on bigger holds.

56   The Lemon Tree   HS 4b   30m
FA P H Stanier, W A Carver 1965

Pleasantly meandering though the crux move could slow you down a while. Start on the sloping pink rock ledge in the left-hand side of the bay. Follow the break of stepped ledges rightwards for 15 metres to its end. Step right, past a flake crack (optional stance), and trend rightwards across a short wall (peg) to a flake (thread). Move left and climb past a borehole to the top.

⭐ 57 Thorndyke VS 4c 25m

FA W A Carver, P H Stanier 1965

Good rock and a fairly direct line, though the protection is spaced above half height. Start under a narrow, left-facing corner in the centre of the bay. Climb the corner and trend rightwards to the left end of a detached block sitting on a long ledge. (So far this is pitch 1 of **Peter** (VD), which belays on the ledge and finishes up a broken corner on the right.) Follow a tricky groove slightly on the left; then climb rightwards up a final slab.

58 Sunset Arête VS 4c 15m

FA D Morrod 1972

This is the steep arête of the bright orange-red wall at the right-hand end of the main face. Climb the arête, step out right, and follow its right-hand side to the top, taking care with the rock.

54 *Khyber Wall* **(E2)**
Matthew Thompson   MARK DAVIES

Bodmin Moor

Bodmin Moor has its own unique charm and provides climbing very different from that found on the granite of Dartmoor. Although a smattering of bouldering and a few routes are found at Rough Tor (OS Ref SX 145 808), the highest concentration of climbing is in the area around Kilmar Tor.

The Trewortha Area

Approach   Leave the A30 at Launceston and follow the B3254 towards Liskeard. Carry straight over at a crossroad junction and on to the hamlet of Middlewood. Turn right into a small lane just after the bridge (over the River Lynher), which is followed for about one mile to its termination at a gate. Parking space on the right (OS Ref 253 758). As you look down the continuation track from the car park, Hawk's Tor is the first on the right (do not approach directly – go down the track and then right, following a wall); Trewortha Tor the second on the right. To the left is the long ridge of Kilmar Tor, and over the other side of this (not visible) is Bearah Tor, home to limited bouldering and a few routes (maps pages 138 and 139).

Hawk's Tor

OS Ref SX 253 764

Hawk's Tor has the highest concentration of routes of all the Bodmin Moor tors and, although these are mostly short, they do pack a punch. There are lines along the tor ranging from Diff to E4; the most obvious is:

59 TDK   E3 6b   11m
FA A Grieve, K Palmer 1986

The brutal roof crack at the left-hand end of the crag provides a safe but testing challenge.

Trewortha Tor

OS Ref SX 246 759

Trewartha Tor is home to the best HVS on Bodmin Moor and a range of interesting bouldering. You are unlikely to meet other climbers here and the place has a special remote charm. The following two routes are found at the eastern end (the right side as seen from the approach) of the tor, on the most obvious 11-metre wall; the approach leads to the top of this.

★ **60** **Just Good Friends** HVS 5a 11m
★ FA M Rescorle, A Grieve 1995
A little treat up the centre of the wall. Some tricky moves to gain the first break are followed by very pleasant climbing up the flakes above.

60 *Just Good Friends* (HVS)
Richard Hudson   BARNEY CARVER

⭐ **61   Merlin**   E6 6b   11m
FA D Henderson 2000

Start up a short crack on the left to gain the first rounded break. Arrange gear; then move out and stretch up to some slopers (the lower half of the next break). Precarious moves lead into the third break (large cams). The technical crux remains – make your way out of the break, move up on undercuts, and stretch for a very rounded finish.

Kilmar Tor

OS Ref SX 252 749

Kilmar Tor offers a selection of climbable features spread along its length and on the boulders below. The main attraction is found on the Western Turret (furthest from car park!) where the following two routes are found on the overhanging north-facing wall:

⭐ **62   Special Llama**   E5 6a   11m
FA K Palmer, C Rees 1990

The central line may well require an abseil clean prior to an attempt but this little gem is worth the effort. Climb the centre of the face to a finish via a small flake.

⭐ **63   Sleepy Hollow**   E2 5b   11m
FA S Hawken, M Rescorle 1995

A steep overhanging line on the right. Start by a small corner, move right, and climb the wall above on excellent holds to finish.

Helman bouldering
(*Ice Cream Soldiers*)
Tom Last   LAST col

Helman Tor

OS Ref SX 061 617

Helman Tor lies about ten minutes from the A30 near Bodmin, making it an extremely convenient stop-off on the route west. There is a good selection of bouldering at all grades from 5a to 6c and also a couple of testing routes for which a rope will be useful.

Approach From the big road junction to the west of Bodmin where the A30 meets the A391, turn left towards Bugle for 400 metres, and take the first left before turning almost immediately right towards Luxulyan. Follow this road until a left for Helman Tor is signed, then another sharp left when you get to a junction. Carry on down the road for a few hundred metres until a right turn, up a narrow lane, leads to the tor and a car park.

The lower part of the tor contains the highest face, taken by:

64 Bloody Helman E4 6a 9m
FA S Hawken, A Grieve 1995

Another 'small but perfectly formed' Bodmin classic. Climb directly up the centre of the face past two small flakes to a tricky, rounded finish.

65 Hell's Tooth E2 5c 9m
FA I Parnell, S Hawken 1995

Climb the rib to the right of *Bloody Helman*: bold to start and moving left to finish.

153

The Culm Coast

Extending from Clovelly in North Devon to Bude Haven in North Cornwall is a unique series of cliffs composed of sedimentary rock having the local name of 'culm'. The culms are actually beds of more resistant, metamorphosed rock which have been upended by folding, and which project out to sea from the general cliff mass. Where the culms meet the coast obliquely they form overlapping slabs, as at Blackchurch and Cornakey, while Lower Sharpnose is a classic example of super-resistant culms set approximately on the vertical and therefore able to remain standing although their surroundings have eroded away.

The west-facing coast from Hartland Point southwards is particularly remote and beautiful. With miles of cliffs, sandy beaches and quiet coves it is an inspiring place to climb, and although the climbing is serious many of the crags are surprisingly friendly and can offer sheltered, sunny climbing even in mid-winter.

Culm cannot be treated like gritstone or Cornish granite and some experience and competence is required to climb safely here. The larger sizes of nuts and cams will be found particularly useful on the cracklines, while microwires give surprisingly good security on some of the open slabs.

5 *Sacré Cœur* (E2)
James Mitchell   DON SARGEANT

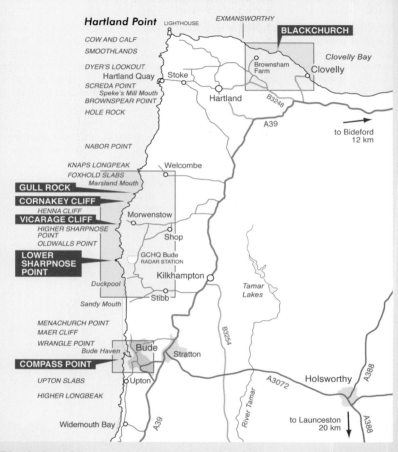

Hartland Point LIGHTHOUSE

COW AND CALF
SMOOTHLANDS
DYER'S LOOKOUT
Hartland Quay
SCREDA POINT
Speke's Mill Mouth
BROWNSPEAR POINT
HOLE ROCK

NABOR POINT

KNAPS LONGPEAK
FOXHOLD SLABS
Marsland Mouth

GULL ROCK
CORNAKEY CLIFF
HENNA CLIFF
VICARAGE CLIFF
HIGHER SHARPNOSE
POINT
OLDWALLS POINT

**LOWER
SHARPNOSE
POINT**

Duckpool
Sandy Mouth

MENACHURCH POINT
MAER CLIFF
WRANGLE POINT
Bude Haven
COMPASS POINT

UPTON SLABS
HIGHER LONGBEAK

Widemouth Bay

EXMANSWORTHY
BLACKCHURCH
Clovelly Bay
Brownsham
Farm
Clovelly
Stoke
Hartland
B3248
A39
to Bideford
12 km

Welcombe
Morwenstow
Shop
GCHQ Bude
RADAR STATION
Kilkhampton
Tamar
Lakes
Stibb
Bude
Stratton
B3254
Upton
Holsworthy
River Tamar
A3072
A388
to Launceston
20 km
A39
A388

Blackchurch

OS Ref SS 298 267

An imposing crag with magnificent rock architecture, somewhat reminiscent of the West Buttress of Cloggy in appearance. The routes on the main cliff are long and serious, having their share of dubious rock and protection. A gloomy northerly aspect heightens this air of commitment but on the routes described the quality of line and impressive situations make up for other shortcomings. In contrast, the single pitch routes on Blackchurch Rock are perfectly solid and well protected, and worth a visit in their own right.

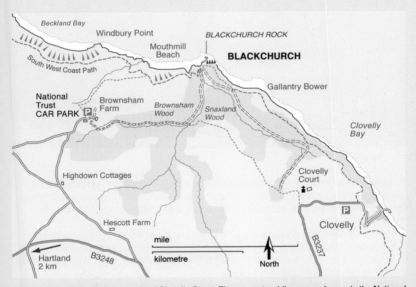

The cliff lies in the private grounds of Clovelly Court. The nearest public access by car is the National Trust car park at Brownsham Farm (OS Ref 286 259), from which a pleasant walk down a forestry track leads to the crag in about half an hour. Only the routes on Blackchurch Rock are seriously affected by tides, other routes being more or less non tidal.

Approach   From the car park, walk down to Lower Brownsham Farm and turn right on the bridleway signposted to Mouthmill. After five minutes or so, bear right at an offset crossroads in the track; then a left turn at the next junction takes you straight down the valley to the rocky cove of Mouthmill. The cliffs are to the east (to the right when facing the sea) of the cove.

157

1   The Verger   E1   83m
FA K Darbyshire, P Buttrick 1974

Despite being somewhat loose and vegetated, this is a 'classic' of the cliff – a splendid route with varied climbing and airy situations. The centrepiece of the crag is a massive smooth slab; the route follows its left edge and starts up the obvious wide crack, left of the big rubble cone which abuts the cliff.

   1 26m 4c Climb over grassy ledges to reach the crack, which begins thin and awkward, then widens to give easier climbing to a good stance (belay on medium cam in slot).
   2 14m 4c Start in a small groove to the left of the belay and climb direct on good but creaky holds to reach a superb stance in a recess.
   3 43m 5a Traverse right to a steep crack and follow it to a small ledge. Continue for 5 metres; then bear left across the overhangs to larger holds on the arête. Climb steadily up the arête to the top.

2   Loose Woman   E1   51m
FA I Duckworth, W Chevrest (aid) 1969; FFA K Darbyshire 1974

The first route on the crag and originally aided – now a worthy climb on solid rock, taking the obvious straight crack at the top of the central rubble cone. The crux can be perfectly protected.
   1 21m 4c Climb the crack to a belay on the left.
   2 18m 5b Climb up into the corner on the right and continue to the roof. Strenuous moves past this gain better holds and a stance.
   3 12m Finish up the loose slab above.

3   The Archtempter   E3   54m
FA P Littlejohn, G Skerratt 1970

One of the great lines of the Culm Coast –
the towering groove which bounds on the
left the smooth triangular slab at the
right-hand end of the cliff. The rock is
reasonable but some holds should not be
used too heavily. On pitch 2 the peg
protection may be supplemented with small
wires and cams, and several large hexes or
cams should be carried for the wide crack
of pitch 3. Below the line a grass ramp rises
from the left into a short chimney.

  1 9m Climb to the chimney and up it
  to a small grass ledge at the foot of the
  groove. Belay here or continue.
  2 24m 5c Climb the groove to a
  bulge (peg), pull steeply round, and
  continue up the groove (two further
  pegs) until harder climbing gains a
  small sloping stance.
  3 21m 5b Climb steeply to the
  overhang. Pull round into the upper
  corner, which gives strenuous climbing
  until difficulties ease near the top and the
  right arête is used for the last few moves.

The right arête of *Archtempter's* groove is
taken by **Lord Bafta** (E5 6a, 6a), an excellent
route (when clean) protected by *in situ* pegs.
Immediately to its right the thin crack in the
face is taken by **Godspell** (E4 6a), another
superb route when thoroughly clean.

1 *The Verger* (E1)
climbers unknown ·DON SARGEANT

Blackchurch Rock

Set in front of the western end of the crag is a pyramid-like foreshore stack whose seaward face
gives excellent climbing on a steep open slab of perfect rock. It is accessible from low to mid tide.

4   Rite of Spring   VS 4c   27m
FA P Littlejohn, P H Biven, A Chadwick, J Hammond 1970

A pleasant route taking the shallow corner which bounds the slab on the left. Climb the corner.

5   Sacré Cœur   E2 5c   34m
FA P Littlejohn, H Clarke 1974

Sheer delight; one of the finest (and most photographed) climbs on this coast. It takes the most
obvious line of thin cracks, towards the left side of the smooth slab. Climb to the slot at
6 metres, move left to the main crack, and follow it until it becomes vague. Move right to some
hairline cracks and climb directly to the summit of the Rock.

★★ **6　Jamaican Dub**　E3　6a　30m
FA P O'Sullivan, P Bingham, J Thompson 1981

Another sustained and intricate slab pitch protected by small wires. Start at a thin crack 5 metres right of *Sacré Cœur*. Climb the crack to a bulge, and surmount this to gain a line of thin cracks, which are followed for 8 metres. Step right to another crack leading to the finish of *Notre Dame*.

★ **7　Notre Dame**　VS　4b　40m
FA K Darbyshire, D Garner 1974

Climbs the stepped arête which bounds the slab on the right. Pleasant and exposed but a little short on protection. Start at the obvious weakness right of the arête. Gain the arête and follow it to a ledge 5 metres from the top. Either continue up the arête or take the crack on the left (easier) to finish.

There are boulder problems and short pitches either side of the pebble beach at Mouthmill, most notably **Eraser Blade** (E1 5a) a knife edge fin on the main cliff side.

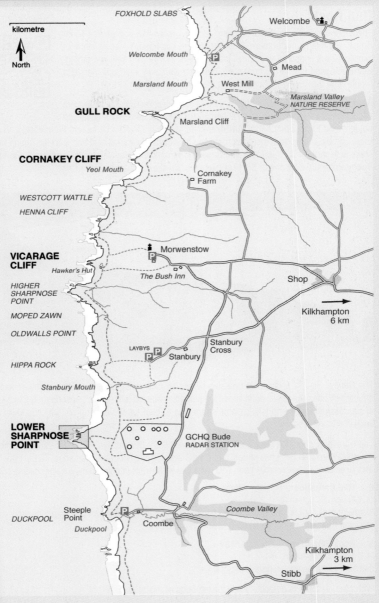

FOXHOLD SLABS

Welcome

kilometre

North

Welcombe Mouth

Mead

Marsland Mouth

West Mill

Marsland Valley
NATURE RESERVE

GULL ROCK

Marsland Cliff

CORNAKEY CLIFF

Yeol Mouth

Cornakey
Farm

WESTCOTT WATTLE

HENNA CLIFF

**VICARAGE
CLIFF**

Morwenstow

Hawker's Hut

The Bush Inn

Shop

*HIGHER
SHARPNOSE
POINT*

Kilkhampton
6 km

MOPED ZAWN

OLDWALLS POINT

LAYBYS

Stanbury
Cross

Stanbury

HIPPA ROCK

Stanbury Mouth

**LOWER
SHARPNOSE
POINT**

GCHQ Bude
RADAR STATION

DUCKPOOL

Steeple
Point

Coombe Valley

Duckpool

Coombe

Kilkhampton
3 km

Stibb

Gull Rock

OS Ref SS 207 172

There are several venues for relaxing, easier grade climbing on the Culm Coast, and this is one of them. It features single-pitch, south-facing slabs of excellent rock peppered with small incuts, sandy coves, and safe swimming. Gull Rock itself is a large, tidal stack between Cornakey Cliff and Marsland Mouth, and the climbing is on the long promontory running out to it.

Approach   The best plan is to time your visit around low tide (all routes are accessible for at least three hours either side of low tide, some for longer) and boulder-hop to the point either from Marsland Mouth or Welcombe beach. Alternatively, to allow more climbing time, take the coast path to Litter Mouth Waterfall and abseil to the beach from a stake just north of it. This takes you down the remarkable 'Baywatch Wall', which is climbed by **Booby Prize** (E6 6b), one of the best pitches of its standard on the Culm Coast.

Welcombe Mouth

Approach

The Central Slab is a clean, impressive sweep of rock rising above a ledge which is scarcely affected by tides. An abseil point above the slab (towards the left) enables several routes to be done in succession. It is worth taking some spare tape to back up the existing tat, which is likely to be weakened by the sun.

There are three good little routes on shorter slabs left of the Central Slab: **Popadom** (VS 4b) climbs the most seaward slab (which is almost a pinnacle) keeping just left of the right edge. To the right, Inset Slab rises above a perfect rock pool. This gives two worthwhile pitches up the parallel slanting cracks:

⭐**8   Red Carnation** HS 4b 21m
FA B Rossiter, P O'Sullivan 1984
Excellent rock, holds, and protection. Traverse left to gain the left-hand crack and follow it, stepping right into its continuation 6 metres from the top.

9   Rock Pool Crack HS 4b 18m
FA C Nicholson, A. Gallagher 1980
Pleasant climbing up the right-hand crack.

With care, descent is possible down the left edge of this slab, or abseil.

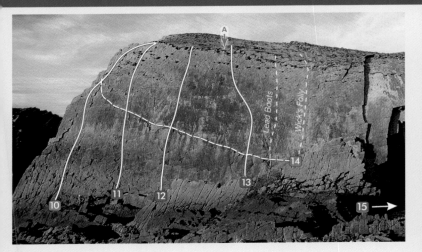

Central Slab

⭐ **10 Seaward Edge** S 4a 27m
FA Unknown

This route follows the crackline some two metres in from the left edge of the Central Slab. Start at the left end of the ledge which runs beneath the slab. Follow the line of cracks for 15 metres; then move up to holds on the stepped arête and climb rightwards to the top, using the arête.

⭐ **11 Solid Air** VS 4b 24m
FA S Chadwick 1973

An interesting pitch with more holds than are apparent from below. Start 6 metres in from the left edge, below an obvious quartz patch. Climb to the quartz and continue straight up to gain a narrow shelf. Step left and up onto another shelf, step back right, and climb direct on widely spaced holds to the top.

⭐ **12 Crazy Streak** HVS 5a 24m
FA I M Peters, G A Jenkin 1981

Fine technical climbing straight up the middle of the slab. Start below a prominent peg about 10 metres up in the centre of the slab. Climb slightly rightwards up a thin crack to reach the peg. Continue in a direct line on well-spaced holds to the top.

⭐ **13 Walking on the Moon** HVS 5a 24m
FA C Nicholson, A Gallagher 1980

A delightful pitch – perhaps the best on the slab. Start about 5 metres left of the shallow corner which bounds the slab on the right. Climb straight up, keeping left of a quartzy patch at 6 metres, until it is possible to move up and left to a narrow ledge (peg – sometimes absent but there is a small wire to the left). Sustained climbing straight up the slab gains the top.

Between *Walking on the Moon* and the shallow corner is **Lead Boots** (E1 5b), which climbs up to a prominent peg and then left above it. The corner itself gives **Wicks' Folly** (VS 4c).

13 *Walking on the Moon* (HVS)
Tom Thorpe   JAMES MANN

14 Magical Staircase S 37m

FA T Colter, S Chadwick 1973

Start at *Wicks' Folly* and follow the obvious gangway which rises across the slab from right to left, passing a prominent peg halfway. Nice situations at the grade.

Landward of Central Slab is a vegetated slab crossed by a ramp (which can be used for a cautious descent). To the right of this is a smooth, inset slab providing the next route. It is the last area to become sea-washed on a rising tide.

15 Haile Selassie E2 5c 24m

FA I M Peters, P O'Sullivan 1984

An immaculate, sustained pitch with just adequate protection (small wires and cams). Follow the continuous thin crack towards the left side of the slab. At the top use belays at the far side of the ridge.

Cornakey Cliff

OS Ref SS 203 165

Cornakey is one of the biggest culm cliffs and provides one of the South West's truly classic climbs. Though sheltered and sunny, the crag is serious as high tide cuts off the approach and the awesome slopes of Yeol Mouth offer no easy escape in case of rain or mishap. The structure of the crag is typical of many on this coast – overlapping slabs with steep intervening walls – but the rock is generally too loose and vegetated to appeal to current tastes. Exceptions are *Wreckers' Slab* (which gets many ascents) and the shorter routes on the Nose – a clean, concave wall whose base is traversed on the approach.

Gull Rock

16 17

18

Approach From the National Trust car park at Morwenstow, walk north on the coast path (above the awesome 150-metre precipice of Henna Cliff) until the huge overlapping slabs of Cornakey Cliff come into view. Descent is by the rocky ridge running down the seaward (northern) edge of the crag, and from low to half tide the cliff base can be easily reached along a boulder beach. At higher tides the boulders are covered and approach (or escape) is made by traversing the seaward slab: **The Nose** (S). This becomes impossible in high seas.

The following two climbs are on the Nose, and could be picked off on the way to *Wreckers' Slab*.

16 Stormy Weather   HVS 5a   24m
FA P O'Sullivan, K Tole 1984
Start 3 metres right of the seaward arête of the Nose. Easy climbing leads to a slanting break. Trend diagonally right to a large flat foothold; then climb the deep cracks above to the top. Belay well back.

17 Sunday Bloody Sunday   E2 5c   24m
FA P O'Sullivan, K Tole 1984
Excellent climbing up the thin crack in the face right of *Stormy Weather*. Start below a scoop at 6 metres. Climb to the scoop (peg), and then up and left to reach the thin crack, which leads to a good foothold on the right. Difficult moves up a thinner crack gain good holds and the top. Belay well back.

18 Wreckers' Slab   VS 4b   120m
FA T W Patey, J H Deacon, K M Lawder 1959
A wonderful outing, having the scale and qualities of a mountain route but in a coastal setting. It climbs the tall, slender slab furthest from the sea. The grade reflects the situation and former looseness – today it barely warrants 4b and the rock is generally solid. Several pegs are in place for protection and belays. Start at the left-hand side of the narrow base of the slab and climb bearing left for some 18 metres to a stance on the edge. Continue to the top in three more pitches, following a shattered crack in the centre of the slab for the most part, and then keeping left on solid rock and excellent holds for the final 30 metres.

left: 18 *Wreckers' Slab* (VS)
Nolan Smyth   PETE SAUNDERS

167

22 *Box of Delights* (HS)
Sam Beaton   MARK DAVIES

Vicarage Cliff

OS Ref SS 197 152

Arguably the most friendly and relaxing of all the Culm Coast's climbing venues, Vicarage Cliff is a long, jagged promontory of solid culm whose south face is seamed with cracks and generously supplied with holds and protection. With plenty of routes in the lower and middle grades it is suitable for less experienced parties, and it also features one very fine harder climb.

Approach   From the National Trust car park at Morwenstowe (where the Rectory Tearooms serve prize cream teas in summer), walk to the coast path, turn south past Hawker's Hut, and in less than ten minutes reach the little stream of Tidna Shute, which drops down into the broad boulder cove containing the cliff. A fisherman's path descends the southern side of the cove. It is steep and slippery and best negotiated by fixing a rope (stake in place). The base of the cliff is accessible for about 3½ hours either side of low tide, giving plenty of climbing time.

Descent from the routes is generally by abseil (there are several fixed points along the top of the promontory), but it is also possible to climb down the far side of the promontory and walk back around it.

19 Pandora   HS 4b   18m
FA P O'Sullivan, M Dunning, D Sargeant 1985
A lovely, varied little climb taking the bottomless, sea-facing groove at the left end of the promontory. Climb up to gain the groove from the right. Follow it for 4 metres; then step right around the arête to a crack leading to the top.

20 Sunstruck   VS 4c   21m
FA B R E Wilkinson, P Wilcox 1989
Start as for *Pandora* and trend right to a point halfway along the leftward-slanting overlap. Pull through and climb the crack above.

24 *Sol* (S)
Dan Barnett   MARK DAVIES

★★ **21 Little Dribbler**   HVS 5a   21m
FA P O'Sullivan, M Dunning 1985

Starting 2 metres right of *Pandora*, follow the continuous thin crack system which runs up and through the overlap to arrive at the left side of a prominent pancake of rock near the cliff-top. Sustained.

★★★ **22 Box of Delights**   HS 4b   21m
FA P O'Sullivan, M Dunning 1985

A perfect little climb which takes the crack that cuts through the highest point of the overlap and finishes just right of the 'pancake'. Start by climbing the face just right of the crack until it can be gained and then followed.

★★ **23 Tombstone**   S 4a   21m
FA C Stripp, D Hillebrandt 1986

Another fine little route at the grade which follows the pronounced crackline going through the lowest point of the overlap (5 metres to the right of *Box of Delights*). The crux is moving past the overlap.

★ **24 Sol**   S   21m
FA B R E Wilkinson, P Wilcox 1989

Pleasant climbing up the cracks immediately to the right of the lowest point of the overlap. Good holds and protection all the way.

26 *Spotted Dick* (S)
Dan Barnett MARK DAVIES

25 *Wellington's Stand* (VS)
Martin Koscis   DAN LANE

25 Wellington's Stand VS 4c 21m
FA R Cope, M Dunning, P O'Sullivan 1985

The furthest right crack system on this wall is a deeper crack running up to a downward-pointing spike at the overlap. Follow this most enjoyably.

A prominent feature in the centre of the cliff is the huge poised block of Vicarage Tower. The cleft running up its left side was the first route ever to be recorded on culm – **Vicarage Tower** (VD) in 1957. It is a bit loose and rattly, and a better route takes the front face of the Tower:

26 Spotted Dick S 24m
FA B R E Wilkinson, M Grapes 1992

Not destined for longevity perhaps, but worth doing while it lasts. Climb the blocky lower wall, pull through onto the face of the tower, and climb it past several curious spots. Belay on top of the Tower. Climb down the back to escape.

27 Harpoon E2 5b 24m
FA B R E Wilkinson, P Wilcox 1989

Impeccable rock and climbing up the concave slab to the right of Vicarage Tower. Start just right of a prominent arête and follow thin cracks past a small overlap to a hidden spike runner (for tape) on the arête at 11 metres. Continue to another overlap, move left, and ascend the concave slab with difficulty (peg) to the top.

Lower Sharpnose Point

OS Ref SS 195 128

Generally considered to be the best crag on the Culm Coast. The rock is top quality culm and there are excellent routes in a range of grades, from classic cracks and corners to modern wall climbs which stand comparison with any in the country.

The structure of the cliffs is remarkable. Three narrow fins of rock project westwards from the general coastline and present sheer north and south faces. The Middle Fin is the most striking, being up to 40 metres high, 60 metres wide, and less than 2 metres thick! The fins are natural windbreaks and make sheltered climbing possible in nearly all weathers, and because the faces take no drainage they dry very quickly, especially the south sides.

Approach On the headland above the cliff is a huge 'listening station', where clusters of tracker discs stand in a high-security compound. These can be seen from miles around. There is limited parking at the metal gate a few hundred metres north of the compound (just past a row of houses). Walk across the disused airfield to join the coast path at the seaward corner of the perimeter fence. The path soon swings seawards and begins to descend gently to some grassy hollows above the crag. An alternative approach is to follow the coast path northwards from the car park at Duckpool – this is slightly longer but more straightforward.

Easy descents exist to the south of the South Fin and north of the North Fin, although after half tide, when the sea prevents one from moving around the promontories, many climbs can be reached by abseil as those nearest the shore are only sea-washed for a couple of hours around high tide.

LOWER SHARPNOSE POINT

North Fin ~ North Face

The smoothest and most compact of all the big faces is somewhat forbidding for much of the year because of its northerly aspect, but nevertheless has superb rock quality.

28 The Devonian E5 6a 34m

FA S Monks, J Wilkinson 1987

Start at a thin crack left of the diagonal quartz break which runs up rightwards to the base of the obvious wide crack of *Mascon*. Climb the crack to gain the rightward-ascending break and follow this more easily to a peg. Climb up and over the bulge and continue straight up the wall above, past another peg, to the top.

29 Mascon E1 29m

FA P Littlejohn, H Clarke 1972

The obvious crack near the right edge of the wall – a good steep route having something of the flavour of *Cemetery Gates*. Start from a large block beside the arête.

  1 9m 4c Follow cracks diagonally left until steep moves gain a spacious ledge.

  2 20m 5a Traverse left across the steep wall to the crack and follow it (strenuous but with good protection) to the top.

North Fin ~ South Face

Excellent climbing, some of it not too fierce, makes this the most popular of the faces. The wall is bounded on the left by the corner of **Hatchet** (HVS 5a), while the most obvious weakness, a leftward-rising traverse-line, is taken by *The Smile*.

30 Diamond Smiles E4 5c 34m
FA C Nicholson, N White 1984

A real gem. Low in the grade but still a powerful lead. Start a couple of metres right of a diagonal crack running up left to the corner of *Hatchet*. Follow the line of least resistance up the quartz-seamed wall, past a remarkable crystal-lined crack, to gain the traverse of *The Smile*. Follow this leftwards almost to the niche; then break rightwards across the wall to a peg. Continue steeply to the top on better holds.

SOUTH FIN

High tide escape routes

BABY FIN NORTH FIN MIDDLE FIN

Hatchet

Wraith

30   31   32

33 *Lunakhod* (HVS)
Alice Martin PETE SAUNDERS

31 The Smile E1 5a 37m
FA P Littlejohn, S Jones 1971

A sustained and strenuous pitch which builds up to an exhilarating finale on the headwall. Very well protected if a large rack is carried. However, rope drag can be severe near the top and should be reduced with long slings. Start below the right-hand end of the obvious slanting fault. Climb to the fault and follow it for some 18 metres to a shallow brown niche. Pull onto the steep wall above and climb directly to the top on improving holds.

32 Out of the Blue E3 5b 26m
FA K Marsden, A March 1980

A lovely pitch – pumpy at first, then full of nice surprises. Start 3 metres right of *The Smile*. Follow the line of weakness, a series of shallow scoops and horizontal breaks trending very slightly left, until about 8 metres from the top. Climb direct to a steep finish.

Just left of *Out of the Blue* is the tenuous line of **Wraith** (E4 6a), another superb pitch.

Middle Fin ~ North Face

This – the biggest face of the cliff – has some striking lines. Two prominent grooves, taken by *Lunakhod* and *Clawtrack*, define a tower which projects above the top of the wall. Just left of these is the superb crack of **Spoils of War** (E4 5c,5b) which is so obvious as to need no further description. The ridge above the fin is unstable and it is best to stay roped and climb this section as an additional pitch if the tide prevents descent by abseil (from the fixed abseil station above *Clawtrack/Lunakhod*).

33 Lunakhod HVS 5a 40m
FA K Darbyshire, P Littlejohn 1971

The long groove running up to the left side of the tower. A big pitch with excellent protection and sustained interest. Follow broken corners into the groove and climb it to the top. Belay round the tower. It is possible to move into the crack of *Spoils of War* from halfway up this pitch, giving a three star route at E3 5b.

34 Clawtrack HVS 4c 40m
FA P Littlejohn, K Darbyshire 1971

The wider corner-crack running up to the right side of the tower. A powerful line giving a strenuous route which requires very large nuts/cams to protect the main difficulties. Start at a ramp beneath the flake cracks leading into the corner. Climb the ramp and leaning flake crack to a ledge beneath the corner (optional stance). Follow the corner-crack to the top.

36 *Pacemaker* (E5)
Adam Lincoln   KEITH SHARPLES

Middle Fin ~ South Face

The impressive scene of the best modern routes is vertical for the first two-thirds, then overhangs slightly. It faces the sun and, with routes which are steep and challenging but not over serious, it has become the Culm Coast's Mecca for higher-grade climbing.

35 Break On Through   E4   42m
FA P Littlejohn, P Amphlett 1986

A steep, fairly juggy, and highly enjoyable line near the left edge of the face. Start at the right-hand end of the sloping ledge at the base.

> **1** 24m 5c Move up and rightwards to some obvious large holds. Climb bearing slightly left until about 5 metres from the top, when bold moves diagonally left gain the crest of the fin.
>
> **2** 18m 4b Climb the ridge until it flattens. Scramble to the top of the headland.

36 Pacemaker   E5   6a/b   30m
FA P Littlejohn, M Hardwick 1986

A superb and very sustained pitch of the highest calibre, one of the best wall climbs on culm. Start at a pointed block 11 metres right of the sloping ledge beneath *Break On Through*. Follow a diagonal crack up to the left for about 9 metres; then move up to a quartzy break and follow this leftwards until below a peg. Climb diagonally right from the peg for 9 metres to another peg in a slanting quartz break and continue steeply to the top.

181

37 Fay (E5)
Adam Lincoln   KEITH SHARPLES

★ 37 Fay E5 6a 37m
★ FA P Littlejohn, M Hardwick 1986
★

The classic central line of the wall gives another outstanding pitch. Unrelentingly steep in the upper half but reasonable for the grade, having positive holds and good protection (the pegs can be backed up with natural gear). Start as for *Pacemaker*. Climb on good holds bearing slightly right to the first quartz break (thread), move up to a big spike, and climb leftwards to the start of a large diagonal crack. With the crack at foot level, move up to its end and climb steeply past two pegs to a good resting jug. Bear rightwards up the thin crack to reach the horizontal break; then swing left and up into the niche. Exit to the top.

Climbing the wall about 6 metres to the right of *Fay* is the challenging natural line of **Coronary Country** (E6 6b), a very strenuous and bold pitch.

South Fin ~ North Face

The smoother left side (taken by *Leprosy*) is bounded on the right by a corner leading to a long ledge, **Blunt End** (HVS 5a). The two rightward-slanting cracks in the wall right of this both give good pitches at E3 5c. The deep corner/chimney to the right again is **Heffalump Trap** (VS 4b).

✪ 38 Leprosy E3 5c 34m
FA S Bell, R Perriment 1983

A challenging pitch following a series of flakes and cracks up the centre of the wall. Climb direct for 5 metres, and then follow a line of sloping footholds rightwards to beneath the first obvious flake. Climb past this with difficulty and continue in the same line to a narrow ledge 6 metres from the top. The crack on the left leads to a tricky finish.

★ 39 Dulcima HVS 5a 27m
★ FA P Littlejohn, K Darbyshire 1973

A delightful pitch taking the obvious leftward-leaning crack and groove in the wall right of *Heffalump Trap*. Start beneath the line. Climb the crack and then the groove, which leads with increasing interest to a finish on the left.

Compass Point

OS Ref SS 199 064

The headland enclosing Bude Haven to the south is a popular and pleasant place to climb, being accessible, sheltered, and sunny.

Approach Park near Bude Canal at the south side of the town and walk in along the narrow road beside the canal to the residents' turning space at the end. The cliff-top is now a two-minute walk away, through a gate and up grassy slopes to the conspicuous Compass Tower. The routes are on the south side of the promontory which runs seawards from the Tower. It is possible to scramble out along the promontory to abseil stakes, or there is an easy descent 200 metres beyond the Compass Tower. From low to half tide, a simple approach is to walk in along the boulder beach from Bude Haven.

At its seaward end the promontory divides into two spurs, with a boulder bridge between. The crest of the northern spur is taken by **North Ridge** (VD), while *Westerlation* takes its south face.

⭐ **40   Westerlation**   S   24m

FA K Darbyshire, H Clarke 1973

A fun pitch with good solid holds. Start at the third boulder in from the edge of the wall. Climb the wall to a broken crack leading up and left to a diagonal break. Move right then straight up to finish. Scramble along the ridge to the abseil point or continue to the Compass Tower.

The wall right of *Westerlation* offers several more pitches in a similar vein, up to VS.

The crest of the southern spur is taken by **South Ridge**, a straightforward scramble at Diff standard. Working rightwards along the south face of the promontory, the wall steadily gains height towards the first big feature, a left-facing corner which runs the full height of the cliff: **Corinth** (E4 5c). The first route takes the wall midway between *South Ridge* and this corner.

41 Sugar Magnolia HVS 5a 18m
FA K Darbyshire, D Garner 1974
A nice little pitch on good rock. Start just right of the jagged overlap 12 metres up and climb a thin crack to a small niche. A shallow ramp leads leftwards above the overlap to a tricky finish.

42 Tydomin HVS 4c 27m
FA K Darbyshire, D Garner 1974
A fine, open pitch taking the narrow face to the right of the corner of *Corinth*. Climb just right of the arête until it curves off left. Continue straight up the slab to the top – on good holds, and with just enough protection.

43 Fruichon VS 4b 26m
FA K Darbyshire, D Garner, H Clarke 1974
The broken corner right of *Tydomin*. Good, interesting climbing but with sparse protection (cams in the cracks just right of the corner). Climb the corner to a small cave. Move left and finish up the layback flake above.

To the right of the grassy descent ramp in the middle of the promontory is a clean open slab, the best sweep of rock at Compass Point.

★ 44 Crimtyphon E2 5c 30m
FA K Darbyshire, D Garner 1974

A pitch with real class, linking a series of pockets on the slab by sustained, delicate climbing. Start to the right of the overhangs, where the slab is continuous. Climb easily to a large pocket and continue to a smaller pocket. Step left and down (peg), and then climb to better holds, which lead leftwards to another large pocket (peg). Climb to a small pocket above (peg) and go straight up the slab above.

⭐ 45 Caravanserai HVS 4c 37m
FA K Darbyshire, A Clark 1975

Some 15 metres to the right of *Crimtyphon* a straight and narrow groove line splits a smooth wall. Sustained at a reasonable standard but the rock requires careful handling at the top. Gain the groove via the sloping ledge on the left and follow it directly to its somewhat exfoliating finish.

44 *Crimtyphon* (E2)
Martin Koscis   DAN LANE

North Cornwall – The Atlantic Coast

The fifty-mile stretch of coastline between Boscastle and St Ives Bay possesses some of the highest vertical sea cliffs on the British mainland. The shale cliffs are the highest, presenting up to 180 metres of vertical rock in places, and providing some of the most committing sea-cliff routes in the UK. These are somewhat esoteric however, and the routes described here are generally confined to more reliable rock, though they are far from tame. Many crags plunge straight into a hostile sea, giving access and escape problems. On the more exposed headlands the sea is rarely calm enough to swim in safety (making some routes very committing), and during winter storms the waves can strike up to 30 metres above high-water level. These factors, sometimes combined with a forbidding northerly aspect, lend the climbing in North Cornwall a particularly adventurous character that is both inspirational and uniquely rewarding.

25 *Darkinbad the Brightdayler* **(E5)**
Andi Turner & Perttu Ollila   MIKE HUTTON

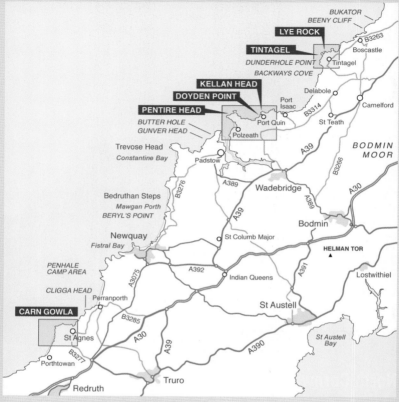

Lye Rock

OS Ref SX 066 899

This sombre and hostile precipice gives one route which is now recognized as a classic of its genre. A mile east of Tintagel Head is the headland of Willapark – the small island of Lye Rock is on the east side of this and is separated from it by a narrow zawn ending in a boulder choke which connects the rock to the mainland at all states of tide. The route takes the intimidating wall above the choke.

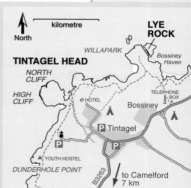

Approach From Bossiney village, take the path to Bossiney Haven and up onto the headland (twenty minutes). The boulder choke can be reached directly by abseil or at lowish tide from the small beach immediately to the west.

1 Bird Brain E4 116m
FA M Fowler, M Smith 1982

A bold undertaking. Hammer and pegs useful, as well as large nuts (in all senses). It takes the most obvious weakness on the face, finishing up a prominent orange flake. The rock is solid on the first pitch but requires care above. Start from the extreme left edge of the boulder choke.

    1 30m 5a Traverse horizontally left for 24 metres to an overhanging crack which leads to a stance.

    2 37m 5b Climb the overhanging flake above until it ends (peg); then move rightwards up a discontinuous crack to a good ledge in the centre of the wall.

    3 37m 5b Follow the obvious line diagonally leftwards and break through the overhangs (peg) to reach the base of the prominent flake crack, which widens to a chimney higher up. Climb the crack and move precariously left over the top of the pinnacle (peg) to a stance close to the top.

    4 12m 4b Climb directly through the overhang in the corner to the top.

From the summit, descend steep grassy ramps and ledges on the west side of the rock and either regain the boulder choke by a difficult sea-level traverse or return via the small beach at low tide.

Tintagel Head

OS Ref SX 047 892

The headland is famous for its castle ruins and their dubious connection with King Arthur. It is virtually a separate island connected to the mainland by a footbridge, and a fee is charged for access. In summer the official visiting hours are 9.00 a.m. to 5.00 p.m. daily; in winter they are shorter. However with discretion it is possible to operate outside these hours.

The authorities are greatly concerned to protect areas of the headland for archaeological reasons and climbers are asked to pay heed to all notices concerning this. Because of this sensitivity the headland is subject to an access agreement between the BMC and English Heritage, and permission to climb can be gained by writing to English Heritage, South West Regional Office, 29 Queen Square, Bristol BS1 4ND. Email: southwest@english-heritage.org.uk. All members of the party need to sign a disclaimer.

The cliff is continuous on the west side, though only attains its full height of 80 metres for a relatively short distance, within which it forms one of the greatest lines in the South of England – the magnificent groove of *Il Duce*. This part of the cliff faces west, gets plenty of sun and takes no drainage. The routes are not tidal but feel especially remote and serious as they are almost impossible to view from anywhere but a boat.

High Cliff

Approach   From the top of the headland, descend grass slopes to the south of the highest area of cliff, and then work northwards to a slabby ramp running beneath a 'dolomitic' wall rimmed with grotesque serrations. The restricted area is to the south of this descent and it is therefore important to keep to the ramp under the wall.

2   Il Duce   E5   78m

FA P Littlejohn, K Darbyshire (1 pt aid) 1972; FFA T Jones, R Hughes 1980

A magnificent route taking a huge hidden groove to the left of the 'dolomitic' wall. The climbing is strenuous, exposed, and committing; the rock is excellent. Belay at the foot of the aforementioned ramp.

   1 18m 5a Step down from the toe of the ramp, traverse left, and swing on to a projecting ledge. Continue leftwards beneath a roof to a platform below overhangs which guard entry into the big groove.
   2 18m 6a Climb the right-hand of two converging cracks and make hard moves to reach holds beneath the roof. Bold climbing across the roof gains a short chimney on the lip. Climb the chimney, and then move leftwards across the exposed wall to a stance at the foot of the groove.
   3 18m 5c Climb the groove for 12 metres to where it starts to bulge; then make difficult moves round the left side of the bulge to a good ledge.
   4 24m 4c Climb the crack on the right for some 10 metres and step left into the groove. Follow the groove to a large thread beneath a roof, traverse right to a huge flake, and finish up the obvious break on the right.

3   Vagabond   E4   102m

FA M Fowler, M Morrison 1978

A superb and committing excursion, again on excellent rock, taking the easiest line up the impressive face to the left of *Il Duce*'s groove. Approach as for *Il Duce*.

2 *Il Duce* (E5)
Peter Telford   DON SARGEANT

1 18m **5a** *Il Duce* pitch 1.

2 18m **5c** From a belay at the far left end of the ledge, move up left into a small groove, and climb it until it closes (peg). Move up then diagonally rightwards to a narrow ledge before trending left to a ledge and nut belays.

3 18m **5c** Climb diagonally rightwards to a slanting overlap and continue beneath it, making difficult moves where it ends, to reach a ledge. Follow the ledge rightwards, past a short step, to a good stance.

4 24m **5a** Climb the corner above to the overhangs, step right onto a rib, and climb to a ledge. This leads rightwards to the final stance of *Il Duce*.

5 24m **4c** *Il Duce* pitch 4.

4   King's Arête   E4   75m

FA A Meyers, M Fowler (VL) 1982

Superb situations and serious climbing up the right arête of the *Il Duce* groove. Start as for *Il Duce*.

1 9m **5a** Traverse left and belay on the projecting ledge.

2 18m **5c** Climb directly for 6 metres; then move left to gain the arête. Follow the arête over a bulge to a narrow ledge leading rightwards to a stance and peg belay at its far end.

3 24m **5b** Climb diagonally left to regain the arête and follow it to reach a short, steep crack on the right leading to a stance in a niche.

4 24m **5b** Pass the overhang above on the right, and then move back left to the arête and continue to reach the huge flake of *Il Duce*. Finish up the break on the right.

North Cliff

A dramatic 25-to-30-metre high wall extends northwards from High Cliff. A pack of fine single-pitch climbs on immaculate rock is on offer – all facing the afternoon sun in readiness for battle.

Approach   From the castle and monastery remains on the hill top, walk north-westwards, descending grass slopes towards a zawn (Black Zawn). Before reaching the zawn, bear leftwards to pick up the northern end of a rock terrace (Dinnerplate Terrace) that runs above the cliff (and which boasts a fantastic vantage point across to *Il Duce* from its far end). There is an exposed step across a corner (the exit of *Astroslide*) to start.

The climbs start from large ledges 6 metres above the sea, and are reached by abseil from Dinnerplate Terrace for which a spare rope (and ascenders!) should be brought. However, climbing here during very rough seas is reserved for noblemen seeking an honourable end.

The first climb is found on the isolated face at the northern end of the wall:

5   Astroslide   E3 5c   40m

FA M J Crocker, D Sargeant 1994

Black and atmospheric; a thrilling pitch with classic qualities. Start at the right-hand end of the ledge under the face, best gained by abseiling from threads 5 metres before the exposed step. Climb up and rightwards above the void to get established on the left arête of a tapering groove above some roofs. Move up the face left of the groove to a break. Step right, climb an overhang, and continue up a steep slab to a second break. Step right and finish up a corner.

Starting as for *Astroslide* is **A Weekend on Mars** (E3 5c), which climbs the cracks to its left via a triangular niche.

Approach
Ramp

3

4

2

★
★ **6   Wicked Gravity** E4 6a 20m
★ FA I Parnell, M J Crocker 1994

Flawless compact rock and a superb line are complemented by some committing climbing.
Climb into the left-facing groove in the centre of the wall past a good thread, and follow it to the
top on frayed nerves. One unconvincing thread should be in place; small cam useful nearby.

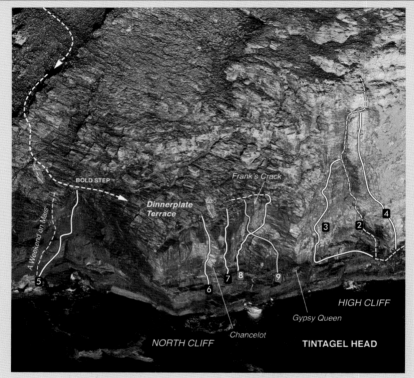

BOLD STEP

A Weekend on Mars

Frank's Crack

Dinnerplate
Terrace

5

6

7

8

9

3

2

4

HIGH CLIFF

Gypsy Queen

Chancelot

NORTH CLIFF

TINTAGEL HEAD

Chancelot (E5 6a) lays siege to the right-hand arête of *Wicked Gravity* while the wall to its right is tackled by the following route:

7   One Stood against Many   E5 6a   25m
FA M J Crocker, I Parnell 1994

An elaborate and super-sustained pitch that seeks a way up the black wall left of the major corner (of *Legend Has It*). Start at a huge thread under the wall. Climb up and stand on a projecting ledge slightly left. Continue direct for 3 metres and gain a good sidehold on the left. Carry on straight up to a flake (bold), and swing right into a slight finishing groove.

At the southern end of the wall, before it turns an arête and merges with High Cliff, is a major corner with a subsidiary roofed corner above half height in its left wall. A short traverse left from the exits and belays of the remaining routes here regains the terrace.

8   Legend Has It   E2 5c   30m
FA M J Crocker, D Sargeant 1994

A noble line with a gallant finish. Climb the corner past ledges at half height and traverse right under its capping roof to exit on good holds.

196

★9 Frank's Corner   E2 5c   30m
FA F Ramsey, M J Crocker 1994

This is the roofed corner left of *Legend Has It* – the crack between the two is taken by **Frank's Crack** (E2 5b). Follow a slim groove right of the corner to ledges on *Legend Has It*. Above on the left is a leftward-leaning corner: take it to the top.

The arête dividing North Cliff from High Cliff is ruled by **Gypsy Queen** (E6 4a,6b,5c), a stunning line that starts from the far right-hand end of the ledges. A wind-worn thread waves forlornly from its crux.

Kellan Head
OS Ref SW 969 812

Kellan Head is the small headland immediately north of Port Quin, a rocky inlet some 1½ miles west of Port Isaac and two miles east of Pentire Head. Its claim to fame is a series of accessible walls of fine pillow lava which provide a feast of short, high-calibre climbs relatively uncompromised by the sea.

Most of the climbs here face west and take the afternoon sun; they are non tidal, but would be affected by rough seas. Note that until the sun gets to work, the ledges under the Hidden Amphitheatre can be very greasy – dangerously so at times – and extracting yourself from the sea below would prove challenging. When conditions underfoot are poor, an alternative means of access to this cliff is by abseil from the terrace under the coast path.

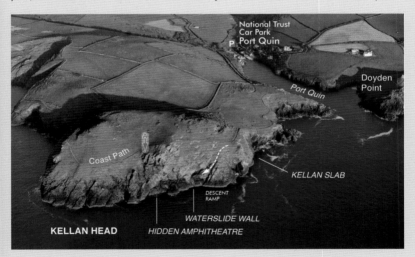

Approach   The cliffs are reached from the National Trust car park in Port Quin in about ten minutes. Follow the coast path north-westwards and, just after passing the top of a large easy-angled slab (Kellan Slab), leave the path and contour across grass slopes to meet the southern end of a descending ramp. The steep grey wall above the ramp is Waterslide Wall. Beyond this, out of sight, is the Hidden Amphitheatre which is reached via a ledge system 10 metres above the sea, left of Waterslide Wall.

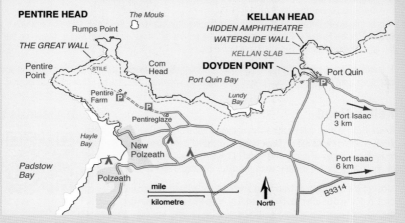

Hidden Amphitheatre

The amphitheatre is divided into two bays by the bulging arête of *Kellan Arête*. Amongst the routes in the left-hand bay is the corner of **Kellan Corner** (E1 5b), an obvious line to the left of the arête. Most climbs described are in its right-hand bay which comprises a large triangular slab right of the arête, overhung by a sloping ceiling.

10 Telekenesis E4 6a 30m
FA D Pickford, E Alsford 2005

The obvious steep V-groove bounding the left wall of *Kellan Arête* gives intricate, technical climbing with good gear, although a little bold to start. Start as for *Kellan Arête*, following the triangular slab to the short corner. Break left here and move up to the base of the overhanging V-groove, which is climbed with sustained interest to a wild finish moving out right. Belays well back.

11 Kellan Arête E6 6a 25m
FA M J Crocker, D Henderson 1995

Witheringly steep and strenuous to protect, this is the towering arête in the centre of the Hidden Amphitheatre – one of the dominant lines of the crag. Start at the triangular slab right of the arête. Climb steadily up and left to a ledge beneath the arête. Using some pockets just to its left, follow the leaning arête to a black-lipped jug and a shake-out. Fighting the pump, launch up a sloping handrail on the arête and make crux moves onto its short headwall. Finish direct.

The sensational ceiling right of the arête is vanquished by **Kellanesis** (E6 6c), which is unfortunately dependent on peg runners dated 1995.

12 Endgame E1 5b 35m
FA K Hosie, I M Peters 1986

A route of character, thanks to a wacky finish. A crack runs leftwards under an impending wall that overhangs the right-hand edge of the triangular slab. Climb a thin crack to reach the crack system under the wall. Take the wide crack leftwards to a small ledge just below the apex of the slab (optional stance – old pegs). Above is a deep chimney-slot; enter and depart from it in as dignified a fashion as possible.

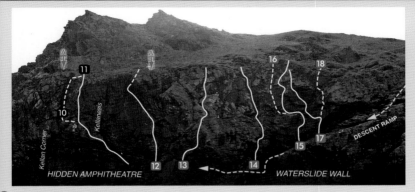

HIDDEN AMPHITHEATRE　WATERSLIDE WALL

DESCENT RAMP

Kellan Corner

Kellaness

⭐ 13　Knight's Move　E1　5b　25m
FA E Heslam, G Williams 1989

An entertaining way up the right-hand side of the Hidden Amphitheatre.

1 12m 5a Work around the left-hand side of a shallow cave to gain footholds above the cave roof. Take the centre of the slab to a terrace.

2 13m 5b Stand on a big flake above the stance, and follow the leaning crack above (peg) to easier ground.

Waterslide Wall

This steep wall is undercut at low level by a line of roofs. Belays at the top are 12 metres back on rock outcrops.

14　Frostbite　E1　35m
FA I M Peters, J Barber (AL) 1985

Very steep for the grade; start at a corner 3 metres left of a short vertical step in the lower end of the ramp under the wall.

1 15m 5b Climb the corner to a roof which caps it. Move right and continue direct to ledges.

2 20m 4c Move up and right and follow a corner-crack to an exit left.

⭐⭐ 15　Zugzwang　E2　35m
FA K Hosie, I M Peters (2 rest points, AL) 1986; FFA S Cardy, N Jowett 1986

The classic of the crag, which provides varied moves up the centre of the wall. Start at a corner under the roofs, where the descent ramp ends.

1 15m 5a Climb the corner, moving rightwards into a niche. Move up and leftwards above the lip of the roofs and take a stance in a horizontal break.

2 20m 5b Climb cracks in the wall above to a circular niche. Step right above the niche into a corner, and then move back left onto a slight prow. Climb the wall above, rightwards at first (peg); then exit direct.

Variation

⭐ 16　Tiger's Eye　E3
FA B R E Wilkinson, E Heslam 1989

2a 15m 5c Climb the face left of the *Zugzwang* cracks past a peg near the top: a fine alternative well worth reclimbing pitch 1 for.

199

HIDDEN AMPHITHEATRE

WATERSLIDE WALL

DESCENT RAMP

⭐ **17   Play It Straight**   E3 5c   25m

FA P Littlejohn 1988

This is the striking curving corner right of *Zugzwang*. Start 4 metres right of *Zugzwang*. Climb the face to a slot at 3 metres. Swing left onto larger holds and gain the slanting break above. Gain the corner with some committing moves and follow it past overhangs to finish up the steep face of *Zugzwang* (peg).

⭐ **18   Rock-a-Bye-Baby**   E3 6a   20m

FA E Heslam, B R E Wilkinson 1989

A great little climb with some bouldery moves over a roof. Gain the slot at 3 metres as for *Play It Straight* and continue direct to the overhang (old peg in overhang, but gear above). Transfer onto the layaways over the lip, and go up the headwall to a sloping ledge. Finish up a groove on the left.

19 *Flying Circus* (E2)
Pete Saunders
SUE HAZEL

20 *Caprice* (VS)
Mun Leung
DUNCAN CRITCHLEY

Doyden Point

An engaging little crag which is one of the most benign of the North Cornwall cliffs – especially on calmer days when it basks in the afternoon sun. It lies just to the west of Port Quin. Leave cars in the National Trust car park at Port Quin and walk out to the point, which is easily distinguished by the unusual folly built above it.

The rock at Doyden is excellent pillow lava, weathered near the sea to resemble Cornish granite. Apart from *Illegal Alien*, which requires low tide for the original start, the routes can be reached at all states of the tide.

Approach   The traditional approach is a traverse of HS standard and some parties may wish to rope up. Descend easy rocks at the north-east edge of the cliff until about 10 metres above the sea, and then traverse in until, just past a black corner, the edge of a slab is reached. Cross the slab to ledges and descend diagonally to a terrace. Above the right-hand side of this is the steep orange corner taken by **Decumanus** (E1 5a/b) while the slab to the left is taken by *Caprice*. Further right, the impressive green corner of **Sick Rose** (E4 6a) rises above the lower, sea-washed terraces. An abseil approach directly down the corner of *Decumanus* is increasingly popular but detracts from the ambience of the crag.

19 Flying Circus   E2 5c   37m
FA I M Peters, K Hosie 1986

Enjoyable climbing up the left arête of the *Caprice* slab. Start on the terrace beneath the arête. Climb leftwards to an overhung niche. Step up and left; then traverse right beneath the undercut arête to a foot ledge below a shallow groove. Move up a little way, and then go leftwards to the arête, which is followed up thin cracks to a large foothold on the left. Climb the rib above then an easier slab to the belay of *Caprice*.

20 Caprice   VS 4c   37m
FA P Littlejohn, S Jones 1971

A very pleasant slab climb which makes an excellent round trip when combined with the approach traverse. Start 5 metres left of *Decumanus*. Traverse left, rising slightly, to the edge of the large slab. Move up to a bollard, traverse left across the slab, and climb via a short crack to a ledge. Climb the thin crack on the left until steep moves gain a series of broken ledges leading out left to belays. (A direct finish through the poised blocks is hazardous, and should be avoided.)

21 Lotus   E1   48m
FA P Littlejohn, I M Peters 1977

Fine positions, good rock and runners, positive holds: this route has a lot going for it! It takes the prominent 'outrigger' crack branching rightwards from the corner of *Decumanus*.

1 37m 5b Climb *Decumanus* to reach good holds above the bulging section at 15 metres. Now take the discontinuous crack across the right wall of the corner to gain the edge of a slab, which is followed up to the right until, after a steep move, the crack ends at a rounded bollard (spike for thin tape). Move right and step down to easier-angled rock. Nut belays, plus spikes on the right.

2 11m 4c Move awkwardly round a rib to gain the next slab on the right. Climb easily to a ledge; then pull leftwards across the final steep wall to the top.

★★ **22 Illegal Alien**   E3   50m
FA M Fowler, S Fenwick 1985

An impressive route taking the very steep rock to the left of *Sick Rose*. At half to low tide descend a steep wall from the platform beneath *Decumanus* to reach the lower terraces. Start about 10 metres left of the corner of *Sick Rose*. (Alternatively, an exciting, non-tidal start can be made by traversing right above the large overhang from the terrace below *Decumanus* at 5c.)

  1 15m 5c Climb steeply to a large overhang, traverse to its right-hand end, and move up onto an overhanging wall (peg). Climb the wall trending slightly left to a ledge and peg belays on the left.

  2 24m 6a Move left into the obvious smooth groove and climb this with difficulty (peg) to a smooth slab. Move left onto the arête and follow a crack into a niche. Exit right, using a dubious flake, to the belay of *Lotus*.

  3 11m 4c *Lotus* pitch 2.

23 *Eroica* (E3)
Niick Cox   GLEN CRAVEN

Pentire Head

OS Ref SW 930 809

The Great Wall at Pentire is probably the most impressive sweep of rock on the North Cornwall coast, and strongly reminiscent of its Cloggy namesake. The rock is very solid pillow lava, nearly black in colour and therefore lending a rather sombre atmosphere to this north-facing crag.

Approach   The headland lies just north of the popular resort of Polzeath and is approached from Pentire Farm, where cars can be left for a small fee payable at the farmhouse. Follow the farm track towards the point until it ends in a large field. Cross to the far side of this and climb over a stone stile onto the coast path. The top of Great Wall is now 100 metres away to the right and is discernible as a rocky knoll protruding from the general cliff-top. A grassy descent on the east side leads to a beach of massive boulders at the foot of the wall. This is well above high-water level, so there are no access problems.

23   Eroica   E3   64m

FA P Littlejohn, G A G Morton 1971 (2 pts aid); FFA P Livesey, J Lawrence 1975

One of the prime routes of the South West and the one that launched climbing in North Cornwall. On the left side of the smooth central wall is a line of cracks culminating in a huge flake. The route follows these, then links with the yellowish, rightward-veering groove in the upper wall. Start beneath a shallow black groove at the left end of the deep rift which undercuts the cliff.

   1 40m 6a Climb the groove to a ledge and continue easily to the first overhang. Move up right and follow the cracks to hollow flakes beneath the double roof. Pass this by a sensational layback and continue to the top of the flake. Difficult climbing above the flake gains a shallow ramp which is followed until it is possible to move right to belay at the base of a long groove.
   2 24m 5b Climb the groove (steep and sustained); then step right to a short gully which leads to the top.

24   Black Magic   E5   61m

FA S Monks, J Wilkinson 1987

Wall climbing sorcery; immaculate, very sustained, yet nowhere too desperate. Take plenty of small wires. Start 6 metres right of *Eroica*, at the obvious line of thin cracks.

   1 43m 6a Follow the cracks for some 14 metres; then move right and up to a peg. Gain a white quartz 'pillow' up to the right, and follow the series of shallow edges running up to the right until just past a further peg, when it is possible to climb straight up the wall to the base of the large impending corner.
   2 18m 5c Climb the corner, or move round to the right and finish up the obvious groove.

25   Darkinbad the Brightdayler   63m   E5

FA P Littlejohn, I Duckworth (6 pts aid) 1972; P Livesey (l pt aid); 1975, FFA R Fawcett, P Gomersall 1976

One of Britain's best. Start 12 metres right of *Eroica*, at a line of weakness where a block abuts the cliff.

   1 43m 6a Climb to the sloping ledge at 8 metres (bold). Climb the steep wall, keeping left of a small overhang, to a crack which snakes off to the left (peg). Traverse left for 6 metres; then move up to a band of overhangs. Climb diagonally right, up a discontinuous crack (peg), Gain the thin crack on the right and follow it (peg) to belay at the base of the groove of *Eroica*,
   2 20m 6a Traverse left into a groove and climb to where it overhangs. Continue with increasing difficulty to a ledge, move left, and climb the exposed final wall to the top.

24 *Black Magic* (E5)
Dave Turnbull MIKE HUTTON

Carn Gowla

OS Ref SW 698 512

These very extensive and serious cliffs make up one of the prime climbing areas of the North Cornwall coast. The crags are continuous for about two miles around St Agnes Head and have all come to be known by climbers as Carn Gowla, although in fact they consist of several different areas. A minor road leaves St Agnes near the church and heads west up on to the headland. Tracks lead off this road to various parking spots near the Coastguard Lookout.

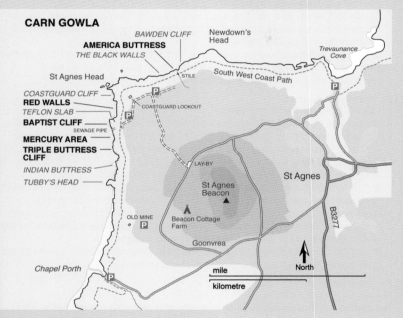

America Buttress

Some 500 metres east of the Coastguard Lookout is an awe-inspiring crag, north-facing and plunging 100 metres into the sea from its summit prow (OS Ref SW 704 517). The climbs are serious, exceptionally so if the original sea-level approach traverse from the north-east is used (which requires low tide, calm seas, and a Tyrolean traverse). The normal approach nowadays for *America* and *The Mausoleum* is to abseil 100 metres on joined ropes from

various anchors on top of the buttress to the foot of the spur of *America* (low tide), or to a ledge partway up the first pitch (higher tide) or indeed to the first stance (this has been referred to as *America Lite* , but is only *'lite'* compared to the original!). *The Mausoleum* can be approached at low tide from the base of *America*, but its magnificent final corner can be enjoyed in its own right by abseiling down it (giving a quick clean en route if necessary) to belays on the slab.

26 America   E4   100m
FA P Littlejohn, K Darbyshire 1973

The epitome of adventure climbing, taking the left edge of the cliff in three big pitches, each offering a different type of challenge. The rock is good but protection is not over-abundant, particularly on the central slab where the grade rapidly escalates in damp conditions. Start beneath the broad rib forming the left edge of the lower wall.

1 27m 5b Climb to a ledge beneath a short groove. Continue up easy rock; then bear right to the edge of a slab (poor peg). Step right, and then climb to the obvious niche. Break right using the wide crack to gain a stance on top of a flake.

2 43m 5b Climb direct to where the slab becomes smooth. Move to the left edge and climb delicately until better holds are reached and the angle eases slightly. Continue up the slab to belay beneath the impending upper wall.

3 30m 5c Climb the obvious groove and enter another groove above. Quit this fairly soon by traversing right to a narrow shelf. Climb up and left onto an exposed arête and make strenuous moves to gain a ledge beneath the final wall. A thin crack leads to the top.

27 Guernica   E6   79m
FA P Littlejohn, H Clarke (1 pt aid) 1982; FFA P Littlejohn, F Ramsay 1987

An unforgettable route taking the impending wall to the right of *America*'s top pitch. The climbing is both serious and technical, and the crux very strenuous. Start on the first stance of *America*.

1 37m 5c Climb easily, bearing right to reach the corner formed by the junction of the central slab and the wall above. Climb the steep slab just left of the corner and continue for 8 metres to belay at the obvious vertical crack formed by a huge block.

2 24m 6b From 3 metres up the slab from the block, climb the wall to a large flat handhold (small wire higher up); then traverse right across the wall to stand on the detached block above the roof. Follow the thin crack and shallow groove to a resting place on the right (peg). Some committing moves leftwards onto the overhanging wall gain a line of flake holds leading up and rightwards to a sloping ledge and various mediocre belays.

3 18m 5b Climb steeply from the left end of the ledge into an exposed bay. Traverse left and move past the next overhang into a short corner leading to the top.

28 The Mausoleum   E3   84m
FA K Darbyshire, P Littlejohn 1973

Two excellent but misaligned pitches. The upper bastion of *America* is bounded on the right by a big 'Cenotaph' corner set 60 metres above the waves. There are good natural anchors above this for an abseil – either to the base of the corner to climb this pitch only, or on joined ropes to the foot of the cliff. Start in the obvious chimney 30 metres right of the start of *America* (a protected but lonely spot on a rising tide, particularly if you have traversed in).

1 30m 5a Climb the chimney and the long, leftward-slanting groove above to a stance on the slab. Peg belay.

2 24m Traverse left on a rising line to belay beneath the corner.

3 30m 5b Climb the corner, strenuous at first, to a small ledge. Continue on better holds to a widening of the crack beneath an overhang; then swing left to a ledge. Reach good holds above the bulge and pull up to more good holds leading to the top.

The impressive left arête of *The Mausoleum*'s final corner is taken by **Ku Klux Klan** (E6 6a/b), a serious pitch protected by two blade pegs (not in place).

Note: At the central slab (reached by the first pitches of *America* and *The Mausoleum*) it is possible to escape from the cliff by traversing right and climbing a groove, **Escapist** (HVS 5a), where the slab ends.

The Red Walls & Vault Wall

From the rocky promontory of St Agnes Head, the Red Walls extend to the south until terminated by a steep black bastion, the Vault Wall, situated directly below the spinal ridge of Carn Gowla itself. Running beneath the walls is a flat platform known as 'the Heliport', most of which is above the high-tide mark (though it is frequently swept with spray). The Heliport is split by a zawn/cave below *Rotwand*. Two different approaches are used. To reach the northern end (for *Chicken Flesh*), traverse in at lowish tide (Diff) from the St Agnes Head direction, or at high tide abseil down the left arête of the Red Walls.

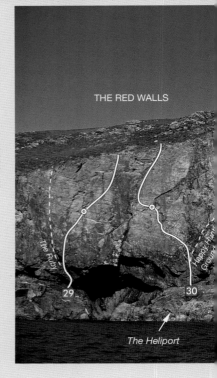

THE RED WALLS

The Ruby

Happy Hour Groove

29

30

The Heliport

★★ **29 Chicken Flesh** E2 64m
FA P Littlejohn, K Darbyshire (VL) 1973

Good climbing and positions on a rightward-trending line above the zawn which splits the Heliport. Start some way left of the zawn, at the obvious entry to the right of a highly stratified, overhanging wall.

1 30m 5b Climb rightwards to an overhung rib and continue steeply until it is possible to break left and rest. Traverse back right into a groove and climb it strenuously to easier-angled rock. Continue slightly rightwards to a small stance and peg belays 5 metres left of a depression.

2 34m 5a Traverse right across the depression and follow a thin crack rightwards to ledges. Continue over grass to exit at a groove formed by a projecting rib. Block belays well back.

Another fine route sharing the start of *Chicken Flesh* is **The Ruby** (E3 5b), which climbs the sheer-looking red face up and to the left of the steep entry.

The southern part of the Heliport (for *Rotwand* and routes on the Vault Wall) is gained by a spectacular 45-metre abseil from above the spinal ridge above the Vault Wall. There are good nut belays and it is best to leave the abseil rope in place (with ascenders attached!). The abseil ends near the base of a tall (90-metre) black slab, Teflon Slab, leaving a short, slippery scramble across and down to the Heliport. The 'escape route' from here, which requires a lot of care in wet conditions, is to make a rising traverse across the base of Teflon Slab to its right edge, which soon leads to the grass slopes.

VAULT WALL

TEFLON
SLAB

33

Helcyon Days

32

The Vault

Escape Route

31

The Baptist Cliff →

⭐ **30 Rotwand** HVS 58m

FA P Littlejohn, S Jones 1972

A popular open face climb on good rock; perhaps the most amenable on the Red Walls. Start at the obvious weakness 5 metres right of the zawn which splits the Heliport.

    1 34m 4c Climb the steep narrow wall for 11 metres, stepping left at the overlap to reach a ledge. Continue up the steep face on the left, on larger holds, to a stance on a large block forming the floor of a niche.

    2 24m 4c Move up and follow a thin slanting crack to a spike. Step right and climb a crystal-filled crack to a ledge; then move right and climb the centre of a red wall to finish. Belay well back on blocks,

Sharing the start of *Rotwand*, **Happy Hunting Ground** (HVS 5a) takes a long, rising line up the walls to the right. Further right the obvious central gash in the Vault Wall is the line of **The Vault** (E1 5a) – the original route of the wall and worthwhile in dry conditions; but a much finer route weaves through the overhangs to its left:

213

31   The Tomb   E3   85m

FA R Perriment, R Broomhead 1974

A splendid route with superb situations. Dry conditions are required. Start left of *The Vault* at the rightward-trending ramp.

1 21m 4c Follow the ramp to a groove. Step up and bear left to the left end of the overhang.

2 18m 5b Climb to the top right-hand corner of the slab (peg); then move right and up (crux) to a ledge and flake.

3 46m 4c Move across into *The Vault* and up this for a short way. Move right across a small slab to a large flake which leads to a ledge. A thin crack on the right leads up to easier-angled slabs and a belay at the abseil point to the right.

Starting 6 metres above and to the right of *The Vault* at a leftward-leaning slab is the sensational line of **Saviourblade** (E6 6a). There are some good but serious pitches near the right arête of the Vault Wall, in the vicinity of the abseil. **Killing Time** (E2 5b) takes two disconnected red grooves left of the arête, and **Halcyon Days** (E3 5b) gives excellent, bold face climbing just right of the arête. The main crackline of Teflon Slab gives the rather mediocre **Tempest** (HS) but its left retaining wall has a more worthwhile offering:

32   Demerara   VS 4c   46m

FA K Darbyshire, D Garner 1974

Solid rock, positive holds, and good gear make this a fine route in its own right as well as a useful escape from more serious climbs in poor conditions. It takes the easiest line on the quartzy wall overlooking Teflon Slab. Start below the arête, in the corner formed by Teflon Slab and its retaining wall. Climb the corner for 6 metres or so to a groove on the left and follow this to a ledge. Move left and climb the face to the obvious ramp, which leads up and leftwards to the abseil point.

Following the initial corner all the way gives **Last Exit to St Agnes** (VS 4b)

The Baptist Cliff

Round the corner from the bottom of Teflon Slab is a wall of orange-coloured rock plastered with overhangs. This is the Baptist Cliff. At its base is a huge sloping shelf, the highest part of which is non tidal. At low tide the shelf can be reached by descending the seaward edge of Teflon Slab, but usually the best way in is to abseil 50 metres down the wall from block belays on the steep grass slope immediately above. The first route traverses the cliff at half height and begins at the start of the 'proper' climbing on the descent of the outer ridge of Teflon Slab (belay peg normally in place).

33   Après-vous   E1   75m

FA R Perriment, D Gough 1974

Great situations, particularly when a big sea is running, and usefully non tidal.

1 24m 5b Descend steeply rightwards for 9 metres to the lower line of overhangs. Move right around the corner and cross the steep slab to a small ledge. Peg and nut belays.

2 21m 5a Continue rightwards beneath the overhang and make an exposed swing to cross an overhanging corner. Continue traversing steeply until the angle eases and a slab is crossed to an awkward belay in the corner of *Diabolist*.

3 30m 5a Traverse right for 6 metres until just before a niche, and take a zigzag line through the overhang above to gain a steep orange slab below a diagonal roof. Follow the line of the roof to the top. Belays well back.

The next two routes are best begun at low tide or just after, giving the rock at the cliff base time to dry out. Roughly in the centre of the cliff is a tapering corner running the full height. This is *Diabolist*. The next route takes the very steep rock between the corner and the sea cave on the left.

★ 34 The Awakening E3 61m
FA R Edwards, M Edwards 1985

Sensational climbing on good rock and surprisingly good holds. Start 8 metres left of *Diabolist* at a slab containing a small V-groove.

1 27m 5c Climb the groove to a small ledge on the right (belay possible). Continue up the slab on the left to a steep wall and traverse left to a bolt. Step down and move left around the overlap to an overhanging corner (peg). Continue traversing to reach a slab (peg) and a small stance further left.

2 34m 5b Climb the groove above, then up a short wall to an overhang (peg). Traverse right to another roof, pull over onto a slab, and climb directly to the top.

★ 35 Diabolist E3 6a 40m
FA P Littlejohn, K Darbyshire 1972

Harder after a rockfall but still a fine natural line giving a well-protected pitch. Dry conditions essential. Climb the corner to the first overhang and pass this with difficulty. Continue to a larger roof and climb it on good holds to the upper groove which is followed to the top.

36 *Silver Dollar* (HVS)
Richard Pullen PATRICK DANIEL

The Mercury Area / Triple Buttress

The great expanse of crag to the right of the Baptist Cliff is known as the Mercury Area (after the huge hidden groove of *Mercury* which dominates the right-hand portion). A prominent feature of the left-hand section is a steep wall with a large shallow cave at its foot. A sill of excellent light-coloured rock slopes up to the right from the cave and provides the first pitch of *Crystal Voyage*.

The first two climbs lie either side of the shallow cave and are approached by traversing southwards along sea-level ledges from the platform beneath the Baptist Cliff. This is possible at all states of the tide in calm seas but requires a lowish tide if there is a swell, in which case one is well advised to rope up.

36 Silver Dollar   HVS   79m
FA R Edwards, P Renouf 1978

A good route taking the easiest line up the impressive rock left of the shallow cave. Start just left of the cave at the foot of a leftward-slanting black slab.
   1 30m 5a Move up to the slab and climb it, following the line of the roof rightwards, until a traverse left can be made onto a good ledge in a niche. Peg belays.
   2 40m 4c Traverse right and climb the wall above before traversing back left to a large patch of quartz (the 'Silver Dollar'). Climb this and the slab above, heading for the left side of a large block on the skyline. From a cave, exit left to reach a stance above.
   3 9m Climb the wall behind the belay.

37 Crystal Voyage   E1   79m
FA R Edwards, S Salmon 1978

A magnificent outing, giving exposed climbing, on generally good holds, in a remote situation. Take several long tapes for threads. Start at the right-hand side of the large cave.
   1 21m 5a Climb rightwards to a roof and traverse right (peg) before pulling over to a crystal-lined crack. Follow the crack for 6 metres; then traverse left along the lip to an exposed stance.
   2 15m 4b Climb straight up for 6 metres and then go diagonally left to a ledge and belays (high and low threads).
   3 43m 5a Climb direct for 8 metres to a smooth wall; then trend diagonally left, passing a small quartz ledge, until beneath the obvious overhang. Climb through the right-hand side of the overhang and up the quartz face above to a ledge, above which easier ground leads to the top.

The next feature to the south (right facing the crag) of the cave of *Crystal Voyage* is the huge arched groove of *Mercury*. It is well viewed from the top of the projecting buttress (A Buttress) 50 metres further south again. During calm seas at low tide it is possible to reach the large ledge at the base of the groove via a committing traverse (5a standard) from the ledges beneath *Crystal Voyage*, but generally it will be necessary to abseil. There are good belays on a small outcrop of rock near the cliff edge just north of the line. Joined 50-metre ropes (or a 90-metre single) are necessary, and the abseil runs down the slabby wall left of the groove until it is possible to swing around the arête and abseil (free) to ledges at the base which are exposed until half tide during moderate seas. At higher tides aim for another good ledge with a thread belay 12 metres higher. Obviously, ascenders should be carried, and some previous experience of changing over at the knot is desirable, as this is perhaps not the best place to learn. The cliff gets the sun from midday onwards.

36

Ledge traverse

37

THE BAPTIST CLIFF

Joined rope abseil from bluff
above cliff edge boulder

39

The Andromeda Strain

HVS 5a traverse

38

THE MERCURY AREA

39 *Mercury Direct* (E2)
Nolan Smyth PETE SAUNDERS

⭐ 38 Mercury E1 82m
FA P Littlejohn, S Jones 1974

A classic of the North Coast taking the first half of the arching groove, then breaking out on to its slabby left arête. Though not hard technically, the route is committing and even with large nuts/cams the first pitch feels rather bold. Start on the lowest ledge at the foot of the corner.

1 43m 5a Follow the corner on generally good holds until the walls become smooth and the crack widens. Awkward moves gain a large jammed flake, and then the crack above is followed until it is possible to move left to an excellent stance.

2 27m 4c Move left around the arête and follow the extreme right edge of the rugged slab, in an exposed position overlooking the groove, to reach a shallow ledge below smoother, lichenous slabs. Peg and nut belays.

3 12m 4b Climb diagonally rightwards on grassy rock to the top.

Variation

⭐ 39 Mercury Direct E2 46m
FA R Edwards and party 1979; Complete: M Fowler, M Hunt 1979

A better and more logical climb taking the upper part of the arching groove of *Mercury*, adding up to one of the finest E2s on British sea cliffs. Sustained and significantly harder than the original; also somewhat slower-drying. Start from the large stance above pitch 1 of *Mercury*.

2a 46m 5b Follow the corner for about 18 metres until past the subsidiary overhang formed where it curves to the right. Traverse right across the slab to a pillar of compact red rock, and climb for a short way to a small ledge and peg (poor belay possible). Climb for 5 metres; then traverse right to a groove and follow this through the final overhangs to the top. Belays well back.

The huge slabby face forming the right wall of *Mercury*'s groove is ascended by **The Andromeda Strain** (E5 6a), a magnificent route with scant protection. Immediately south of the Mercury Area is Triple Buttress Cliff, its northernmost buttress (A Buttress) being some 100 metres from the rocky projection marking the top of its southern buttress (C Buttress – a comfortable spot to gear up for the next routes described). Crossing A and B Buttresses is an enjoyable high-level traverse which is easy of access and unaffected by tides:

40 Journey to Ixtlan HVS 124m

FA R Perriment, C Owen 1978

A high traverse of the two buttresses, giving steep and exposed climbing, mainly on good holds. A fantastic trip on a blustery day when big seas deny access to routes beginning from the base of the cliff. Start above the narrow, easy-angled ramp which descends on the north side of C Buttress.

1 21m Climb down to the ramp and descend it until it steepens at a good ledge. Nut belays.

2 21m 4c Descend the ramp for a further 5 metres; then move left onto the wall and climb diagonally left to gain a small ledge level with the belay. Move up left; then traverse steeply to the arête and around it to peg and nut belays.

3 21m 4c Descend slightly to traverse past two grooves into a corner. Move across the corner and descend diagonally left to nut and spike belays on the arête.

4 37m 4c Traverse into the corner formed by the junction of the buttresses and continue across the left wall, rising slightly, until exposed moves gain the arête. Climb the arête for 6 metres to peg and block belays (high up).

5 24m 4c Climb the arête; then move left and follow the obvious weakness which runs diagonally left across the wall. Climb directly to the top just before the big corner.

A Buttress

With C Buttress and the area immediately south of it (the South C Walls) Carn Gowla provides a friendlier and more relaxed climbing experience (provided the sea is not too lively!). The routes are single pitch and non tidal; the rock is solid and the cliffs start to get the sun before midday. The seaward face of C buttress is a sheer pink wall – approach by abseiling down this (plenty of good anchors atop the buttress) to a good ledge just above the high-tide mark.

B Buttress

C Buttress

TRIPLE BUTTRESS CLIFF

⭐ **41 Looking for a Rainbow** S 4a 34m
FA D E Hope, A Camm 1990

Traverse left from the ledge to the obvious chimney/groove and climb this to a large platform. Climb the wall on the right and continue easily to the top of the buttress.

⭐ **42 Sunny Delight** E1 5a 30m
FA L Pavey, S Palmer 2003

Delightful climbing up the left arête of the sheer pink wall. A tricky start gains good holds, after which the climbing is 'pure heaven' all the way to the juggy finish.

C Buttress   South C Walls

43 Rainbow Games   E2 5b   30m
FA D E Hope, A Camm 1990

A stunning pitch beginning at the left-hand of two thin cracks in the lower part of the pink wall. Climb the thin crack until a better crack on the left can be gained. Climb this directly and continue in the same line (peg) to the top of the buttress.

The right-hand crack is **Four for Texas** (E2 5b), also excellent.

44 Sundance   HS 4a   27m
FA S Harry, R Perriment 1978

A sweeping line up the right-hand side of the buttress gives enjoyable climbing. From the right-hand end of the ledge, follow the black slab to the right of the sheer, pink wall until it narrows to form a rib. Climb the rib, and then trend leftwards, following a band of quartz, to reach a notch and the top.

left Carn Gowla north; *above* Carn Gowla south

Just around the corner to the south of C Buttress it is possible to descend to sea level. This is straightforward in the dry but treacherous when wet. Descend towards the red back wall at first; then cut back rightwards (facing out) on an old miners' path until slabs lead on down to sea level and a non-tidal platform below the South C Walls. There are two prominent cracklines, of which the left is **Chimney Route** (S 4a), while the right gives:

45 Crackline HS 4b 15m
FA J Cheshire, D Ryden 1996
A fine little route – just climb that crack.

46 Feline VS 4b 15m
FA J Cheshire, D Ryden 1996
Follow the red ramp immediately right of *Crackline*.

47 Fine Line D 21m
FA J Cheshire, D Ryden 1996
The 'gully' in the centre of C Walls.

48 Bee Line HVS 5b 21m
FA J Cheshire, D Ryden 1996
Right of *Fine Line* is an obvious groove. Gain and follow it to a steep wall. Step left and climb directly to the top.

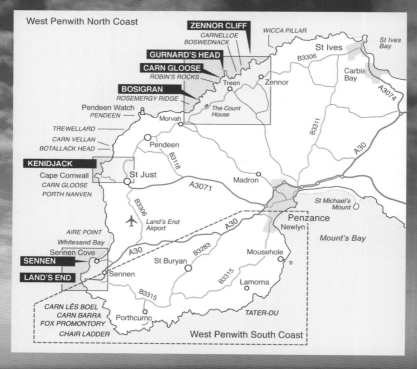

West Penwith North Coast

ZENNOR CLIFF
CARNELLOE
BOSWEDNACK
WICCA PILLAR

GURNARD'S HEAD
CARN GLOOSE
ROBIN'S ROCKS

BOSIGRAN
ROSEMERGY RIDGE

Pendeen Watch
PENDEEN

TREWELLARD
CARN VELLAN
BOTALLACK HEAD

KENIDJACK
Cape Cornwall
CARN GLOOSE
PORTH NANVEN

AIRE POINT
Whitesand Bay
Sennen Cove

SENNEN
LAND'S END

CARN LÉS BOEL
CARN BARRA
FOX PROMONTORY
CHAIR LADDER

St Ives
St Ives Bay
Carbis Bay
Treen
Zennor
The Count House
Morvah
Pendeen
Madron
St Michael's Mount
Penzance
Newlyn
Mount's Bay
Land's End Airport
Mousehole
St Buryan
Lamorna
St Just
Sennen
Porthcurno
TATER-DU
West Penwith South Coast

B3306
B3311
A3074
A30
B3118
A3071
B3306
B3283
B3315
B3315

West Penwith – North Coast

West Penwith is the part of Cornwall to the west of St Ives and Penzance, culminating in Land's End. Its coastline provides one of Britain's richest traditional climbing areas with wonderful classic climbs in all grades, some of them first done a century ago. Most of the cliffs are granite of the very best quality, but there are also excellent crags of greenstone and killas slate. The climbing areas are described anticlockwise round the coast, starting with Zennor Cliff, which is five miles west of St Ives along the northern coast road.

16 *Suicide Wall* (E1)
Dave Coley SEAN KELLY

Zennor Cliff

OS Ref SW 447 393

This small but attractive cliff, in a commanding position on top of the headland and above the impressive Horse's Back Zawn, is an ideal place to round off a day and watch the sunset before retiring to the *Tinner's Arms*. It is reached by a short walk from Zennor village (pay car park), along a path beginning behind the house opposite the church. On top of the headland is a rock outcrop containing a National Trust plaque. Descend to the left of this until a small path leads around rightwards to the foot of the tier (map page 232).

The crag is split by an obvious chimney towards its left side. This gives **1923 Route** (VD). The climbs described are to the right of this on the steepest part of the crag.

1   Rosebud in June   VS 5a   24m

FA W A Carver, R Nadin 1973

A sustained pitch mainly following the thin crack 3 metres right of *1923 Route*. Start two metres right of the chimney at a crack. Climb for a short way, step right, and move up with difficulty to a small niche at 8 metres. Move up and left to the thin crack and climb it on positive but widely spaced holds to the top.

2   The Royal Forrester   VS 5a   23m

FA W A Carver, P Turner 1973

Steep and enjoyable climbing with good protection. Start at a shallow, square-cut groove 5 metres right of *1923 Route*. Climb the groove to the overhang and layback boldly into the crack above. From the top of the crack, move left and up to a small ledge. Climb the left side of the face above, with interest, to the top.

Gurnard's Head

OS Ref SW 432 385

Gurnard's Head is the most popular and accessible of the greenstone crags in West Penwith, offering several classic routes on rock which is hardly less solid than Cornish granite. It consists of a narrow promontory jutting out northwards from the mainland, and having some impressive cliffs on its west side. Low tide and afternoon sun provide the ideal climbing conditions, but *Right Angle* is possible at any state of the tide unless a big sea is running, when the situations can become a little too impressive (map page 232).

To reach the headland, leave vehicles on the broad verge opposite the *Gurnard's Head Hotel* and walk down the lane beside the pub and Coastguard Houses. Continue straight on across fields to the Head. At the neck of the headland is Kittiwake Zawn, which offers some mediocre climbing. The *Right Angle* cliff is a little further out along the promontory and is unmistakable, consisting of two great planes of rock which intersect to form the huge corner of *Right Angle*.

3   Right Angle   HS   72m

FA I M Peters, J Gerber 1966

A classic route which ascends a great natural feature and offers superb situations for the grade. It starts by traversing in along the belt of slabs forming the left wall of the corner, then climbs the corner in one big pitch. Start by descending a short, rounded gully near the seaward end of the belt of slabs to a stance about 12 metres above the sea.

  1 17m Traverse along the obvious break to a large ledge just beyond a groove.

  2 18m 4a/b Continue traversing at the same level to the top of a vertical crack. Descend this, awkward, to a stance below the great corner.

  3 37m 4a Climb slabby rock into the corner proper. Move past a small overhang and follow the corner to the top, mainly on good holds.

3 *Right Angle* (HS)
Richard Wheeldon, Bob Peters,
& Jorn Knusted   DON SARGEANT

★★★ **4　Behemoth**　E2　48m
FA P Littlejohn, S Jones 1969

The great sweeping weakness in the impressive wall to the right of *Right Angle* gives a fine serious route – difficult to retreat from during a rising tide and requiring low tide to approach. Dry conditions required. Start by climbing the first two pitches of *Right Angle* and then descend to the big cave platform just below the second stance of that route.

　1　18m　5c　Climb the two overhanging corners which lead up and out onto the main face, to a semi-hanging stance just around the arête.

　2　30m　5b　Climb diagonally right on good holds to a rounded spike; then move up and right to enter the obvious smooth groove. Climb this and the larger groove above to a pedestal, above which an easy corner leads to the top.

The *Behemoth* face is bounded on the right by the clean-cut corner of **Shark** (E1 5b), a good pitch reached at lowish tide by abseiling down the short corner to its right, which gives **Probe** (HS), and traversing back along a sea-level ledge. The next route starts at the foot of *Shark*.

★★★ **5　Mastodon**　E3　55m
FA R Edwards, S Salmon 1978

The outstanding route of the wall, offering superb, sustained climbing on perfect rock. At higher tides it is worth abseiling in to start the route from a hanging stance partway up the first pitch (and climbing from there to the second belay).

　1　20m　5b　Climb leftwards into a scoop, then left again to another scoop beneath a long crack. Follow the crack, exiting left at the top to a semi-hanging stance.

　2　23m　5c　Move left to a ledge and climb the crack above until it becomes smooth. Move up and right, then back left into the crack, which is followed to its top. Traverse right to belay at a pinnacle.

　3　12m　5c　Climb the steep crack above to the top.

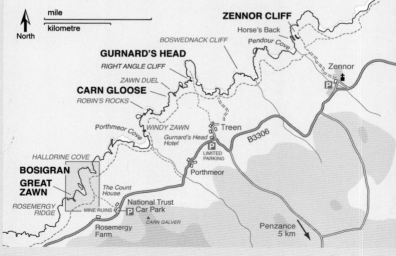

3

4

5

Shark

233

Carn Gloose

OS Ref SW 428 383

A very impressive greenstone crag in dramatic surroundings. Approach by taking the path towards Gurnard's Head but turn left (west) along the coast path just before the neck of the headland. After a few minutes the narrow chasm of Zawn Duel appears on the right. Just beyond is Carn Gloose, the first significant headland west of Gurnard's Head, prominently notched near the top of its ridge.

Descend the ridge to reach the bottom left edge of the crag, which is now seen as an amphitheatre with a line of big overhangs at one-third height. The following route takes a spectacular rising traverse-line between the roofs:

6 Astral Stroll E1 70m
FA R Edwards, C Bryan 1980

A stunning route with situations to match any in Cornwall, best enjoyed in the afternoon when the crag catches the sun. It is not greatly affected by tides but high seas can add considerably to the atmosphere. Start at the base of the ridge.

1 15m 4b Climb around the corner and traverse right to a slab. Cross the slab into a corner and continue to a less steep slab. Belay at the far end, below a leftward-leaning groove. If the sea is too high, the belay can be reached via a higher line at a slightly harder standard.

2 15m 5b Move down a groove and traverse right until it is possible to step down again and traverse to a stance in the far corner – 'the Bidet'.

3 20m 5a Climb to the roof and follow the break diagonally rightwards to a black wall. Traverse the wall across some grooves to reach a flat ledge above the roofs.

4 20m 5a Climb the overhang above and finish up the obvious corners.

West Penwith – North Coast

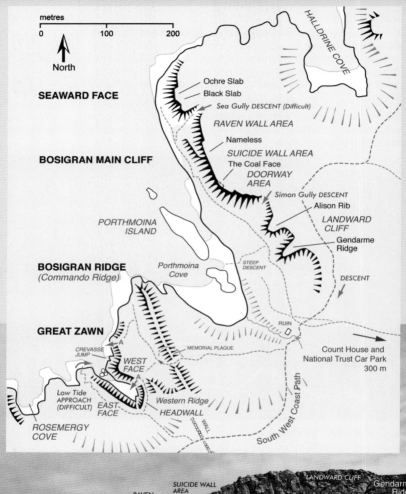

metres

0   100   200

North

SEAWARD FACE

BOSIGRAN MAIN CLIFF

BOSIGRAN RIDGE
(Commando Ridge)

GREAT ZAWN

HALLDRINE COVE

Ochre Slab
Black Slab
Sea Gully DESCENT (Difficult)
RAVEN WALL AREA
Nameless
SUICIDE WALL AREA
The Coal Face
DOORWAY AREA
Simon Gully DESCENT
Alison Rib
LANDWARD CLIFF
Gendarme Ridge

PORTHMOINA ISLAND

Porthmoina Cove

STEEP DESCENT

DESCENT

CREVASSE JUMP
A
MEMORIAL PLAQUE
RUIN
Count House and National Trust Car Park
300 m

WEST FACE
A
Low Tide APPROACH (DIFFICULT)
EAST FACE
Western Ridge
HEADWALL
WALL
South West Coast Path

ROSEMERGY COVE

RAVEN WALL AREA
SUICIDE WALL AREA
LANDWARD CLIFF
Gendarme Ridge
Black Slab
Ochre Slab
Alison Rib
PORTHMOINA ISLAND

SEAWARD FACE   **BOSIGRAN MAIN FACE**   *Start of BOSIGRAN RIDGE*

Bosigran

OS Ref SW 416 368

The Bosigran cliffs are perhaps the most important in Cornwall in terms of popularity and on several other counts. They offer a tremendous concentration of top-quality climbs throughout the grades, all on flawless granite and mostly without tidal problems.

The cliffs are approached from a car park at the conspicuous mine ruins one mile west of the Gurnard's Head Hotel on the B3306. Adjacent to this is the Count House, a Climbers' Club hut with its own parking area for members. A well-marked path leads down to the large blunt headland of Bosigran, which stands 100 metres above the sea and presents the impressive profile of the Main Face on its west side. This overlooks a slender sea stack, Porthmoina Island, set in a beautiful cove, beyond which are the long, pinnacled Bosigran Ridge and the Great Zawn.

The routes are described from **right to left**, as approached.

The Main Face

The path to the cliff descends gently to the remains of some buildings beside the stream running into Porthmoina Cove. From here, the first real feature of the cliff can be seen – **Gendarme Ridge** (a pleasant Diff). The path passes beneath the ridge, then continues below the Main Face on a terrace 45 metres above the sea.

Western Ridge

Bosigran Ridge

HEADWALL

WEST FACE

SEAWARD FACE

GREAT ZAWN

Left of *Gendarme Ridge* are some broken slabby rocks, and the first feature of real significance is a prominent rib leading up to a large platform at 30 metres:

⭐ **7　Alison Rib**　D　50m
FA D G Romanis 1923

An enjoyable route, frequently soloed and perfect for beginners. Start just right of the foot of the rib.

　1 18m Climb on large holds for 3 metres; then step left and follow the true arête to a stance.
　2 14m Climb the steep wall above on good holds to the platform.
　3 18m The less distinct, upper section can be climbed in a variety of ways, the most usual being up cracks on the left.

⭐ **8　Oread**　VD　57m
FA P Jaynes, E Byne (VL) 1955

Pleasant and popular. Left of *Alison Rib* is an obvious groove. Start below the rib just left of this.

　1 34m Climb the rib to reach a large sloping ledge at 20 metres. Continue up the wall above to a stance.
　2 23m Scramble to the foot of the crackline just left of *Alison Rib* and climb the slim groove above to the top.

Left of *Oread* are more discontinuous crags offering several routes in the VD to S grades, but the Main Face proper begins to the left of an obvious descent gully where, just above the path, a slender slab of rock leans against the cliff.

⭐ **9　Ledge Climb**　VD　52m
FA A W Andrews, J B Farmer 1905

The first route to venture on to the Main Face. Safe, low in its grade and ideal for novices. The slender slab on the edge of the face forms a crack on its left side. Start here.

　1 9m Climb the crack to a ledge with numerous belays.
　2 20m Climb leftwards over some broken ground; then move up a slab and over some blocks to a stance beneath an overhang.
　3 14m Move right beneath an overhanging nose and enter a chimney. Climb this to a good stance at the foot of the 'Ledge', which runs up left.
　4 9m Follow the Ledge, which is in fact a shallow trough, diagonally left to the top.

10 Anvil Chorus VS 58m
FA P H Biven, H T H Peck, B M Biven 1956

Despite a broken middle section, this is a truly great climb featuring a challenging layback and an exposed final mantelshelf. Start just left of *Ledge Climb*.

1 34m 4b Climb a thin crack in the centre of the face to a ledge. Move up into the groove above and climb around the right-hand side of the small overhang to more ledges. Scramble left and up to belay beneath the prominent double cracks.

2 24m 4c Climb the cracks by steep laybacking, facing right at first, then left (and not forgetting to place protection), to good holds at the top. Traverse right along the break until an awkward move gains a ledge. Either finish up the corner on the right or, more excitingly, via thin cracks on the left (HVS).

11 Doorway S 58m
FA J Simpson, W J Hutchinson 1949

One of Bosigran's venerable classics – disjointed in line but with excellent climbing on the final pitch – which takes the large, roofed corner right of the steep central area of the Main Face. Some 6 metres left of *Ledge Climb* is an inset groove having a smooth black slab as its left wall. Start here.

1 21m Climb either the slab or the groove itself and continue in the same line over more slabs and ledges to a stance and large chockstone belay.

2 11m Scramble leftwards and up to belay beneath the big corner.

3 26m 4a Climb the wide corner crack (much harder in wet conditions) until just below the roof, where an exposed leftwards traverse leads round the arête to a short crack which is climbed on excellent holds to the top.

12 Little Brown Jug VS 60m
FA B M Biven, P H Biven (VL) 1955

A varied climb of impeccable quality, with each pitch sustained at its grade. About 10 metres left of the inset slab of *Doorway* is a smooth, light-coloured face having a shallow corner in its centre. Start below and to the right of the corner.

1 21m 4a Make a rising traverse on small flakes into the corner and climb it until steeper moves gain a good stance on the left (common with *Doorpost*).

2 18m 4a A line of holds runs across the slab on the right to a large block on the skyline. Follow these, and then move up over large blocks to a stance beneath an overhang.

3 21m 5a Above is an obvious break in the overhang. Climb a steep rib and move on to a sloping ledge. Step up left onto a rounded bulge; then make delicate moves up to the right to gain better holds leading to the trough of *Ledge Climb*. Finish directly up the obvious overhanging crack.

To the left of the first pitch of *Little Brown Jug* is a smooth wall of superb orange granite. A thin seam running up the centre gives the delectable first pitch of **Thin Wall Special** (E1 5b). The route finishes by pulling dramatically around the big overhang which shrouds the corner of *Doorway*.

RAVEN WALL
AREA

★ **13 Doorpost** HS 60m
★ FA B M Biven, H T H Peck, P H Biven 1955
★ The perfect Cornish climb, tracing a great
  sweep up the cliff just right of the impending
  central section. Left of *Little Brown Jug* is a
  broken corner, just above the point where the
  path is lost among boulders. Start here.

  1 22m 4a Scramble up the corner and
  move right onto the obvious rightward-rising
  traverse-line, which is followed to its end.
  Climb up to a stance and nut belays.
  2 12m 4b Climb the twin cracks above the
  left side of the stance, first in the left-hand
  crack then the right, to the large ledge below
  the corner of *Doorway*.
  3 26m 4a Move up the rib above the left
  edge of the stance to a good hold (and
  thread). Continue up the rib on large
  knobbly holds to an easy final crack.

13 *Doorpost* (HS)
Alberto Rampini SEAN KELLY

14 Bow Wall E2 51m
FA Pitch 1: J Brown 1957; pitch 2: B M Biven, H T H Peck (2 pts aid) 1958

A steep, challenging, and iconic climb taking the impending, light-coloured wall which arches up to the right-hand side of the central overhangs of the Main Face. Start by scrambling up the broken corner of *Doorpost* to block belays beneath the wall.

1 24m 5b Climb diagonally right to an obvious spike above a shallow groove. Climb directly up the wall until a strenuous move up a rounded crack gains the 'pancake', a tongue of rock slightly detached from the face. Follow the crack round to the right and transfer to an obvious foothold on a sloping slab. Move up and through a slanting break in the overhang to belays and a tiny stance on the left.

2 27m 5b Traverse left along the lip of the overhang to a ledge beneath a wide crack running up right. Follow the crack for 8 metres; then climb directly up the slab to easier ground.

Beyond the start of *Bow Wall* the path drops down a rocky step and continues beneath a large, leaning flake (Cave Flake) at the base of the cliff. Cave Flake and the walls to its left provide good bouldering.

15 The Ghost E3 60m
FA P H Biven, H T H Peck (aid on traverse) 1956; FFA E Drummond, T Proctor 1973

An airy spacewalk through the central overhangs, described with the first pitch of *The Phantom* as the best combination. Start 6 metres right of Cave Flake, beneath a long ramp sloping up to the right.

1 27m 5a Follow the ramp for 8 metres; then move up into a V-groove and follow it, past a ledge, to a stance on the 'Pedestal' on the right.

2 24m 5c Step right and climb to the top of the 'Coal Face'. Move up into a small groove, step left, and climb a bulge to reach a recess beneath the roofs. Traverse right between the overhangs until it is possible to break through to a small stance 5 metres above.

3 9m Climb easily to the top.

The obvious crack splitting the left side of the central overhang is taken by **The Phantom** (E4 6a), which climbs boldly up to the roof from the Pedestal then traverses left to the crack. **Morgawr** (E6 6c) goes directly through the roofs from the recess beneath them via the obvious black dyke.

16 Suicide Wall E1 64m
FA P H Biven, H T H Peck, B M Biven 1955

The original line of ascent of the central wall – a varied route of great character and tradition. Small cams and wires protect the crux pitch. Start as for *The Ghost*.

1 38m 4b Climb easily up the rightward-sloping ramp into the corner formed by the Coal Face. Move up, and follow the obvious diagonal crack across the face, stepping down at its end to a stance on the Pedestal.

2 18m 5c Follow the line of thin flakes leftwards, up and across the wall, and make awkward moves to gain the rounded ledge. Climb the smooth, technical groove directly above to a large platform.

3 8m 5a Climb the corner above for a short way; then swing right on a good jug into a pod. Break right and finish easily.

Morgawr (E6)
Jiri Sefl
14 *Bow Wall* (E2)
Heather Clark
SCOTT TITT

17 Beowulf E2 60m

FA P H Biven, H T H Peck (3 pts aid) 1966; FFA P Gordon 1967

A delicate and technical climb taking a series of grooves left of *Suicide Wall*. Start just right of Cave Flake.

1 27m 5a Follow the hold-plastered rake up to the left for 6 metres and then climb directly into an overhung bay. Break steeply right from here to thread belays at some blocks.

2 18m 5c Traverse left above the lip of the bay and move up into an open groove. Climb the groove to the break; then move up left into another groove leading to the large platform.

3 15m 5b From the left end of the platform, climb leftwards and up into a scoop on small holds. Move up to a small overhang which is passed on the left to easier ground.

The knobbly ramp to the right of Cave Flake runs more than halfway up the cliff and provides the first pitch of *Nameless*, which leads to a stance shared with *Autumn Flakes*.

18 Paragon HVS 62m

FA P H Biven, H T H Peck 1956

More a series of pitches than a natural line, but a very popular route giving consistently high-quality climbing in inspiring positions. Start 3 metres left of Cave Flake.

1 18m 5a Climb a steep wall slightly leftwards to a ledge at 6 metres. Follow the series of black corners on the right to belay on the knobbly rake (of *Nameless*).

2 21m 4c Make a rising rightward traverse to an exposed rib and move up to a large crystal-filled pocket. Take the overhang above on good holds and then climb diagonally left to belay in an open bay.

3 9m 5a On the right side of the bay is an obvious layback crack: follow it to a large stance below a steep corner.

4 14m 5a Climb the corner, using holds and a crack on the right wall where it bulges. Finish more easily.

19 Autumn Flakes/Nameless HVS 51m

FA R Goodier, P C Henry 1955; D Kemp, N E Morin 1953

This combination provides interesting climbing to a stiff finish which can feel much harder in less than perfect conditions. Care should be taken to arrange good protection and belays for the upper pitches, since accidents have occurred through reliance on old pitons. Start 9 metres left of Cave Flake.

1 27m 4a Climb the crack in the initial wall to a ledge. Follow a series of flake cracks up and slightly right to a small stance where the line meets a rugged rake (the true first pitch of *Nameless*, which rises to this point from further right). Good natural belays.

2 9m 4b Move up right for a short way, and then climb leftwards into a bay. Traverse left to belays beneath twin cracks.

3 15m 4c Climb the twin cracks to a small ledge and continue up the corner above, where a series of moves on poor holds gains a gritty scoop. Climb more easily but still with care to the cliff-top.

Variation

Taking the true continuation of *Autumn Flakes* rather than the *Nameless* finish gives a worthwhile route of HS standard.

2a 27m 4b Climb up a couple of metres; then traverse left and follow the left slanting break to the top.

23 *Kafoozalem* E3
Dave Turnbull PETE SAUNDERS

The left side of the Main Face, known as the Raven Wall Area, rises above a terrace which is separated from the path along the cliff base by a short, steep tier. A path leads up to the left side of the terrace and the initial wall of *Autumn Flakes* leads to its extreme right-hand end. The routes here are shorter but more sustained, technically hard, and on immaculate rock. It is the last part of the cliff to get the sun and the left-facing grooves are often slippery (and harder) until they have dried out in the afternoon sun.

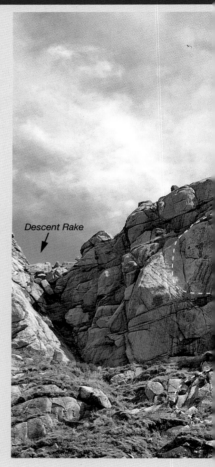

Descent Rake

⭐ 20 Zig Zag VS 45m
FA J Simpson, W J Hutchinson 1948

The original route to breach this part of the cliff is well worth doing, and although the difficult sections are quite short, they are well positioned and feel quite challenging. Start by a prominent spike at the right end of the grass terrace.

1 21m 4c Move up blocks until a move right across a steep wall gives access to a black-veined break, which is followed to a niche below the overhang.

2 24m 4c Climb up left beneath the overhang, and take the line of weakness up to the right to gain the final section of *Autumn Flakes* (a left-slanting break).

⭐ 21 Raven Wall E3 5c 37m
FA J H Deacon, R Goodier (some aid) 1955

Climbs the largest of the black corners, starting 6 metres right of the huge pointed block at the base of the wall. Climb to a large ledge and continue up the steep corner to a bulging section. A difficult move up the right wall gains a good crack. Step back left and climb the continuation groove to the top.

⭐ 22 Evil Eye E5 6b 37m
FA P Littlejohn, C King 1978

A brilliant sustained pitch taking the slim groove immediately left of *Raven Wall*. Start at the overhanging corner beneath the groove. Climb the corner and move up into the groove (thread). Climb the groove and continue direct until it is possible to move up and left onto a slab. Climb to a bulge, and then up the wall above to a rounded ledge. Finish leftwards.

⭐ 23 Kafoozalem E3 6a 37m
FA F E R Cannings, P Badcock (aid) 1964; FFA J Moran, D Banks 1977

A stunning line giving superb climbing. It takes the thin crack splitting the diamond-shaped wall left of *Evil Eye*. Start at a corner 5 metres right of an obvious faultline. Climb the corner, traverse

248

right, and make difficult moves leftwards to enter the crack. Follow the crack to a scoop on the left and continue in the same line to a ledge. A crack on the left leads to the top.

The slanting fault itself is taken by **The Armchair** (HVS 5a) and also gives the problematic first 9 metres of **Beaker Route** (HVS 5a), which then slants away up the steep attractive slab on the left. The Main Face is terminated by a wide rake running the full height of the crag. This is the usual descent from routes on the Seaward Cliff and the left side of the Main Face, but it requires care, especially in wet conditions.

The path which runs beneath the Main Face continues down left to ledges beneath the Seaward Cliff, from where the next routes begin.

Descent

27 26

25

24

The Seaward Cliff

This area of cliff, though for the most part not influenced by tides, is sprayed by the sea during heavy weather and thus has more of a sea-cliff atmosphere than the Main Face. A prominent feature is the unmistakable Black Slab (a bigger 'coal face'), and routes are described in relation to this.

⭐ 24 Ding HS 49m
FA J H Deacon, B Grey, M E Banks 1957

Delightful climbing and sustained interest. Halfway between *Black Slab* and the right-hand edge of the cliff is a slanting dyke. Start at the foot of this.

1 26m 4b Climb up to a scoop; then move rightwards and make a difficult move onto a ledge. Step up to a horizontal crack, traverse right, and pull over an awkward bulge. Continue up a crack to a stance.

2 23m 4b Climb to a prominent spike, and continue up a light-coloured scoop on the left to the final overhang. Pull straight over on good holds and in a fine position.

⭐ 25 Black Slab D 32m
FA C F Kirkus, P S Fallows 1938

This climb, magnificently situated with large friendly holds, provides a good introduction to the adventurous quality of sea-cliff climbing. Start from a platform 6 metres down from the base of the slab.

1 23m Climb up to the pinnacle on the left side of the slab; then step right and follow the left edge of the slab to belay under the roof.

2 9m Escape left to an easy gully leading to the cliff-top.

Left of *Black Slab* is a triangular slab of wonderfully rough granite – the Ochre Slab. It gives two excellent climbs.

⭐ 26 Ochre Slab Route I VS 39m
FA H T H Peck, P H Biven 1956

Delicate slab work followed by a spectacular finish through the overhang. Start at the toe of the slab.

1 27m 4c Trend rightwards up the slab until it steepens to a wall. Traverse right and move over onto the upper slab, which is climbed direct via a thin seam to the stance of *Black Slab* under the roof.

2 12m 5a Climb up into the V-groove which splits the overhang above and bridge out to good finishing holds on the right. Go easily to the top.

⭐ 27 Ochre Slab Route II S 33m
FA Unknown

Very pleasant climbing and situations, taking a rising line from left to right across the slab. Start near the foot of the shallow chimney which bounds the slab on the left.

1 24m 4a Climb to a flake at 5 metres and continue diagonally rightwards over a lip onto the main slab. Climb bearing slightly right to the ledge beneath the large overhang.

2 9m 4a Climb the wall just left of the overhang on small positive holds.

The only true sea-cliff section of the Bosigran cliffs is further to the left and lower down and offers three quite serious climbs: **Boldfinger** (E3 5b), **Geronimo** (E2 5b), and **Hopeless Slab** (HVS 4c). These perhaps are best left to the Bosigran habitués.

31 *The Dream/Liberator* (E3)
Rob Greenwood   MIKE HUTTON

Bosigran Ridge

This is the long ridge that encloses Porthmoina Cove opposite the Main Face. It gives a unique expedition for Cornwall and can be great fun in all weathers. The route mainly follows the crest but many variations are possible and only a general description is given.

Approach   Take the path leading to the Main Face until it is possible to cross the stream running into Porthmoina Cove, either down at the ruined buildings or more directly by a vague path higher up. The path crosses Bosigran Ridge at the first distinct notch at the landward end and after this it is possible to scramble down beside the ridge to reach shelving slabs near sea level.

⭐ 28 Bosigran (Commando) Ridge   VD   210m
FA A W Andrews, E Andrews 1902

Start directly beneath the nose at the base of the ridge. During high tide or heavy seas one should belay earlier, or even gain the ridge higher up if the sea is really threatening. Move round the ridge onto a sloping platform above a deep zawn. Move up left onto the wall and climb to a ledge. Continue up the cracked face on enormous holds to a platform. Climb the chimney behind to the true crest of the ridge and follow this in five or six more pitches, tackling problems direct or skirting them either side, until the ridge fades into the slope.

The Great Zawn

OS Ref SW 414 366

An intimidating canyon with walls that provide some of the South West's finest routes, all in the higher grades. It lies to the west of the Western Ridge, which is adjacent to Bosigran Ridge.

The Zawn presents four faces, each with its own character and style of climbing. The outermost, seaward face is Green Cormorant Face. This is open and relatively quick drying but affected by tides, particularly in rough seas. It is reached using the path that crosses Bosigran Ridge, from where it leads down to a sloping ledge above the lowest walls of the zawn. A 20-metre abseil gives access to a large sea-washed platform beneath the face, from where *Variety Show*, *Dream/Liberator*, etc. can be reached.

Climbs on the interior walls of the zawn are reached by walking west along the top of the cliffs, to just beyond Bosigran Ridge, then descending the steep grass and bracken slope via a small path until the zawn is encountered on the right. Turn right and take the path above the headwall to its flanking corner, where a prominent spike is used for a 24-metre abseil onto the upper end of the sloping zawn bed.

⭐⭐ 29 Variety Show   HVS   45m
FA H T H Peck, B M Biven (VL), C Fishwick (aid) 1957; FFA P Littlejohn, F E R Cannings 1970

Superb climbing with plentiful protection – a good introduction to the zawn. The wall to the right of the abseil line, **Exit Route** (HS), is split by a prominent thin crack. Start beneath this.
   1 27m 5a Climb to the start of the crack and follow it until a move right at 23 metres gains another short crack leading to a large sloping stance above a horizontal break.
   2 18m 4b Climb the slab to a short, overhanging corner and move up to gain easier rock above.

253

At the back of the platform is a huge tapering cleft, **Great Zawn Chimney** (E1 5a), below which is the 'Crevasse' separating the platform from the ledge at the foot of Green Cormorant Face proper. A well-aimed jump gains belays on the far side – a badly-aimed jump doesn't.

⭐ 30 Green Cormorant Face E2 45m

FA J H Deacon, M E Banks (aid) 1957; P Littlejohn, F E R Cannings (VL, l pt aid) 1969

This, the first climb to breach the Zawn's defences, has reassuring stances but a nice air of commitment. Start on the smooth ledge beyond the Crevasse.

1 18m 5a Move up to the overhang from the right and climb directly to a large flake. Step up to a horizontal crack and climb up on the right or the left to the spacious stance above.

2 9m 5c Move up left to a sloping ledge beneath a smooth groove. Step right and make steep moves to better holds at the top of the black diagonal crack which rises from the right. Good stance above. Alternatively, the smooth groove itself may be climbed by a fierce layback (E3 6a) or by its left arête gained and followed to the stance (E2 5c).

3 18m 4a Climb the groove above to the top.

The sheer black slab right of the second pitch of *Green Cormorant Face* is taken by **Déjà Vu** (E4 6a), a tense piece of climbing which traverses on to the face from the 'spacious stance', and then ascends boldly to a shallow ramp running up left.

⭐ 31 The Dream/Liberator E3 60m

FA M J Guilliard, R O'B Wilson (aid) 1968; P Littlejohn, F E R Cannings (VL, 3 pts aid) 1970/72; FFA R Fawcett, P Livesey (VL) 1976

An impeccable route, basically following the magnificent seaward arête between the Green Cormorant and West Faces. Start as for *Green Cormorant Face*.

1 9m 5a Traverse right and move round into a corner (often greasy). Climb 3 metres to a small ledge and belay.

2 24m 6a Climb the groove above, move right, and follow another groove with more difficulty to its capping roof. Make a long reach to holds on the left edge of the roof and pull round onto a steep slab. Follow a weakness up to the left for 5 metres; then climb straight up thin cracks to the horizontal fault. Traverse right, and step down around the arête to a small stance.

3 27m 5c Climb the steep cracks above for 6 metres; then traverse right, beneath the roof, to a large incut foothold. Follow the thin slanting crack and a wider continuation crack to the top.

The imposing west-facing wall of the inner zawn is dominated by the magnificent central groove of *The West Face*. Once an aid-climbing extravaganza for winter days, it is now a free climb of the highest calibre requiring dry spring or summer weather to come into condition. To its right the face changes character and forms the steep slab of *Desolation Row*. This is less enclosed and dries out more quickly,

⭐ 32 The West Face E5 54m

FA P H Biven, H T H Peck (VL, aid) 1957; P Livesey, J Lawrence (l pt) 1975; FFA R Fawcett 1976

An inspiring line with bold and strenuous climbing on the first pitch, and technical moves in exposed situations on the second. Start beneath the obvious layback crack in the lower groove.

1 21m 5c Climb the black wall (peg) and move right to gain the crack. Follow this to a stance on the right.

2 24m 6b Move back left into the groove and follow it with increasing difficulty (peg) to the first roof. Climb past the roof to a restricted corner beneath a second roof (peg). Move right to pass this and climb the crack above to a cave stance.

3 9m Continue easily up the crack.

Bosigran Ridge

'Crevasse' Jump

29 30 31 32 33 34

33 Desolation Row E2 5b 46m
FA F E R Cannings, P Littlejohn 1969

A sustained and delicate pitch which can be well protected with small wires. It follows a line of thin cracks near the left edge of the steep slab. Start at a shallow groove below the cracks. Climb the groove to a small overhang; then step left and up a rib to the right-hand end of the large roof. Step right and make delicate moves to some good footholds. Continue up the obvious line to the top, and belay higher on the grassy slope.

The crackline in the centre of the slab is **Candy Man** (E2 5b) and the cracks just left of the abseil corner give **Shape Shifter** (HVS 5a). Right of the corner is the sheer headwall of the zawn, which suffers a little from seepage but gets a good deal of afternoon sun. The cracks in its centre give **Omen** (E2 4b,5b), which belays at the prominent finger of rock pointing to the line. The thin black seam running diagonally left from the finger provides the excellent **Fated** (E5 6b). The next route ascends the East Face of the zawn.

34 Xanadu E2 60m
FA P Littlejohn, I Duckworth 1970

The compelling line of the East Face is a long groove which curves left. An outstanding climb, generally dry only in the summer months. Start at the initial groove.

1 30m 5b Climb the groove to a sharp flake at around 20 metres (steering clear of a nest on the right at 15 metres if the cormorant is in residence). Continue on better holds to a stance in the niche beneath the overhang.

2 30m 5b Move up and left past a blunt spike to the foot of a black seam. Pull rightwards across the overhang into a wide crack and follow this to the top.

Kenidjack

OS Ref SW 354 323

This excellent little crag of sound killas slate lies just to the north of Cape Cornwall, near St Just. Approach by taking the narrow lane which runs seawards down the steep-sided valley on the north side of St Just. There is a parking spot on the right just before the main track divides. Continue on foot taking the left fork to reach small grassy quarried bays above the cliff.

The main cliff is an impressive sheet of slab, bounded on the left by the broken corner of *Gneiss Gnome* and on the right by a smooth open groove – **Thane** (E1 5b). Right of *Thane* the cliff becomes a steep, stratified wall crossed by two obvious diagonal breaks, the upper one being **Slanter** (VS 4b).

The cliff is only slightly affected by tides, and even at high tide routes such as *The Shield*, *Thane* and *Stormbringer* can be reached by abseil. The normal descent is via the ridge which runs down the seaward edge of the cliff, cutting back left down a quartz ramp to the base.

⭐ 35 Gneiss Gnome HS 4a 27m
FA K Darbyshire, P Littlejohn 1971

Worthwhile as an introduction to the crag and the rock. Start below and right of the corner, on the ramp which undercuts the left side of the slab. Climb the quartz-covered wall on good holds to the foot of the corner. Steep climbing up the corner gains a grassy ledge and belays.

⭐ 36 Rock Dancer E1 5b 46m
FA R Edwards, M Edwards 1979

Excellent climbing throughout. Start 5 metres left of *Saxon* at a scoop in the overhang. Climb straight up to the traverse of *Saxon*, continue up the right wall of the shallow groove, and then climb direct to gain the sloping ledge left of the big groove in the middle of the face. Move left until it is possible to climb directly to the top past a horizontal break.

⭐ 37 Saxon HVS 5a 46m
FA P Littlejohn, S Jones 1974

The classic of the slab – an intimidating line which unfolds to give beautiful sustained climbing. Start just left of the enormous block which abuts the base of the slab. Climb to a ramp and follow it up to the left for 9 metres before moving up into a niche. Step left and climb the steep wall to better holds on the left. Continue slightly leftwards up a depression until steeper moves right gain the obvious horizontal line. Finish direct from here (or to follow the easier original line: hand-traverse along the break to a stance, and then take the wall above).

⭐ 38 The Shield E1 46m
FA P Littlejohn, K Darbyshire 1971

A satisfying route climbing to the apex of the slab via a bold second pitch. Start on the huge block which abuts the cliff.

  1 21m 4c Climb to a horizontal break, and then bear left to a patch of quartz. Climb straight up to the short corner formed by a huge block, and move up to a stance and peg belay on top of the block.
  2 15m 5a Move up, and then right onto the upper face. Climb diagonally rightwards almost as far as the groove of *Thane*; then take a fairly direct line, on small holds, to the top.

⭐ 39 Stormbringer E3 46m
FA R Edwards, S Salmon 1979

A steep and impressive line on the back wall of the zawn. Start at the foot of the slab below a leftward-sloping ramp.

  1 12m 4b Climb up to the ramp and belay just above the block.
  2 34m 5c Climb up, and then right into a corner. Step right on to the arête, climb to the roof, and make difficult moves rightwards gain the lip of the next roof and a sloping ledge. Move back left and climb the steep wall to the top. Peg belays.

40 *High Street Blues* (E4)
Alexis Perry   SIMON CARDY

The Sennen Cliffs

OS Ref SW 346 262

Though of little more than outcrop height, the Sennen cliffs have great charm and offer scores of steep, gymnastic climbs on beautifully sculptured granite. They are situated beneath the Coastguard Lookout on the headland to the west of Sennen Cove, and cars should be left in the most westerly of the official car parks, leaving a walk of a few minutes to the cliff-top.

At low tide the crag can be approached along sea-level terraces from Sennen, but it is usually more convenient to descend from the cliff-top. The easiest descent is via the gully just to the left (south) of the lookout. A more direct descent uses the deep re-entrant gully, **Griptight Gully** (D), 100 metres north of the lookout. The top of this can be identified by a depression which runs down to a prominent break in the cliff edge.

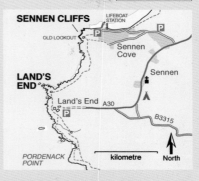

The cliffs rise above a wide platform which inclines gradually to disappear into the sea at its northern end. Only the lower end of the platform (below *Zig Zag* etc.) is tidal, but on stormy days waves can engulf the whole cliff. At the northern end of the platform is a black zawn whose left wall is split by the very prominent crack of *Zig Zag*. The thinner crack 6 metres left of this is **Delilah** (E1 5b).

40 High Street Blues   E4 6a 17m
FA R Edwards, M Edwards 1987

Superb climbing. Start just left of *Delilah*. Move up onto the block on the right, and step left onto the wall. Climb via a faint weakness to the break, and follow faint cracks to another break. Finish up the steep wall above the roof.

41 Zig Zag   HVS 5a 18m
FA M E Banks 1955

The striking crack gives a good tough pitch. Gain the sentry box; then follow the steep crack to a sloping ledge. Move right and climb on good holds to the top.

The impressive wall to the right of *Zig Zag* gives two desperate testpieces – **Tears of a Clown** (E7 6b) and **29 Palms** (E6 6c). The slab forming the right wall of the zawn is **Slippery Slab** (VS 5a), a good delicate pitch. The most obvious break in the steep wall further right, above a step in the terrace, is **Genge's Groove** (HVS 5a).

42 A Swift Flight of Fancy   E3 6a 23m
FA R Edwards, M Edwards 1984

Start 3 metres right of *Genge's Groove* below an impending crack. Climb the crack and continue, via a black-streaked wall, to the big horizontal break. Move right along the break, and climb directly up the centre of the overhanging face above.

Unfortunately, the impressive wall to the right has been desecrated by bolts and chipping, a source of great shame on this fine sculptural cliff. The wall is terminated by an elegant arête whose seaward side is taken by:

⭐ 43 Samson Arête   E2 6a   23m
FA R Edwards, I Pomfret 1974

Climb the wall just right of the arête, and pull up to a crack leading to an overhang. Step left, and follow the rounded cracks above to a larger overhang. Pull through this on the right to a final short slab.

The fine wall to the right of the arête gives Sennen's best-known route:

⭐⭐⭐ 44 Demo Route   HS   24m
FA J F Barry 1943

A great little climb, famous thanks to its photogenic appeal. Start at the foot of a flake roughly in the middle of the wall.

1 15m 4b Climb the flake, a groove, and finally an awkward wide crack to a good ledge.
2 9m 4b Step up; then move left and down using the undercut nose to gain a juggy slab leading to the top.

⭐ 45 Corner Climb   D   21m
FA Commando party c.1943

The corner which bounds the wall of *Demo Route*, some 20 metres left of *Griptight Gully*. A steep pitch on big jugs and sinking jams. It is also a satisfying descent route for the experienced.

Griptight
Gully

47 48   49 50

Step in
platform

46

⭐ 46 Banana Flake VD 26m

FA Commando party c.1943

Pleasant climbing on good holds throughout. To the right of the lower part of *Griptight Gully* is a large pointed flake with a yellow top. Start beneath the shallow, stepped groove to the right of this.

    1 14m Climb the groove, bearing left to the top of the flake and a good ledge.

    2 12m Climb the corner above the right-hand side of the ledge, or the face just to its left, both on excellent holds.

About 60 metres right of *Griptight Gully* is a 5-metre step in the platform.

⭐ 47 Staircase D 18m

FA Commando party c.1943

A fun pitch on perfect holds taking the narrow black slab some 10 metres left of the step.

⭐ 48 Overhanging Wall VS 4c 20m

FA V N Stevenson, C B Wilson 1962

Fine climbing and good protection. Start as for *Staircase*. Climb the steep slab to the foot of the overhanging corner on the right. Move left and ascend twin overhanging cracks to a spike. Pull over onto a small ledge and continue more easily to the top.

The corner just right of *Overhanging Wall* gives another good pitch at a similar standard:

⭐ 49 Africa Route VS 5a 18m

FA R Flemming 1955

Interesting and varied, with a problematic start. Start 8 metres left of the step in the platform, beneath a steep wall with an obvious pocket hold at 4 metres. Gain the pocket with difficulty and continue steeply to a small ledge. Step left and up the rib into the bay; then move up and right to a junction with *Double Overhang* at the base of its final crack. Climb the rounded cracks on the left, awkwardly, to the top.

★ 50 Double Overhang HS 4b 18m
FA J F Barry 1943

A local favourite; steep and juggy. Start just to the left of the step. Climb directly to the base of a leftward-slanting slot, and follow this to a pinnacle (possible stance). Step left and climb an overhanging corner to easy ground.

★ 51 Vertical Crack HS 4c 21m
FA J F Barry 1943

A powerful line which is steep and strenuous but very well protected. It takes the large corner roughly 20 metres right of the step in the platform. Climb the corner, mainly by bridging, to a ledge at 12 metres. More wide bridging up the rounded groove above gains the top.

★ 52 Gillian E3 5c 21m
FA A Mahoney, P de Mengel (aid) 1972; FFA R Edwards, M Edwards 1977

Excellent technical climbing up the left-hand of the two cracklines in the impressive wall to the right of *Vertical Crack*. Climb the steep wall, and move left into the leftward-curving crack. Follow it to a pocket, and continue to the second of two horizontal breaks. Move right over a bulge and finish up twin cracks.

★ 53 Golva E2 5c 23m
FA M B McDermott, S Bemrose (aid) 1966; FFA R Edwards, M Edwards 1976

Steep and varied climbing up the more obvious right-hand crack. Follow the crack, over a difficult bulge, to the second horizontal break. Move up right and follow a crack, below the roof, to a shallow groove leading to the top.

★ 54 Dolphin Cracks HVS 24m
FA T Genge 1947; Complete J H Deacon, R Goodier 1955

A good tough climb, this old favourite takes a strong natural line up the steep Coastguard Face. The first pitch – Genge's Crack – is the main challenge. Start near the lower left edge of the face at a wide corner-crack.

1 9m 5a Climb the corner, making an awkward exit to a good ledge.

2 15m 4c Above the corner, a crack leads up and past the left side of an overhang. Follow the crack and the groove above to the top.

★ 55 Superjam E5 6b 27m
FA R Edwards, M Edwards (VL) 1984

An amazing roof crack – fierce, spectacular, and photogenic. It takes the split in the overhang to the right of the top pitch of *Dolphin Cracks*. Gain the ledge below the overhang from the right and belay below the line. Climb the right-hand crack to the roof. Swing out left into the roof crack proper and traverse horizontally left until it widens (peg). Follow the crack around the left side of the roof to a corner which leads to the top.

Sennen also provides a lot of good bouldering. Recommended areas are the sea-level tiers at the western end, the short wall below *Gillian* and *Golva*, and below *Africa Route*.

43 *Samson Arête* (E2)
Richard Waterton   SIMON CARDY

Land's End

OS Ref SW 341 253

Because of its status as a tourist attraction, Land's End is unlike any other climbing area in Cornwall. The whole headland is privately owned and run as a holiday centre with all sorts of amenities and amusements. Climbers are welcome and get a discount on car parking in summer provided they use only the toilets, shops, and cafe and avoid the other 'attractions'.

Though generally single-pitch, the routes here are very impressive, being steep and sustained and in a very dramatic setting. The granite can be rather friable in places, but poor rock is not a problem on the routes described.

Land's End itself (Dr Syntax's Head) is the broad headland furthest north of the *First and Last House*, some 400 metres from the large car parks (towards Longships Lighthouse).

Dr Syntax's Head

The cliff on the south side of this headland is known as Entrance Wall, being at the entrance of a big sea cave (the Great Cave) which goes right through the head. To approach, abseil down the wall to ledges (lowish tide) and traverse into the zawn (VD standard) towards the Great Cave until below the overhanging wall at the entrance. **Blitzkrieg** (E1 5b) climbs the obvious wide crack on the left side of Entrance Wall while **New Waves** (HVS 5b) shares the same start, and then takes the wall to the right.

56   Edge of Time   E4   44m

FA R Edwards, M Edwards 1985

A superb route with an isolated atmosphere. It can be climbed as one pitch but rope drag is a problem. Start at a right-slanting crack at the cave entrance.

1 14m Climb the crack to a ledge which leads into the cave.

2 30m 6b Traverse back left to the arête, and climb the steep wall to the roof (peg). Move left round the arête into a shallow groove, which leads to a square recess. Climb up to a flat ledge, and move right to finish.

267

Cormorant and World's End Promontories

The large, boulder-filled cove below the *First and Last House* is bounded to the north by the pinnacled Cormorant Promontory, and to the south by the less prominent World's End Promontory. At low tide, the latter gives a descent route to both areas, but if an abseil descent is preferred the best one for Cormorant Promontory is down the steep grey slab (*Cormorant Slab*) forming its seaward face. This gains a platform from which both *The Cormorant's Bill* and the main pitch of *Last Dancer* can be reached at high tide.

★ **57   Cormorant Slab**   S 4a   24m
FA D M Holroyd, A Blackshaw, J H Deacon 1957

Pleasant, friendly climbing in a wonderful location. Start towards the left of the slab at a shallow, left-facing corner. Climb the corner and crack above to a ledge; then move right to another crack leading to good finishing holds. Belay; then scramble off along the promontory.

★ **58   The Cormorant's Bill**   HVS 5b   27m
FA J H Deacon, C Fishwick (some aid) 1971; FFA P Littlejohn 1972

A steep and technical pitch taking the conspicuous groove on the tip of Cormorant Promontory. Start at the right-hand end of the platform beneath *Cormorant Slab*. Climb to a ledge, and then gain another ledge beneath the groove proper. Continue with interest to the overhang, and make strenuous moves through the V-shaped cut to reach a good hold on the left wall. Better holds now lead to the top.

> **58** *The Cormorant's Bill* **(HVS)**
> **Ken Palmer**   PETE SAUNDERS

★★ **59 Last Dancer** E5 38m
FA R Edwards, M Edwards (VL) 1985

Sustained, technical climbing up the slender tower to the right of *The Cormorant's Bill*. Start at the base of the buttress, just left of a wide crack, and below an all-too-obvious peg.

1 9m 6c Climb the pock-marked wall to the peg. The obvious crack leads to a stance (this can be reached more easily via the start of *The Cormorant's Bill*).

2 29m 6b Climb the wall on the left and swing round the arête (peg). Continue to traverse, and then move up into a shallow groove. Climb the steep slab above to a horizontal fault, and go over an overlap to another steep slab (peg). Continue to another faultline; then ascend rightwards to the arête and thence to the top. This pitch can be climbed at high tide by moving right and up to the shallow groove from the ledge at the foot of *The Cormorant's Bill*.

The climbing descent to the cove begins from the lowest point of the path above World's End Promontory. Descend a groove to a large prominent ledge; then climb down the chimney on the left (facing out) which runs down beside the steep face taken by *World's End* to an area of large, non-tidal ledges (Diff in descent, and avoidable by abseiling from the prominent ledge). To reach Cormorant Promontory from here, descend a little further and cross the boulder-filled cove which drains at low tide.

60   Johnstone's Route   S   30m
FA J H Deacon, D M Holroyd 1957

A route of character in impressive surroundings; steep and exposed towards the top. Start about 10 metres right of the end of Cormorant Promontory, below a large triangular niche.

1 15m 4a Climb bearing slightly right on good holds before breaking left to a stance and belays in the corner.

2 15m 4a Climb the right-hand corner behind the stance to a narrow ledge. Move left to the start of a steep crack and climb this to the crest of the promontory.

Towards the back of the zawn, but still on Cormorant Promontory, is a corner formed by a rounded, undercut buttress. Just left of the corner is the line of **Tide Race** (HS 4b), while the buttress itself gives an impressive climb:

61   Day Tripper   E4   40m
FA R Edwards, M Edwards (VL) 1981

A brilliant route which, after a strenuous start, gives sustained, technical climbing up the thin cracks on the arête of the buttress. Start beneath the roofs at the base of the buttress.

1 34m 6a Climb the steep wall to the first roof and move round into an overhanging V-groove. Climb the groove to reach holds high on the left and pull over onto the wall above. Continue to the next roof; then climb rightwards until a finger crack on the left can be gained. Follow this with increasing difficulty to a small triangular ledge, and then step left into a thinner crack which leads to a good ledge.

2 6m 4c Climb into the wide crack on the left and up this, with care, to the top.

On the opposite side of the zawn, just right of the back wall, is a buttress split by an obvious crack, **Virgin on a Crisis** (E6 6c), a stunning pitch on good rock with some bold climbing near the top. The left edge of the wall is taken by the excellent **Edge Control II** (E5 6b).

62   World's End   E1   5a   26m
FA J H Deacon, D M Holroyd, A G Day 1957

This excellent pitch takes the obvious leftward-slanting line on the steep wall to the right of the descent chimney. Start beneath the large overhang at the bottom right corner of the wall. Climb to the roof and traverse left to clear it. Follow the shallow cracks bearing left, and then climb straight up the face on the obvious line.

63   Zawn Face Route   HVS   25m
FA D M Holroyd, J H Deacon 1957

A unique climb with its hardest moves in an exposed position above the deep zawn beside the promontory. Start as for *World's End*.

1 17m 4c Crawl rightwards along the slot and establish an upright position in a short open groove. Climb the groove; then break left to easier rock and follow the obvious fault leftwards to a large ledge.

2 8m 4a Climb the crack above the left end of the ledge.

Diff chimney
downclimb

Low tide approach to
Cormorant Promontory

The Parasite

Initiation

62
63
64

On the opposite side of the zawn from the last two routes are two obvious grooves. These are, from the right, **Initiation** (HVS 5a) and **The Parasite** (E2 5b), the latter reached using the obvious ramp. The next route – *Voices* – is even further to the left. These climbs, best viewed initially from the World's End side, are reached by an abseil down the front of the next buttress to the south.

64 Voices E3 5b 30m
FA P Littlejohn, D Roberts 1977

A fine route in a spectacular situation. Start at a triangular ledge at the edge of the zawn, opposite *Zawn Face Route*. Move left along a tilting ramp to below the corner of *The Parasite*. Step left on to the back wall of the zawn and climb cracks to just below the overhang. Move right and climb a chimney for 3 metres, until a good foothold on the left can be gained. Climb the face to a line of handholds, and from their left-hand end, move up to finish up the cracked face on the right.

Longships Promontory

From the top of the rambling buttress in front of the hotel, Longships Promontory is visible slightly to the north as a narrow finger of rock pointing seawards. It lies about 100 metres south of the island of Dollar Rock. On the south side of the promontory is a conspicuous wall of black schorl – Longships Wall. The usual approach is to abseil down this to a sloping platform which is covered at high tide, thus making an abseil rope available should escape be necessary. However, between low and half tide, descent is possible by climbing down a short steep groove on the south side of the end of the promontory (Diff standard).

65 Longships Wall E3 6a 23m
FA J H Deacon, M B McDermott (aid) 1959; E. Grindley (l pt) 1973; FFA P Littlejohn, I M Peters 1977

A popular route with some good face climbing. Start beneath the obvious thin crack towards the right-hand side of the wall. Climb the crack – sustained and with the crux moves around 12 metres up.

An equally fine route (not affected by seepage and slightly bolder but less technical) takes the first 8 metres of *Longships Wall*, and then traverses to the left edge of the wall before going directly to the top – **Antenna** (E4 5c). The groove immediately to the right of *Longships Wall* gives the excellent **New Editions** (E4 6b).

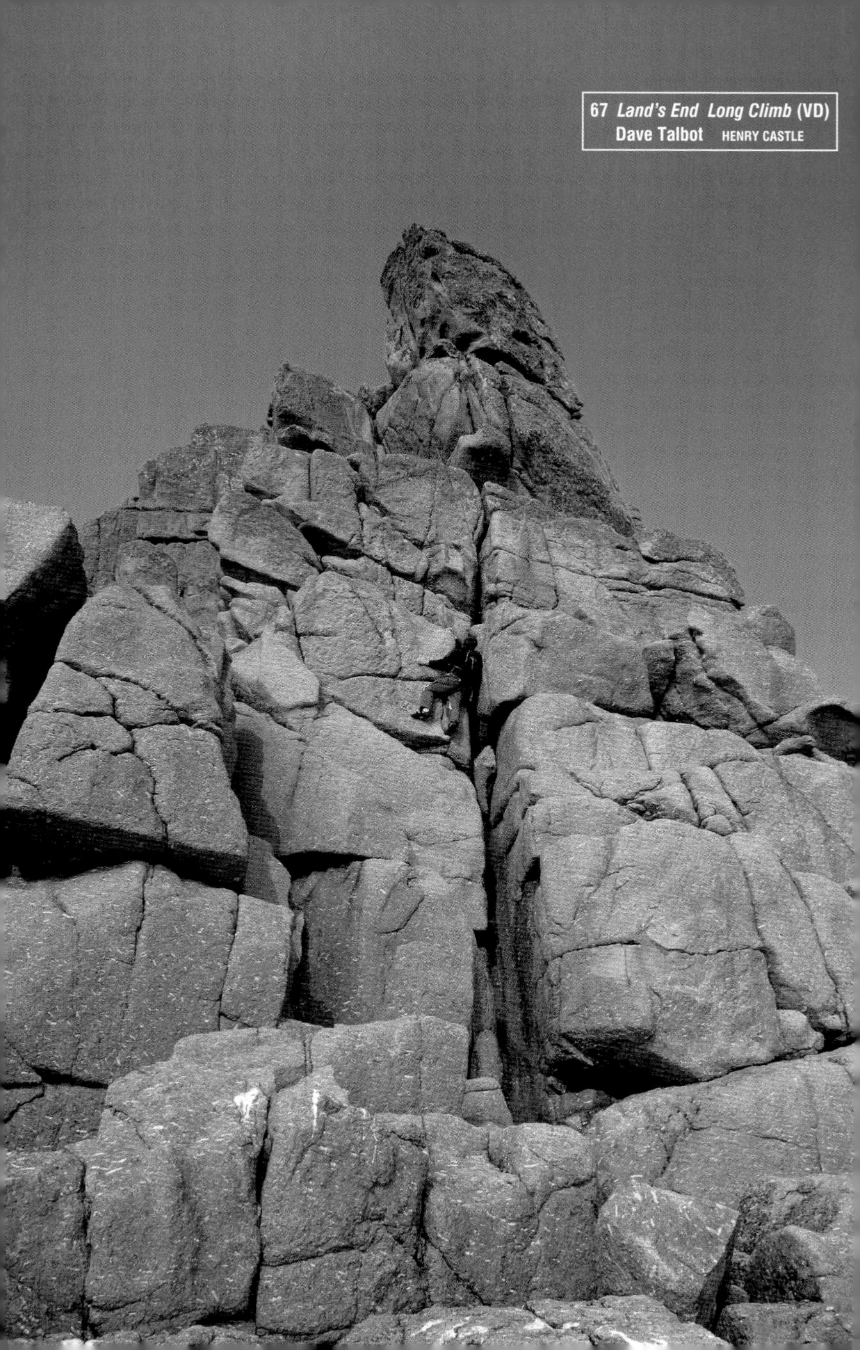

67 *Land's End Long Climb* (VD)
Dave Talbot HENRY CASTLE

66   Atlantic Ocean Wall   E5   68m
FA R Edwards, M Edwards (VL) 1981

A major undertaking up the highest wall at Land's End. At the time of writing there are several bolts in place for protection, but take a full rack. The granite is rather friable in places, especially towards the top, and be prepared to encounter some wet rock. Start at mid to low tide at the far end of the platform south of *Longships Wall*, below a chimney.

1 6m Move round rightwards to a good ledge beneath the corner which bounds the wall on the left.

2 8m 6a (in the usual wet conditions) Climb the corner to the first horizontal break and traverse right to a sloping ledge.

3 24m 6b Climb the thin crack to a slanting break and follow it to a reddish wall. Steep climbing up the wall gains a poor resting place. Climb the narrow corner on the left to reach an undercling flake on the right, and continue up and rightwards to a good flake. Step right across some poor rock to a narrow, sloping ledge, and cross this to a stance at the foot of the main groove.

4 30m 6a Climb the groove to the roof, move round into the continuation groove, and climb to the next roof. Move left and climb the steep wall to a small groove above a roof. Follow the groove to a crack leading to the top.

One route in particular at Land's End escapes the seriousness of the other climbs and is ideal for inexperienced parties. It ascends the high, rambling buttress (Hotel Buttress) in front of the hotel, the foot of which is approached by scrambling down the path on its south side, and then working back north and crossing a gully to reach ledges 9 metres above the sea.

67   Land's End Long Climb   VD   67m
FA Royal Marines 1946

The crest of the buttress is climbed in five or six short pitches, taking the various pinnacles and blocks. The final steep wall is the crux and stiff for the grade. Many interesting variations are possible and almost any section can be avoided if one feels inclined to miss it out.

Traversing southwards from the foot of Hotel Buttress brings one to a zawn containing two obvious cracklines. The left is **Aberdeen Angus** (E1 5b) and the right is **Iron Hand** (E2 5c), both being well worthwhile. The impressive buttress to the right of these cracks provides the real gem of the zawn:

68   Crystal Fingers   E3   6b   30m
FA R Edwards, M Edwards 1984

Safe, technical climbing on perfect granite. Start on the large ledge below a wide crack on the right. Climb the wide crack, and then a thinner one on the left which leads to a roof. Traverse the obvious fault (two pegs) to a thin vertical crack which leads, via a groove, to the top.

West Penwith – South Coast

From Land's End, granite cliffs of various sizes extend eastwards along the South Coast for some six miles, interrupted only by sandy beaches and boulder-filled coves. In fine weather the area is a sea-cliff climber's dream. Apart from Pordenack Point, which is approached from Land's End, all the crags described here are approached from Porthgwarra, a secluded fishing village with a large car park, public toilets, teashop, and safe swimming in the summer.

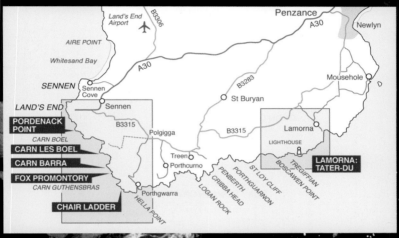

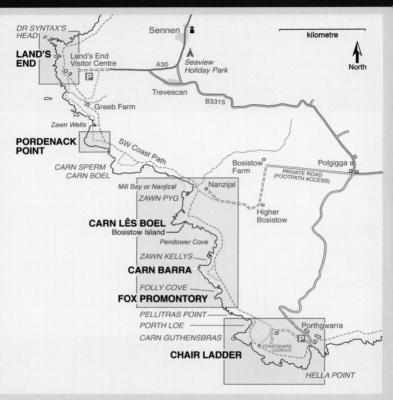

Walk north-westwards along the coast path from Porthgwarra, bypass Chair Ladder, and Fox Promontory is reached in about ten minutes. It lies 100 metres beyond a low stone wall running inland from the rounded headland enclosing Porth Loe Cove to the north. It can be seen as a narrow curtain of rock running out to sea. Beyond this is Folly Cove, enclosed to the north by the massive headland of Carn Barra, with its clean, sea-washed lower walls and a jumble of broken, lichenous tiers above. Half a mile further on, and roughly one and a half miles from Porthgwarra, the next major projection is the headland of Carn Lês Boel, distinguished by steep walls on its southern side rising behind a spectacular 30-metre-high stack (Bosistow Island) which is separated from the main cliff by a narrow channel. Carn Lês Boel can also be approached by footpaths from Polgigga.

Pordenack Point
OS Ref SW 345 242

Lovely clean granite and a south-facing aspect make this cliff an attractive climbing venue, both for high-quality single-pitch routes and for longer 'classic' expeditions.

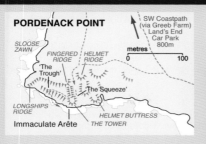

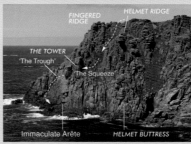

Approach from the car park at Land's End and follow the coast path south-east past Greeb Farm for approximately ten minutes to the top of the first prominent headland. A descent gully drops down left (east) from the seaward tip of the headland. After descending easily for 35 metres turn right through a narrow slot behind some towers (the Squeeze) to reach a sloping, low-angled fault (the Trough) which gives an easy scramble down to the cliff base. The main climbing area is back to the left (east) from here along sea-level platforms exposed from low to mid tide in moderate sea conditions. With big seas, waves can sweep the cliff base at any state of the tide. The left side of the cliff is slabby at first, but rears up to form the impressive buttress taken frontally by *Immaculate Arête*.

⭐**1   Economist's Climb**   VD   62m
FA Royal Marines 1940s
A fine multi-pitch outing taking the full height of the headland. Start beneath a distinctive red seam/vein in the steep slab, directly below the upper part of the Trough.
    1 18m Climb the seam. The last few moves can be taken direct (slightly harder) or on the left, and lead to belays in the Trough.

279

2 18m Follow the groove just left of a big wedged boulder; then climb a short rib on the right to a large stance.

3 16m Continue easily for 5 metres, and bear right, past a rounded chockstone, to belay beneath the final light-coloured buttress.

4 10m The buttress is split by a whitish groove – climb it to a steep and exposed finishing move.

⭐ 2   Nut Route   VS 4c   20m
FA Royal Marines 1940s

Nice climbing up the slabby rib immediately right of the slab of *Economist's Climb*. Start at the crack which runs up just right of the rib and follow it, using hidden holds on the right, to pass a harder section at 3 metres. After reaching a sloping ledge on the rib itself, pleasant climbing up the cracks above leads to the top.

⭐ 3   Vietnamerica   E1 5b   21m
FA G Gibson, D Beetlestone 1982

Steep, open climbing taking thin cracks which zigzag up the wall above the right-hand end of the first platform (6 metres before it drops 3 metres to a second platform). Climb up into a sentry box and exit steeply from this to gain the cracks, which lead past the left end of a long ledge on the right to a short finishing groove.

⭐ 4   Zeke's Route   HS 4b   23m
FA J H Deacon, R Goodier 1955

An enjoyable climb of character. Beyond the 3-metre step is a narrow buttress bounded on the left by **King Crab Crack** (VS 4c) and on the right by **Muscle Chimney** (HS 4b). Start at the corner of *King Crab Crack* and climb it for 5 metres until it is possible to pull out left to a small ledge, and then onto a bigger ledge. Move up and make an awkward move to gain a large flake, above which easier climbing leads to the top.

⭐ 5   Stone Boom   E2   30m
FA R Edwards, R Perriment 1980

Friendly at the grade and ever popular. A treat of a climb which makes a sidelong attack on the narrow buttress. Start as for *King Crab Crack*.

1 18m 5b Follow the wide rounded crack to reach a big horizontal fault crossing the right wall. Traverse along the fault, swing around the arête, and then step up to a good stance.

2 12m 5c The open groove above is technical but well protected. Step right at the small roof, and finish direct.

⭐ 6   Sea Fury   HVS 5b   28m
FA B M Biven, H T H Peck, P H Biven 1955

To the right of *Muscle Chimney* is a wide, crooked crackline giving a worthwhile challenge – safe and strenuous. Follow the crack to a niche below an overhang. Pull over into the crack above and battle on to a good ledge, above which easier climbing gains the top.

⭐ 7   Immaculate Arête   E4 6a   32m
FA R Edwards, M Edwards 1981

Forceful, brilliant climbing that lives up to its name. It takes the blunt nose of the impressive leaning buttress. Start just right of the arête. Climb past a small roof and up the steep crack above to reach a horizontal break. After more difficult moves, bear left to some small ledges before stepping back right and following the arête to a good ledge. The thin crack to the right of the corner leads to the top.

The Squeeze

The Trough

King Crab Crack

1

2

3

4

5

Muscle Chimney

5
6
7
8
9
10

⭐⭐ **8   Cain**   E3 6a   30m
FA P Littlejohn, C King 1978

Another compelling line, steep but very well protected. It takes the rugged, right-slanting crack in the steep face right of *Immaculate Arête*. Start at the groove below the right-hand end of the mid-height overhang. Climb for 6 metres, and then move left beneath a lower overhang to reach good holds beneath the bottomless crack in the main overhang. Follow the crack with interest until it eases; then finish via a thin crack right of the capping nose.

⭐ **9   Nothing Much**   HVS   31m
FA D Wiggett, A J Smythe 1965

A modestly named route originally graded VS but featuring some meaty climbing! Start at the groove below the right-hand end of the main overhang, as for *Cain*.

1 5m 5a Climb the corner and move up into the recess beneath the roof. Break up right with difficulty to a sloping ledge, and climb an obvious groove to the capping nose. Move easily left to a stance and belay.

2 6m Finish up the short layback crack on the right.

⭐ **10   Wrist Climb**   VD   40m
FA R Goodier, R Shepton, R Bisley 1955

A varied and entertaining route with well-positioned climbing. The 'immaculate' buttress is bounded on the right by a reddish-coloured chimney/break. Start here.

1 22m Climb the chimney to the overhang, move right, and climb a corner to a stance on top of the large block on the left.

2 12m Traverse left across the gully, step down, and continue leftwards below the nose to a block belay in a corner.

3 6m Climb the fine little layback corner above to the top. If wet, an easier alternative may be found to the left.

Carn Lês Boel   OS Ref SW 356 233

The main attractions of this cliff (which is not to be confused with Carn Boel to the north-west) are the classic *Excalibur* and routes on the Paradise Wall (a south-facing suntrap offering very steep and sustained climbs). The cliff is popular with cormorants and most routes should be avoided during the nesting season. However, *Interspace* and *Burning Gold* are still possible with due consideration (using the *Scabbard* abseil approach).

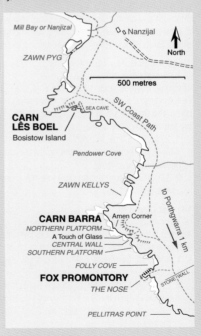

Mill Bay or Nanjizal

Nanjizal

ZAWN PYG

North

500 metres

SEA CAVE

SW Coast Path

CARN LÊS BOEL
Bosistow Island

Pendower Cove

ZAWN KELLYS

CARN BARRA   Amen Corner
NORTHERN PLATFORM
A Touch of Glass
CENTRAL WALL
SOUTHERN PLATFORM

to Porthgwarra 1 km

FOLLY COVE

FOX PROMONTORY
THE NOSE

STONE WALL

PELLITRAS POINT

A prominent feature of the cliff behind Bosistow Island is a huge triangular pinnacle taken on the left by *Excalibur* and bounded on the right by the obvious groove of **The Scabbard** (HVS 5a), to the right of which is the impressive Paradise Wall.

Approach   Left of *Excalibur* the crag is broken by a large gully which gives an easy descent to a large ledge some 6 metres above the sea. *Excalibur* starts here, and its first pitch also gives access to the ledges below Paradise Wall, although these can be approached more directly by abseiling down *The Scabbard*.

11 Excalibur   HVS   33m
FA J H Deacon, D M Holroyd 1957

An excellent climb in impressive surroundings. Start from the ledge at the foot of the descent gully.

1 15m 4b Step across onto the smooth-looking wall and climb, bearing rightwards, to a ledge. Continue easily up to the foot of a corner on the left.

2 18m 5a Climb the corner formed by the huge pinnacle, past a sloping ledge, to the ledge on top of the pinnacle. Climb the steep wall above to the top.

12 Interspace   E4 6a   43m
FA R Edwards, M Edwards 1982

A superb wall climb; strenuous and sustained but nowhere too technical. Start beneath the groove of *The Scabbard*. Climb the groove until the first crack on the right can be gained. Step right into a second crack, move up, and follow the thin diagonal crack running up rightwards across the gently overhanging wall. Increasingly difficult climbing gains a niche below a triangular overhang (peg). Pull left around the overhang to a sloping ledge, and finish easily.

13 Burning Gold   E5   42m
FA P Littlejohn, C King 1978

The most obvious line on Paradise Wall is a rightward-slanting break leading to a groove which cuts through the final overhangs. Once an aid route of obscure origin, this is now a powerful free climb and the classic of the wall. Start to the right of the black (and often wet) groove forming the lower part of the break.

1 27m 6a Climb to a niche; then move left and up into the groove (old bolt). Continue with difficulty to better holds at the rightward-slanting break, and follow it strenuously to a stance beneath the overhang.

2 15m 6a Move up and right into the groove and climb it very steeply to easier ground above the overhang.

14 Hot Line   E5   48m
FA M Edwards, R Edwards 1982

Another superb route taking the wall to the right of *Burning Gold*. Start from the lower ledge 9 metres right of *The Scabbard*, below a smooth slabby wall.

1 11m 6a Climb the wall via a shallow depression to the ledge beneath Paradise Wall proper.

2 37m 6b Climb straight up to a horizontal break; then move up and slightly left to a line of weakness which leads up rightwards to another horizontal break. Climb up and slightly leftwards to the stance of *Burning Gold*. Traverse left into a very steep groove and climb this to the top.

The Scabbard

11

12
13

14

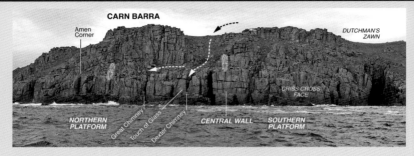

CARN BARRA

Amen Corner · DUTCHMAN'S ZAWN · CRISS CROSS FACE

NORTHERN PLATFORM · Great Chimney · Touch of Glass · Dexter Chimney · CENTRAL WALL · SOUTHERN PLATFORM

Carn Barra

OS Ref SW 358 226

A fine headland ringed by relatively short (up to 27 metres) but impressive cliffs with powerful natural lines. They offer a concentration of high-quality climbs which are mostly non tidal except in high seas.

Approach Take the coast path north-west from Porthgwarra until, after about half a mile, a stone wall is crossed. Some 150 metres beyond this, just before the last rocky mass of the headland, a grassy slope leads down to the top of the crags. The obvious promontory directly beneath the slope gives a good viewpoint for the Central Wall immediately to

Amen Corner

15 · 16 · 17 · 18 · 19 · 20

the south-east (to the right when facing the cliff) and also provides a way down via grooves and ledges on its north-west side to a huge sloping platform (the Northern Platform), above which is the main part of the crag. The most popular descent to the climbs is to fix an abseil rope to one of the many anchors along the cliff edge, thus enabling several routes to be climbed in succession.

Northern Platform

The best area of the cliff, characterized by sheer faces and striking crack, corner, and groove lines. At the left end of the cliff is the obvious **Amen Corner** (E1 5a), which has a thin crack beginning part way up its left wall:

15 Crack in the Sky   E1 5b   26m
FA R Edwards, M Edwards, C Bryan 1980

Less enjoyable since a rockfall, but still worthwhile. Start from the huge block right of the base of *Amen Corner*. Gain the corner and climb it to the first small ledge on the left wall. Move left and climb a short corner, followed by a steep wall to gain a ledge. Finish easily.

16 Mean Street   E4 6a   27m
FA R Edwards, M Edwards 1984

High quality throughout. Start on the block as for *Crack in the Sky*. Follow the thin, staggered crackline just left of the rib to reach a large notch in the arête. Move slightly left, gain the wall above, and climb it to the top.

18 Grande Plage (E4)
Stu Bradbury JOHN REDMOND

17 Sunny Corner Lane   E3 5c   27m
FA R Edwards, M Edwards 1980

Excellent sustained climbing. Start below the steep corner 6 metres right of *Amen Corner*. Climb the corner to the start of the slanting roof; then move left into the open corner and follow this to the next roof. Move up into the overhanging groove above and follow it around the overhang to the top. The slanting roof itself is taken by the fierce **Powerflex** (E4 6a).

18 Grande Plage   E4 6a   27m
FA R Edwards, M Edwards 1980

An immaculate sustained pitch with good protection. Start 9 metres right of *Sunny Corner Lane*, where a thin crack splits an impressive wall. Climb to a flake. Difficult moves up and to the left gain the crackline, which is followed until it is possible to traverse left into a corner. Climb the corner and finish rightwards.

19 Golden Brown   E4 6a   30m
FA G Gibson, P Gibson 1982

Beautiful climbing up the golden face to the right of *Grande Plage*. Follow *Grande Plage* for 5 metres; then climb diagonally rightwards on the obvious ramp to a flake. Move up and climb the superb thin crack in the headwall.

20 Geireagle II   E1 5b   27m
FA R Edwards, M Edwards 1980

Steep climbing, nice rock. Start 5 metres right of *Grande Plage*. Follow the grooves until difficult climbing gains the impending headwall. Climb this to the top.

This wall is terminated by Great Chimney, to the right of which some less continuous walls form a slight amphitheatre, bounded on the right by another deep chimney – Dexter Chimney. **Socket Wall** (S 4a) is a fine little pitch up the pock-marked wall in the centre, while towards the right **Slant Crack** (HS 4b) is also obvious.

★ **21　A Touch of Glass**　E4　6b　24m

FA R Edwards, M Edwards 1983

Takes the steep crack in the centre of the impressive wall to the right of *Slant Crack*. Move up to the crack and climb it direct to the horizontal break. Continue up the wall to a ledge, and another short wall which leads to the top.

The right arête of the wall gives an equally fine pitch – **Glass Arête** (E3 5c).

Central Wall

Some 20 metres right of Dexter Chimney is the very distinctive Central Wall, which plunges 30 metres into the sea and is split by a wide ledge at 12 metres (where all the climbs begin). Above the ledge are three striking corner-lines. The most convenient approach is to abseil to the ledge, although at low tide it can be reached by VS climbing.

★ **22　Ra**　HVS　5a　18m

FA P de Mengel, C Bartlett, B Hocken 1972

A meaty pitch up the wide, left-hand corner crack, which may have been affected by rockfall. Take large nuts or cams. Climb easily to the main crack, which leads to a ledge. The wide crack above demands more effort.

★ **23　Illustrated Man**　E2　5b　21m

FA R Edwards, M Edwards 1979

An impressive pitch. Follow *Ra* to the first horizontal break; then traverse to the next crack on the right and climb it to the roof. Pull past the left side of the roof, and then climb the steep groove above to the top.

The central corner system is **Dialectic** (HVS 5b), which starts with difficult climbing up the thin crack in the arête. The following route takes the right-hand corner:

⭐ **24 Axis** VS 5a 18m
FA A McFarlane, I Duckworth, B Hocken 1972
Pleasant climbing on lovely granite. Start at the short wall below the corner. Difficult climbing up the wall gains a ledge. Continue to the corner and follow it to the top.

⭐ **25 Fourteen Fathoms** E1 5b 20m
FA G Gibson 1982
Fine open climbing up the face immediately right of *Axis*. Climb to the ledge as for *Axis*; then climb the right arête to the break. Traverse 3 metres right to a triangular niche, move up and left onto the face, and climb it via a thin crack to the top.

Fox Promontory OS Ref SW 360 223

A narrow granite promontory whose seaward end provides a cluster of short but worthwhile climbs. It is only five minutes walk from Chair Ladder and combines well with a day's climbing there, as the best routes on Fox Promontory may be accessible at high tide in calm conditions.

25 *Fourteen Fathoms* (E1) Heather Ohly SOPHIE WHYTE

Descent south-east side of promontory

A

THE NOSE

26

27 28

29
30

Approach   To reach the cliff, walk north-west along the coast path to the long stone wall running inland (ten minutes from Porthgwarra). The descent begins about 100 metres beyond this.

Scramble down to reach a line of stepped corners running down the south-east face of the Promontory and ending near the seaward tip – the Nose. Descend the corners; then move left and up into a short corner leading on to a narrow platform beneath the Nose. The striking crack which splits the Nose centrally gives *The Muzzle*. Round the corner is the shadier north-west face, whose left side is sea-washed at high tide. It is sometimes damp early in the day and is at its best in the late afternoon sun.

★ **26 Sunshine Cracks**   HS 4b   26m
★ FA J H Deacon, A Blackshaw 1956
The obvious natural line of the face is a chimney/crack system approximately 15 metres from the right-hand (seaward) edge. Climb the short chimney and the corner-crack above to a ledge. Continue to a chimney which leads to the top.

★ **27 Reveille**   VS   27m
★ FA J H Deacon, A Blackshaw 1956
A good steep pitch taking the north-west face towards its seaward end. Start about 5 metres from the seaward arête, at a line of quartz holds running up to the left.
  1 21m 4b Follow the line of holds and continue up to the left until beneath a wide, rounded crack. Traverse left to easier rock leading to the base of a chimney.
  2 6m Climb the left wall of the chimney to finish.

28 The Curtain Raiser   HVS   26m
FA V N Stevenson, D Bateman, D Brown 1963

Climbs a thin white vein just to the right of *Reveille*. The excellent first pitch is a sustained piece of face climbing on small holds.

   1 20m 5a Climb the wall, following the vein, to a small niche at 9 metres. Continue to a scoop, and move up right to gain a slab which leads to a ledge.

   2 6m 4a Climb the steep nose above.

29 The Muzzle   HVS   26m
FA A Blackshaw, J H Deacon (VL) 1956

The impressive crack splitting the Nose gives a steep and exposed pitch. Start at the right-hand corner of the narrow platform.

   1 8m Step up right and climb to the top of a narrow slab. Move left and down to belay beneath the main crack. (It is possible to climb directly up the steep wall to here at 5b.)

   2 18m 4c Climb the double cracks to the overhang, and move out left around this to easier ground leading to the top.

30 The Whisker   VS   26m
FA V N Stevenson, D Bateman, D Brown 1963

A pleasant route skirting the Nose on the right.

   1 8m *The Muzzle* pitch 1.

   2 18m 4c From the top of the belay pinnacle, move up onto a gangway leading up to the right. Traverse delicately round onto the slab, and climb its left edge to a large perched block. Mantelshelf onto the block, and climb the short twin cracks on the right to the top.

FOX PROMONTORY
SOUTH EAST FACE

THE NOSE

The girdle traverse of Fox Promontory – **The Vixen's Embrace** (VS 100m) is a very entertaining, if slightly contrived expedition, sustained at an amenable standard. Starting on the right it links the routes at roughly mid height and includes a 12-metre abseil down the upper part of the first pitch of *The Curtain Raiser*.

Chair Ladder

OS Ref SW 364 217

The crag which epitomizes the traditional image of Cornish climbing. Its base is tidal, so climbers often find themselves high on a buttress of rough, sun-baked granite with the sea crashing in directly below. These situations, combined with an abundance of good holds and cracks, give Chair Ladder probably the best low-to-middle-grade climbing in the South West.

Approach From Porthgwarra, walk up the tarmac road to the Coastguard Cottages and turn left up a path to the Coastguard Lookout on top of the headland. The cliff is directly beneath and extends for some distance in either direction. It is complex in structure but basically consists of a series of buttresses and faces separated by gullies and chimneys. The main problem for first-time visitors is locating the correct descents. The broad Ash Can Gully is immediately in front of the lookout, and to its right (facing seaward) is the lichen-covered summit of the Main Cliff. Fifty metres to the east another easy-angled gully (Pinnacle Gully) leads down to the back of the Pinnacle, from where a descent can be made on the left (facing out) to ledges at the base of Bishop Buttress. Most parties abseil the lower part of this descent.

The wide couloir running down behind the Main Cliff is cut off at its foot and is no use for descent. Further west the crag is bounded by a large rotting zawn with a jammed boulder at its mouth. This is Zawn Rinny, either side of which may be descended to reach the Bulging Wall area. All the above descents have tricky sections and care is required to find the easiest line, which can be quite devious. Except during high seas, the base of the cliff can be traversed at low tide by linking up a number of ledges.

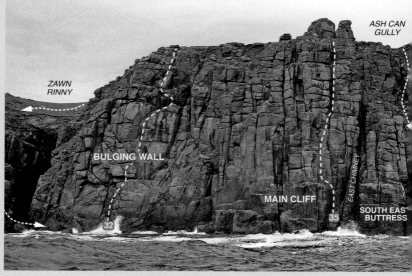

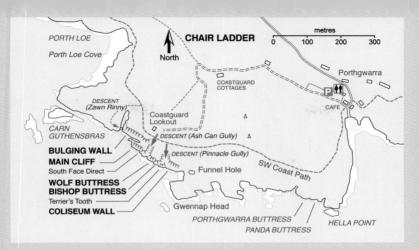

Bulging Wall

Around low tide the easiest descent is on the west side of Zawn Rinny, crossing large boulders in the zawn bed to reach the cliff. If these boulders are sea-washed, descend the path on the east (Chair Ladder) side of the zawn, keeping right to reach ledges at the entrance. Pick a way down the

BULGING WALL

various walls and ledges (Moderate if the easiest route is found) to large platforms beneath the cliff which are exposed until half tide. At higher tides, when the sea is not too rough, it is possible to traverse in about 6 metres above the platforms to reach the climbs. The first obvious line on the left of the face is **Overhanging Chimney** (VS 4c) and to its right the steep face is breached by the somewhat undervalued **Kittiwake** (HVS 5a). The next line on the right is:

31 Seal Slab VS 58m
FA G Smith, J H Deacon (VL) 1955

Reasonable at the grade and most enjoyable, with short-lived and well-protected difficulties. It takes the large inset slab, followed by some steep cracks above. Start in the centre of the foot of the slab, 3 metres left of the initial groove of *Pegasus*.

1 23m 4c Climb the slab, trending right into the corner when it steepens. Follow the corner until a difficult move gains a ledge at the foot of a ramp sloping up left.

2 23m 4b Move up to the obvious layback crack overlooking the ramp. Climb the ramp and continue up a narrow slab, just left of a wide crack, to reach some ledges beneath a short chimney/groove.

3 12m Climb the chimney/groove to a big ledge beneath the lichen-covered final wall. Either finish easily on the left, or move right for 5 metres and climb the slab pleasantly to the top.

32 Pegasus HS 56m
FA J H Deacon and party 1955

Chair Ladder's answer to *Doorpost* – a fine line with excellent sustained climbing. It takes the grooved arête just right of *Seal Slab* and the obvious curving corner higher up. Start beneath the steep corner-crack immediately right of the corner of *Seal Slab*.

1 21m 4b Climb the corner until a move right gains a ledge. Continue straight up and over an overhang on large holds to reach the ledge that crosses the face.

2 20m 4a Move right and climb the black wall to a ledge below the curving corner. Climb the corner, and then the slab on its right to a large belay block.

3 15m 4b Move left across the black wall and mantelshelf with difficulty onto a small ledge. Climb up left again to a large ledge and easier slabs on the right which lead to the top.

Main Cliff

From the cliff-top, this is approached most directly via Ash Can Gully (the broad gully immediately in front of the Coastguard Lookout) which is easy until about 18 metres from the bottom. From here, either abseil or descend chimneys and cracks a little on the right (facing out); then move back left into the gully which leads steeply down to the sea-level ledges. At high tide it is possible to reach *Pendulum Chimney* and *South Face Direct* by abseiling down a narrow subsidiary gully (East Chimney) to the right (facing out) of the steep lower section of Ash Can Gully. This gains some higher ledges in a bay.

The Main Cliff is the large mass of rock to the left (facing in) of Ash Can Gully. Towards its left side, some 30 metres left of the gully, is an obvious square recess. The wide crack in the back right-hand corner of the recess gives a challenging pitch – **Central Route** (HVS 5a), while the narrow back wall is taken by **Centrepiece** (E2 5c). The following route takes the red face forming the left side of the recess:

33 Red Wall HS 48m
FA J Simpson, E Stones 1947

An interesting and varied climb. Start by scrambling up easy rocks to ledges below the square recess.

1 18m 4b Move up into the recess, and climb steeply up the narrow red wall near its left edge to the ledge above.

2 12m 4a Climb to the top of the tower, and make awkward moves up a rounded crack to gain a large ledge above.

3 18m 4a Climb the steep cracks in the wall behind the ledge, then some wider, easier cracks on the right-hand side of a lichenous face, which lead to the top.

Immediately left of the foot of Ash Can Gully is a compact buttress split by an obvious crack – **South East Face Direct** (HVS 5a) – and bounded on the left by East Chimney. The next four routes start at the bay just left of East Chimney.

34 Excelsior E1 58m

FA V N Stevenson, J H Deacon (VL) 1959; pitch 4: V N Stevenson, B Wake 1961

A slightly discontinuous route but with some memorable climbing, especially on the top pitch which was the 'big lead' of the cliff for many years and still commands respect. Start below a groove in the seaward face of the flat-topped pedestal of *Pendulum Chimney*. At high tide the first stance can be reached from ledges in the bay on the right after an abseil down East Chimney.

1 12m Climb the groove to the ledge on top of the pinnacle.

2 15m 4c Move up into the twin cracks on the left and climb steeply, via a continuation crack, to belay near the top of two pinnacles.

3 20m 5a Climb easily to a large recess capped by an overhang. Move up to the overhang and traverse right to a ledge.

4 11m 5b Gain the obvious black runnel in the upper face and follow it to a horizontal break. Enter the undercut groove above and climb it to the top.

35 Pendulum Chimney S 50m

FA J Littlewood c.1930; J Simpson, E Stones (pitches 1 to 3) 1947

A classic, direct route up the Main Cliff, best avoided during the nesting season.

1 8m 4a Climb the left wall of the bay, or the wide crack, to gain the top of a pedestal.

2 12m 4a Climb the V-chimney, step right, and continue to ledges.

3 12m 4a Traverse to the steep crack on the right and follow it to the bed of the gully above.

4 18m 4b Climb the chimney until some awkward moves gain a ledge. A steep wall on the left leads to the summit pinnacles.

Neptune (VS 4c) works an intricate and interesting line between *Excelsior* and *Pendulum Chimney* and is worthy of attention on a repeat visit. The following route takes the wall above the bay:

36 Detergent Wall HVS 45m

FA V N Stevenson, J H Deacon (VL) 1959

The steep pocketed wall right of *Pendulum Chimney* gives exposed and exhilarating climbing. Start as for *South Face Direct*.

1 12m 4b Climb to a niche in the wall left of the crack, and continue straight up to a horizontal break. Move right to the first stance of *South Face Direct*.

2 15m 5a Move back on to the wall left of the crack, and climb to a layback crack which leads to a block belay in *Pendulum Chimney*.

3 18m 4c The steep wall right of *Pendulum Chimney* is climbed, first on the left, then moving right, until harder moves gain a ledge. The short wall on the right leads to the top.

37 South Face Direct VS 52m

FA J Simpson, E Stones 1948

A grand climb, steep and exposed, taking the obvious cracks in the right-hand side of the Main Cliff. Start at a wide crack just to the left of the foot of East Chimney.

1 11m 4b Climb the crack to a prominent, square ledge. This can be reached from East Chimney and is a useful starting point at high tide or when seas are rough.

2 18m **4c** Climb the crack above to a niche. Continue up the crack, and move right to a ledge featuring a mushroom-shaped boss. Step right and climb a short V-chimney to a stance below a steep crack.

3 14m **4b** Climb the crack to a corner which leads more easily to a large ledge beneath the summit block.

4 9m **4a** Climb the crack in the slab to a niche and continue to the top of the tower.

38 Mermaid's Route/Dexter S 45m
FA A J Smythe 1948; L S Powell 1937

A hybrid route that constitutes a most entertaining way up the South East Buttress, with an optional continuation to the top of Wolf Buttress. The first pitch has been substantially changed by rockfall resulting from the winter storms of 2014. Start below the slab at the right corner of the buttress, just left of Ash Can Gully.

1 18m Climb the slab, and continue up a short crack onto the newly exposed ledge (optional stance).Move up the right edge of the rock scar before traversing left onto a small ledge known as the Pulpit stance.

2 18m Make an awkward step left across the gully, step up, and climb the crack and wall above on good holds until an obvious traverse leads left to flakes and a ledge.

3 9m Move up to the right and climb a bulge to gain a ledge from where short steps lead to the top of the buttress. (From here, it is possible to move across to the side of Wolf Buttress and continue up a chimney on the right, and then cracks to the summit notch of Wolf Buttress, to complete an interesting itinerary.)

Wolf Buttress

This is the slender buttress right (facing the cliff) of Ash Can Gully, characterized by its smooth lower wall which gives some of the hardest climbing on the cliff. This wall is split centrally by the line of incipient cracks taken by **Caliban** (E3 6a), just to the right of which is the thin vertical crack of **The Tempest** (E6 6b). **Animated Wall** (E5 6b) takes the smooth-looking face to the left of *Caliban*.

39 Aerial VS 68m
FA H T H Peck, P H Biven 1956; V N Stevenson, E T Rook 1962

A delicate, open climb which rises across Wolf Buttress on the lowest natural line, giving two short, well-positioned sections of difficulty. Being easily accessible, it is a particularly useful route when the tide is in. At low tide, start at a thin crack 9 metres right of the base of Ash Can Gully.

1 11m 4b Climb the thin crack and make an awkward move left to a ledge. (At high tide this ledge can be gained by traversing out of Ash Can Gully.)

2 20m 4c Traverse delicately right and make an awkward mantelshelf to gain a step. Continue rightwards more easily on the seaward face of the buttress to the foot of twin cracks. Climb the right-hand crack to a large ledge.

3 17m 4c Climb the crack above the left side of the ledge and make a delicate move left beneath an overhang. Climb the steep crack above to a ledge, and then a steep wall which leads to a platform.

4 20m Climb easily over blocks to the top.

Bishop Buttress / The Pinnacle

To the right of Wolf Buttress, the next two bastions are split by the dank corner of Mitre Gully. Bishop Buttress is the most impressive and continually steep section of Chair Ladder. The period of access is longer than for most parts of Chair Ladder, extending to within two hours of high-tide in calmish seas. At such times the best approach is from the east. Descend Pinnacle Gully (the top of which is 50 metres east of the Coastguard Lookout) and continue easily down the east side of the Pinnacle until steeper rock is met at a rounded chimney. Most parties choose to abseil from here, but to climb down take the rib on the right (facing out) of the chimney for 5 metres, then cross it and descend short walls to regain the chimney fault where it becomes easier lower down (Diff standard). The base of the elegant Bishop Buttress is marked by a deep pool on the left and a deep trench on the right.

41 *Diocese* (VS)
Rik Gibbon   MIKE HUTTON

40 Flannel Avenue   HS   56m
FA Royal Marines 1949

A classic of the cliff, having a tricky start and superbly situated climbing in its upper reaches. Start at the obvious deep chimney on the left side of Bishop Buttress.

1 18m 4b Climb the chimney by bridging up near the outside. At about 14 metres move onto the left rib and climb to a stance.

2 9m Move right onto the buttress proper and climb a steep wall, on perfect holds, to a niche.

3 21m 4a Move up and traverse right above the overhang to a flat-topped flake. Climb the slab above on small but positive holds, bearing slightly left to a huge block belay on the ledge above.

4 8m 4a Step onto the steep wall from the right-hand end of the block and climb strenuously, on good holds, to the top.

41 Diocese   VS   63m
FA M J Ridges, G F Lilly 1951

A wonderful climb with varied challenges and weaving through fine architectural features. It takes the left-facing corner-crack/chimney to the large central overhang of Bishop Buttress which it turns by a delicate traverse. Start below the corner.

1 23m 4c Climb easily to the right-hand end of a long ledge. Make moves up the short slab on the right, heading back into the corner at 6 metres. The wide crack leads (with difficulty varying with technique) to a cave stance beneath the overhang.

2 11m 5a Traverse left, either using the crack under the roof, or face climbing below it, to gain cracks at the left end of the overhang. A fine pitch.

3 21m 4a Move up to cracks in a steep slab, and climb to a large ledge and block belay.

4 8m 4b Climb the shallow groove in the steep wall 3 metres right of the block.

42 The Spire   E3   51m
FA P Littlejohn, W A Carver 1971

Immaculate climbing up the thin crack just right of the arête of the corner of *Diocese*. Start at a faint crack 5 metres left of the greasy corner (Mitre Gully) which bounds Bishop Buttress on the right.

1 21m 5c Follow the crack, past a good finger slot, until a small ledge is gained after 8 metres. Step left and climb the cracks to a shallow corner leading to a small stance and belays on the left.

2 30m 4b Move up into the crack on the right and follow it to a ledge below the top. Finish easily.

43 Bishop's Rib   E1   58m
FA J H Deacon, J W Oates 1956; M B McDermott and party 1963

An inescapable route of great quality taking the easiest line up the front pillar of Bishop Buttress. Small wires required. Start at the foot of Mitre Gully above an ankle-snapping crevasse.

1 14m 5b Move up, and make a leftward-rising traverse to a small ledge below an overhang. Pass this on the right and continue on better holds to a stance on the right beneath an overhang.

2 21m 5a Move left and climb the steep wall to the obvious leftward-rising traverse-line. Follow this to better holds leading over the bulge to a sloping ledge. Step left into a crack and follow it on excellent holds, up the yellow face, to a recessed ledge.

3 23m Climb the lichen-covered tower above to the top.

The first pitch of **The Mitre** (VS), in Mitre Gully, has been affected by rockfall. The second pitch takes an enthralling line up the right edge of Bishop Buttress, ending with an exposed traverse to the left. This pitch can be done at high tides by starting at the foot of the easy-angled upper gully.

WOLF BUTTRESS

BISHOP BUTTRESS

The Mitre

39
Animated Wall
Caliban
The Tempest
40
41 42
43

★ 44 Terrier's Tooth   S   39m

FA J Mallory, M A Roster, A Greenwood, B Donkin 1940

A terrific climb up the centre of the Pinnacle. The description and grade reflect changes caused by a huge rockfall in the winter storms of 2013/14. Start at the base of the Pinnacle, at a vague ramp in newly exposed rock, which leads rightwards to a prominent left-facing corner.

   1 20m 4a Climb the ramp and corner to ledges on the right (pinnacle belay up left).
   2 19m Climb a corner-crack on the left to ledges. Go up over blocks and then right to a narrow ledge beneath the slab. Pull onto the slab and climb it to the top. The descent into the gully on the left is tricky and best treated as a final pitch.

44 *Terrier's Tooth* (S)
Zoe Clegg   SIMON CARDY

Coliseum Wall

This is the hidden wall at the south-eastern end of Chair Ladder, forming part of the large zawn between Chair Ladder and Hella Point. It is slower to dry out than other parts of the cliff and at its best during dry weather in the afternoon sun. Approach via Pinnacle Gully to the ledges above the steeper rock; then traverse left (facing out) along the narrowing ledges until they peter out. Either abseil from here or climb fairly easily down a rake to the boulder-filled zawn (lowish tide).

45 Private Performance HVS 49m
FA R Edwards, M Edwards 1984

Start at the foot of the descent rake.
> **1** 14m 4a Climb directly up the wall to a belay ledge.
> **2** 35m 5a Climb the wall, starting 5 metres left of the corner, to reach an overlap. Move right and over the overlap, and climb a thin crack to the top.

46 Midnight Runner E1 49m
FA M Edwards, R Edwards 1984

At the extreme right-hand end of the wall is an obvious overlap at the base of the buttress. Start at the right-hand end of this.

309

1 14m 5a Climb the overlap, and follow the faultline to a sloping ledge below a short wall. Climb this to the belay ledge.

2 35m 5b Climb the wall, starting 3 metres left of the corner, trending left to the overlap in the centre of the face. Take the ramp on the right and follow a crack to the top.

Lamorna: Tater-du

OS Ref SW 438 231

This is an interesting greenstone cliff just west of the Tater-du lighthouse, one mile south-west of Lamorna Cove. The access position is delicate and for this reason the coastal path approach is de rigueur, either from St Loy or Lamorna. Climbers must also observe seasonal bird restrictions from 1 March to 31 July. The cliff is quick drying, south facing, and sheltered, but affected by tides. The descent begins well to the west of the lighthouse working back to

below the cliff down rocky steps. The cliff boasts several worthwhile climbs and one outstanding route, *Martell Slab*, which takes an obvious line up the highest section of cliff (situated left of the right-angled corner at its right end). The climb is accessible from mid to low tide.

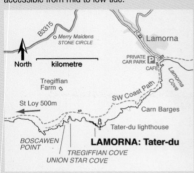

47 Martell Slab VS 46m **R**

FA J H Deacon, D M Holroyd 1957; Direct Finish P O'Sullivan, C Woodhead 1979

One of the best climbs of its grade in Cornwall. It takes the steep slab on the left of the main face and continues up a steep groove on the upper wall above mid-height ledges. The Direct Finish will suit those looking to 'up the ante' but both finishes are very worthwhile.

1 20m 4c/5a Climb a scoop, and then gain the slab with a long step. Continue up its centre until a delicate move left leads to a stance and belay.

2 26m 4b Move right and up to ledges; then go right to a steep chimney. Climb this and the left-hand corner. Turn an overhang on the left, and then move right to where good holds lead directly to the top.

The Direct Finish HVS

2a 18m 5a From the first stance, climb directly to the roof and pull through to an obvious groove that leads entertainingly to the top – airy and strenuous.

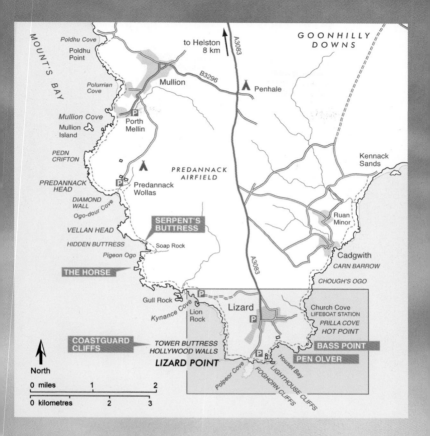

The Lizard

The most southerly point of mainland Britain is now an important climbing area and well worth inclusion on a visitor's agenda. The whole Lizard peninsula is ringed with cliffs, and the coastal scenery (especially around Vellan Head and Kynance Cove) is some of the most spectacular in the region. Most of the crags described here are composed of firm volcanic rock and are generally quick-drying, taking little or no drainage. However, sunshine or a breeze is sometimes required to eliminate salt moisture on the rock, so climbing plans should take account of these factors.

Approach   From the small market town of Helston, take the A3083 southwards towards Lizard village. For the National Trust car park at Predannack Wollas Farm (OS Ref 669 162) turn right into the village of Mullion, continue towards Mullion Cove, and then turn left along a lane leading to the farm. The turning to Kynance Cove is about 2½ miles past the turning to Mullion.

Serpent's Buttress

OS Ref SW 674 146

Approach Walking south on the coast path from Predannack Wollas, after twenty minutes one reaches an extensive area of high slabs – Chameleon Slabs – bounded on the right by a very prominent rib – **Chameleon Rib** (D). Serpent's Buttress is the buttress formed where the cliff swings into the first deep gully to the right (south) of this rib. It is south facing. On the apex of the buttress is a leftward-sloping pillar, while higher up to the right of this is a clean-cut groove of silvery serpentine taken by the following climb:

⭐ **1   The Serpent's Tail**   HVS   39m
FA F Ramsay, P Littlejohn 1987

A striking line and worthwhile climb, although the rock demands care initially. Approach by abseiling down the line (giving it a quick clean if necessary) to the start of the crack leading to the open groove.

   1 27m 5a Follow the faint crack until it becomes deeper and steeper, leading to a stance and belays (peg and nut) beneath the groove.
   2 12m 4b Climb the soapstone groove to the top – slippy!

Half a mile south of Serpent's Buttress is the gigantic, sea-filled cauldron of Pigeon Ogo, and beyond this the great rocky promontory known as the Horse.

left: 1 *The Serpent's Tail* (HVS)   Emma Alsford   DON SARGEANT

The Horse

This bold headland of tougher-than-average rock may be approached by walking southwards along the coast path from Predannack Wollas (forty minutes) or northwards along the coast path from the car park at Kynance Cove (thirty minutes). It offers a cluster of excellent routes which are best enjoyed later in the day once the sun has dried the rock (not necessary during breezy weather). The crest of the headland gives an easy scramble to the airy 'summit'. Dropping away on the south side is a silver wall taken by **Paleface** (E4 6a) while the west side forms an impressive bowl-shaped cliff. Approach this by abseiling 50 metres down the ridge forming the northern edge of the cliff (right facing seawards). The best anchors are block and nut belays 10 metres down the ridge, and the abseil gains non-tidal ledges below the left side of the cliff.

⭐**2   The Amazing Mr Ed**   VS   4c   30m
FA K Tole, P O'Sullivan 1984

A good but rather short-lived route taking the slabby buttress where the crag swings round to the north. Start from the far left end of the ledges reached by abseil. Climb up and rightwards until steep moves gain the base of a slab. Follow the clean-cut groove to reach ledges on the left and easy ground.

⭐**3   Tie That Crittur Down**   VS   45m
FA P O'Sullivan, K Tole (VL) 1984

A strong line, good steep climbing and plentiful protection make this a worthy objective. Above the ledge reached by abseil, at the left side of the west-facing section of cliff, is a chimney/crack.
　1 25m 4c Climb the chimney to a large ledge at 10 metres; then follow the prominent crackline in the wall above, exiting right to a ledge beneath a bulging wall.
　2 20m 4b Move right to pass the bulge, and climb steeply to easier ground leading up leftwards to join the ridge.

The massive arch above the through-cave forms a huge bottomless corner, left of which is the striking groove-line of *Sport of Kings*. The open face to the left of the groove is taken by:

⭐**4   Queen of the May**   HVS 5a   45m
FA P Littlejohn, D Garner 2007

A pitch which looks a little daunting from below but unfolds beautifully. From the ledges reached by abseil, climb up and rightwards (solo or roped as preferred) to gain the ledge below the crag proper. Belay beneath a little groove ending at a pedestal (some 7 metres right of the obvious crack of *Tie That Crittur Down*). Climb to the pedestal; then move up and left to a flat bollard, before trending right to meet the groove of *Sport of Kings* (perfect nut runner). Break left immediately and trend slightly leftwards to the edge of the face. Finish directly up the yellow rib leading to the apex of the groove of *Sport of Kings*.

⭐**5   Sport of Kings**   E3 5c   50m
FA P Littlejohn, D Garner 2007

A full-on treat of a pitch – sustained and absorbing. Right of *Queen of the May* is a groove running almost the full height of the cliff. Belay 4 metres down and to the right of the initial groove of *Queen of the May*. Traverse right for 6 metres to a good microwire placement, and climb the wall above into an open bay below the groove. Step left, and then up to a good crack at the start of the groove. Now follow the groove, sometimes on the left wall, all the way to the top – superb.

Lizard Point

OS Ref SW 694 116

These crags give a good introduction to climbing on the Lizard, being friendly and accessible, and getting plenty of sun (south-west facing). From the car parks at the 'Southernmost Point', walk down to the coast path and follow it west to a bench near the site of the old Coastguard Lookout above the point. One hundred metres beyond this a dry stone wall runs out to the cliff edge at the top of Tower Buttress. Descend easy rock on its north-west face; then cross a broken corner to a narrow ramp running down beneath a large roof to sloping slabs at the foot of the buttress, well above high-tide level. A line of flakes crossing the roof to the obvious fang is taken by **Aboriginal Sin** (E3 5c), while the roof itself is bounded on the right by a corner formed by white quartzy rock.

left: 6 *Sirius* (HS)
Henry Castle CASTLE col

★★ **6 Sirius** HS 48m

FA I M Peters, P O'Sullivan (VL) 1985

Steep, juggy, and very photogenic. Start directly below the corner.

1 18m 4a Move up left, swing rightwards into the corner, and climb it on huge holds to a ledge. Move right to belay at the foot of a large ramp running up left.

2 30m 4a Above is a short corner capped by a pointed overhang. Climb to the overhang, move left across the slab, and then continue up another groove to reach easier rock leading to grassy ledges beneath the summit block. Climb the groove on the right side of the block to finish.

The large complex cliff extending north-westwards from immediately below where the Coastguard Lookout once stood is known as the Hollywood Walls. Its highest point is 50 metres west of the lookout, directly in front of the bench. From here, descend easily on the right side (facing out) of the buttress to a flat terrace (beside a prominent overhang) which overlooks the central section of the cliff. This is the place to leave gear. A low-angled gully is followed down to the right, and then a ramp cuts back left (facing out) beneath a grey overhanging wall and leads to slabby rock beneath the crag (not tidal). A prominent feature is a diamond-shaped slab inset into the centre of the cliff.

★★ **7 The Goldrush** VS 4c 24m

FA I M Peters, P O'Sullivan 1985

An excellent climb which goes boldly up the overhanging grey wall and takes the smooth red face above. Start 6 metres right of the left edge of the wall, on a small orange ledge. Climb steeply on good holds for 5 metres, and then move right between the two bands of overhangs to

a small ledge. Step back left above the bulge, and move up to a big pocket. A difficult move gains a leftward-slanting crack which is followed to the top.

8 Limelight HVS 5a 24m
FA I M Peters, P O'Sullivan 1985

Steep and dynamic. Start about 3 metres left of the diamond-shaped central slab, at three pointed flakes running up left. Swing up left along the flakes, and move up into an open groove (the left-hand of two). Climb steeply to a good hold above the groove and continue straight up the yellow slab above to the top.

9 Mae West HVS 4c 27m
FA P O'Sullivan, J Barber 1985

Steep and exposed but with good holds. Start at the rightward-slanting groove formed by the junction of the inset slab with the wall to its left. Follow the groove for 8 metres; then break leftwards to reach a crack. Climb steeply up to and over a roof to another roof. Traverse right to the rounded arête and finish direct.

The obvious chimney/groove right of the inset slab is **Rendezvous Manqué** (S) and beyond this is a much steeper face split by the prominent crack of **The Big Heat** (E3 5c). The corner-line to the right again is **Casablanca** (E2 5c).

7 *The Goldrush* (VS)
Ed Walker   DON SARGEANT

Pen Olver

OS Ref SW 712 118

A very pleasant, friendly crag having enjoyable routes in the VD to VS grades as well as a cluster of brilliant extremes on Amnesty Wall. On a fine summer's day there can be few better 'family' crags, and provided the sea is reasonably calm access is easy except for about three hours around high tide.

Approach   From Lizard Village (ample parking), walk to the *Housel Bay Hotel* and join the coast path. Turn left and walk for a few minutes until 50 metres short of the rocky outcrop above Pen Olver. A faint track descends rightwards to flat ledges beside a prominent tower (the summit tower of *Blind Pew*). Gear up here; then descend Moderate rock to sea-level ledges beneath the cliff. Moving back towards Housel Bay along the ledges, the first rock of note is the relatively high Slab Wall, beyond which is an obvious squat pinnacle.

10   Songs from a Gentle Man   VS   4c   25m
FA D E Hope, D Issit 1996

Behind the pinnacle on the north side (left facing in) is an attractive arête with deep corners either side of it. Start from a large flat ledge 3 metres above high tide mark. Climb the arête – delicate but with adequate holds and protection.

The next two routes climb the pinnacle, descent from which is by down-climbing the landward arête with care (Diff).

11   Lying Eyes   S   15m
FA D E Hope, D Issit 1996

Start below the seaward face of the pinnacle and follow a ramp up to the left until stopped by an overlap. Make a teasing move leftwards to pass the overlap, and follow the friendly edge to the top.

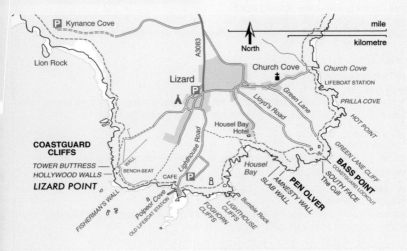

left: **11** *Lying Eyes* (S)
Jill Sumner   DON SARGEANT

★★ **12 Pilot's Song** HS 4b   15m
FA D E Hope, D Issit 1996

Steep but with perfect protection, this takes
the compelling crack in the seaward face of
the pinnacle. Start just left of the prow on the
lower wall. Climb the wall to a ledge, and follow the crack with interest to the top.

Slab Wall

★ **13 Great Slanting** VD   15m
FA D E Hope, D Issit 1996

A strong natural line. Five metres right of the edge of the wall is a huge flake crack running up to
the left. Climb this to join the arête, which is followed to a good belay ledge.

14 Saltheart VD   15m
FA D E Hope, D Issit 1996

Starting 2 metres to the right of *Great Slanting*, climb the wall into an open groove, which is
followed to the belay ledge.

★ **15 Mile End** M 20m
FA D Issit, D E Hope 1996

The easiest climb in the book and a safe excursion for complete beginners. It follows the
rightward-slanting crack/fault in the middle of Slab Wall.

★
★ **16 Blind Pew**   VD   25m

FA D E Hope, D Issit 1996

A route of substance attaining the highest point of the cliff. Start 5 metres right of *Mile End*, below a groove which begins 3 metres up. Gain the groove and follow it to its end. Pull out right to a ledge, and climb the front face of the tower to the summit. Belay here; then climb down on the north ide (left facing in) to reach easy ground.

A Little Gemma (VD), takes the less-defined groove to the right of *Blind Pew*.

Amnesty Wall

On the west side of the rocky outcrop of Pen Olver, at sea level, is a very steep black wall below a flat-topped promontory. Facing north-west, in the mornings it can be a bit damp and forbidding, but when low tide combines with afternoon or evening sun it comes into its own as a prime venue for 'mid-extreme' climbing, the steepness being mitigated by positive holds, plentiful protection and immaculate rock. The best approach is to abseil in from various belays on top of the promontory.

16 *Blind Pew* **(VD)**
Mark Grantham DON SARGEANT

17 Cian E4 5c/6a 25m

FA D Henderson, C Hill 2001

Nice climbing up the left side of the wall, just a shade steeper and with holds a little smaller than on neighbouring routes. Start at the left edge beside the chasm. Move up and climb a left-facing runnel, before stepping right and going directly up the steepening wall to reach good finishing holds.

18 International E4 5c 25m

FA M Raine, S Ohly 1995

As enjoyable as *Amnesty* and as safe – just a touch more strenuous! It takes the centre of the wall, starting at a little left-facing groove 2 metres left of *Amnesty*. Climb the groove; then make a move up the left-slanting crack before heading up and rightwards to good holds. Blast up the steep wall on the left, using a left-slanting crack for the last few moves.

★
★
★
19 Amnesty E3 5c 25m
FA P O'Sullivan, C Pretty 1986

The classic of the wall taking the obvious weakness towards the right-hand side. Start at the obvious crack running up to the left. Follow the crack for 5 metres; then trend right before climbing to a deep horizontal slot (large cam). Continue up the discontinuous crack (sustained – but the holds keep coming!) to the top.

The right arête of the wall is taken by **Alabama Thunderpussy** (E3 5b), another worthwhile pitch.

Bass Point

OS Ref SW 715 119

A tremendous array of short walls, zawns, and buttresses extends eastwards for nearly a mile from the vicinity of the lighthouse, but the main attraction of the area is the superb wall at Bass Point taken by *The Cull*. From Lizard village, walk to the *Housel Bay Hotel* and follow the coast path eastwards for half a mile to a very prominent white building just before the Coastguard Lookout on Bass Point. The Cull Wall is at the end of the ridge running down to the sea from in front of the white building. It is well-viewed from a parallel ridge to the west.

Below the right-hand side of the wall is a ledge just above the high-tide mark, from which all the routes start. This is generally reached by abseil, though at low tide it is possible to scramble down into the cove to the west and reach it by crossing boulders.

★
20 Dawn E4 36m
FA P O'Sullivan, S Bell 1986

The second pitch gives superb bold climbing up the left side of the wall. Start on the ledge.

1 18m 4c Traverse left for some 5 metres to a crack in the slab and follow this to ledges beneath the steep headwall.
2 18m 5c Climb past a rusty peg to a horizontal break, and move right into the middle of the wall (good cam slot). Step up to a pocket, and make difficult moves to another horizontal crack, after which good holds on the left lead to the top.

right: 21 *The Cull* (E3)   Andi Turner   MIKE HUTTON

★ 21 The Cull E3 5b/c 30m
★ FA S Bell, P O'Sullivan, S Bishop 1986
★ A brilliant pitch – very steep and sustained but,
for the most part, on good holds. It takes the
compelling crackline just right of centre. An
open corner slants up left from the ledge to
another big ledge. Make a few moves up the
corner, gain some flakes on the right, and
follow them steeply to more broken ground at
mid height. Move up and right into the base of
the crack and follow this strenuously, passing
a difficult section towards the top.

The obvious, challenging line up the right-hand
side of the wall gives a very demanding pitch:
Lazarus (E6/7 6b).

South Devon Coast

18 *White Rhino Tea* (S0 F7a)
Adrian Baxter KEITH SHARPLES

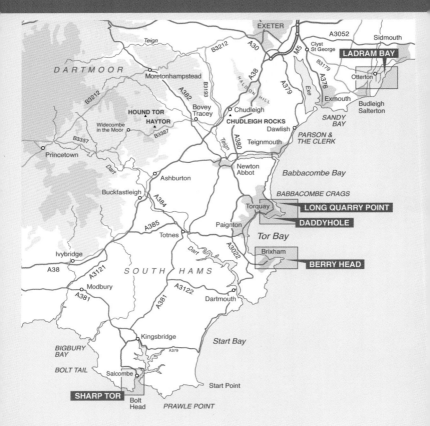

The South Hams

Between Plymouth and Torbay the Devon coast swings southwards around the South Hams, a large region of undulating hills and narrow winding lanes. The area feels 'remote' even for locals, partly because of the time it takes to get anywhere. However, it has a lush charm and the coastline has a rugged unspoilt beauty which contrasts sharply with Torbay.

Sharp Tor

OS Ref SX 728 367

Sharp Tor is a unique climbing venue offering mainly lower-grade climbs on primordial rocks which have been weathered into striking towers and pinnacles. The outlook across Salcombe Bar is beautiful; the climbs are sheltered from westerlies and enjoy the morning sun. There has been climbing at Sharp Tor since the 1960s but in the early days few records were kept. The first ascent details given here are the first recorded ascents.

SHARP TOR   Four Strong Winds   The Eye and The Needle
Flying Arête
Salcombe
Coast Path
Starehole Bay
Bolt Head

Malborough   A381
kilometre   North
Salcombe
Salcombe Harbour
South Sands
National Trust CAR PARK
YOUTH HOSTEL
SW Coast Path
SHARP TOR
Starehole Bay
Mew Stone
Bolt Head

3 *The Eye and the Needle* (D)
Pete Saunders   DON SARGEANT

Approach   Salcombe is the major resort of the area, reached by the A381. For Sharp Tor turn right to South Sands just before Salcombe, and then follow the narrow lane which hugs the coast southwards until it ends at a National Trust property (car park and YHA). The coast path starts 150 metres back down the road, where there is roadside parking for half a dozen cars. After a ten-minute walk along the flat coast path the bizarre rock formations of Sharp Tor loom above. The main buttresses rise above stone steps where the path rounds a ridge.

The routes are described from **right to left**.

1   Flying Arête & Continuations   VD   54m
FA Pitch 1: N White (solo) 1993

Three good, if disjointed pitches. The buttress right of the steps contains a deep corner taken by **Hades** (S). Start here.

  1 18m Climb the corner for 5 metres, traverse right on a line of pockets, and follow the arête to the terrace below the next pinnacle.

  2 12m Starting 4 metres left of the arête, climb the wall for 3 metres, and traverse right along a ledge to a shallow groove which leads to the top of the tower. Belay here, descend the far side, and walk across to the next buttress, which has a white quartzy area at its base.

  3 24m Climb the rib until it bulges; then step left into a shallow crack which leads to ledges. Climb the final rib, taking a crack on the left at the summit nose.

2   Erazor Flake   S   17m
FA N White (solo) 1993

Steep and exciting with big holds, it takes the obvious flake crack in the left wall of the *Hades* corner. Climb the wall to reach the crack and forge on optimistically until the steepness eases and the top is reached.

The arête left of *Erazor Flake* is taken by **Look Sharp** (VS 4c). At the top of the stone steps the path passes beneath the next ridge which is distinguished by an impressive pillar forming a 'needle's eye'. Grooves in the front face of the pillar are taken by **Hair of the Dog** (E2 5b) – a fine pitch, while the ridge itself gives:

3   The Eye and the Needle   D   45m
FA Unknown

Start at the grassy gully to the right of the pillar.

    1 21m Climb the right wall of the gully to the 'eye' and continue to the top of the tower.
    2 6m Climb the seaward side of the 'needle' (making sure your photographer is in position further along the path) and descend the same way. Belay beneath the next buttress.
    3 18m Follow the crest of the buttress on huge holds. A nice variation (VD) is to traverse right at 5 metres and follow a rightward-trending flake crack to the top.

Further along the path a stone bench is reached, high above which is a buttress characterized by a square-cut overhang jutting from its right-hand side. A faint path leads up to the buttress.

⭐ 4   Four Strong Winds   S   4a   37m
FA R Warke, A King, C Solway 1992

A substantial pitch well worth the 'long' approach. Starting left of the jutting overhang, climb the quartzy wall to reach a prominent rightward-slanting groove. Follow this and exit through a hole to the top of the buttress.

6 *Moonraker* HVS
Sarah Goodman MARK DAVIES

Torbay

The Torbay sea cliffs have something for everyone, from single pitch-climbs on sheltered, sunny crags to some of the longest and most serious undertakings in the region. If bad weather should strike during a climbing tour of the South West, Torbay is invaluable. It lies in the rain shadow of Dartmoor, its cliffs face in many different directions and some of them (notably the Great Cave area of the Old Redoubt and the Sanctuary Wall) are so steep that they can remain largely dry in moderate rain. Once you get to know the crags of Torbay, it is fair to say you need hardly ever abandon a day's climbing, whatever the time of year.

The rock is Middle Devonian reef limestone and, in contrast to the uniformity of other limestone sea-cliff areas like Dorset and Pembroke, the Torbay crags vary so much in structure, angle and aspect that no two cliffs give similar climbing. As it is easy to move from crag to crag in the Torbay area, a very varied climbing day may be enjoyed, with each new venue giving fresh inspiration and renewed energy!

The southerly aspect of many crags makes Torbay one of the best venues in the UK for climbing in the winter months. Cliffs in the sun virtually all day include Anstey's Cove, the Sanctuary Wall, Meadfoot Quarry, Telegraph Hole, and the Coastguard Cliff at Berry Head, whilst Daddyhole Main Cliff catches the sun until just after midday. Mild sea breezes often make winter climbing tolerable even on the north-facing cliffs, and at the height of summer the shadier walls at Long Quarry Point and the Old Redoubt are a welcome refuge from Torquay's 'Mediterranean' climate.

The sea temperature affects the seriousness of the traverses and approaching or retreating from certain climbs. Through summer and autumn one can take to the water with little discomfort if a section of a traverse proves difficult or if forced to retreat from the Old Redoubt. At other times of year, and especially on cold windy days, a soaking can be serious and a longer swim dangerous. Due to this and other variable factors, such as the height of the tide and sea conditions, the grades of the traverses should be seen as a rough guide only. When traversing above the sea to reach the start of a climb, even strong swimmers should carry their equipment on a bandolier so that it can be jettisoned in an emergency.

Many of the cliffs have prominent 'No Climbing' signs above them. These are intended to deter tourists and to indemnify the authorities should an accident occur. Currently the only cliffs with seasonal restrictions are at Berry Head, the Old Redoubt in particular being an important auk colony. However, climbing should not take place where holidaymakers could be put at risk from falling rock.

There have been several serious accidents in Torbay, caused mainly by rock and protection failure. Experience and sound judgment are essentials for safe climbing in this area.

Berry Head

OS Ref SX 940 563

The headland lies just to the south of Brixham, from which it is well signposted. Its major cliff is the Old Redoubt, Torbay's finest crag giving big adventure routes as good as any in the South West. There are also smaller, south-facing crags of excellent sea-washed limestone which offer a more relaxing day.

Note: to protect nesting birds there is **No Climbing** on the Old Redoubt and much of the Rainbow Bridge Cliff from 1 March to 1 August. Climbers ignoring

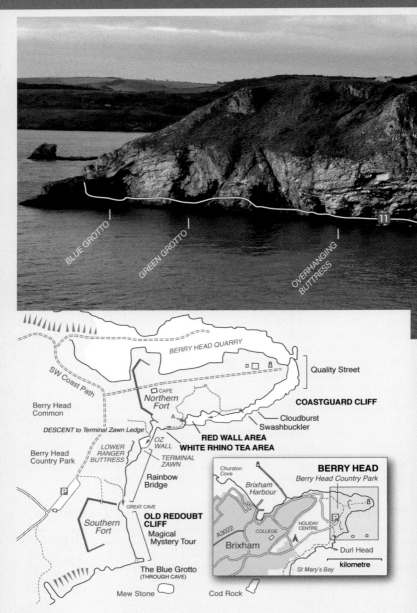

BLUE GROTTO

GREEN GROTTO

OVERHANGING BUTTRESS

11

BERRY HEAD QUARRY

Quality Street

SW Coast Path

CAFE
Northern Fort

COASTGUARD CLIFF

Berry Head Common

A

Cloudburst
Swashbuckler

DESCENT to Terminal Zawn Ledge

RED WALL AREA
WHITE RHINO TEA AREA

Berry Head Country Park

LOWER RANGER BUTTRESS

OZ WALL

TERMINAL ZAWN

P

Rainbow Bridge

GREAT CAVE

OLD REDOUBT CLIFF

Southern Fort

Magical Mystery Tour

The Blue Grotto
(THROUGH CAVE)

Mew Stone

Cod Rock

Churston Cove

BERRY HEAD
Berry Head Country Park

Brixham Harbour

A3022

COLLEGE

HOLIDAY CENTRE

Brixham

P

Durl Head

St Mary's Bay

kilometre

336

Moonraker

Car Park

Gearing up spot

THE GREAT CAVE

17

DWS ROUTES
12 TO **16**

CRYSTAL CAVE

this ban risk a £1000 fine. Also, when deep water soloing it is greatly appreciated if you inform Brixham Coastguard. The telephone number is on the gate on the descent to the Old Redoubt and Rainbow Bridge Cliff.

Old Redoubt (Southern Redoubt)

This is the towering cliff below the fortress immediately on the right as one leaves the car park. The base of the crag is reached by descending the grassy slope left of the first broken rocks, and then bearing right down a ramp to a wall dropping sheer to the sea. Traverse this on good holds to a platform at the mouth of a huge cave. Viewed from here, the most obvious line is the vertical crack system of *Moonraker*, which lies at the junction of the hanging face above the great cave with the main mass of crag to its left.

The climbs are reached by a traverse some 100 metres in length, about Severe standard, for which poor swimmers are advised to rope up. This is only passable for about two hours either side of low water and for a much shorter period during neap tides. However, if one is prepared to climb at a higher level (VS, strenuous) the period of access is extendable by an hour or so. Once the traverse is impassable, the only means of escape from the climbs is to abseil into the sea and swim for the platform. Hence all routes on the Old Redoubt are serious undertakings.

7

8

5

6

9

10

Tricky down climb

11

5   Goddess of Gloom   E1   66m   R

FA F E R Cannings, P H Biven, M Springett 1968

Especially fine on the first and last pitches. It takes the thinner crack immediately left of *Moonraker*. Start at a large ledge below an obvious slanting corner, 8 metres beyond the *Moonraker* stance. If this is awash, belay a little higher.

1 21m 5a Climb easily to an overhang (peg), and move right and up into the corner. Climb to the capping roof; then break right and move up to a small stance on the first shale band.

2 18m 5a Climb straight up the wall left of a vegetated crack, and then right to the second stance of *Moonraker*. A serious pitch.

3 27m 5a From the left side of the stance, move steeply into the groove above and follow it to a cave. Break right to a small ledge; then make some difficult moves up to the thin crack on the left, which leads to better holds and a final grassy groove.

6   Moonraker   HVS   75m   R

FA P H Biven, P Littlejohn (VL) 1967 (starting up *Goddess of Gloom*); pitch 1 added by F E R Cannings, 1968

Torbay's showpiece and a regional classic. The climbing is steep and exposed and the line inescapable. Start at a restricted stance just above the high-water mark, a short way to the left of the crackline.

1 27m 5a Make a rising traverse to the right to reach the start of the crackline. Follow discontinuous cracks up the steep wall above to a large chockstone in a corner. Climb diagonally left for 8 metres to ledges at the foot of another crack. Peg and nut belays.

2 18m 4c Climb the steep corner-crack to a small cave at 12 metres. Traverse left and move up to belays left of the leaning groove.

3 30m 5a Climb the steep groove, and above it move left on ledges to a clean-corner crack, which leads directly to the top.

The big crack system right of the upper part of *Moonraker* is taken by **The Hood** (E3 5c R).

7   The Seventh Circle   E1   79m   R

FA F E R Cannings, P Littlejohn, P H Biven 1969

The 'circle of suicides' in Dante's *Inferno*. The main pitch links *Moonraker* and *Dreadnought* to provide a technically reasonable but outlandishly exposed way up the cliff.

1 27m 5a *Moonraker* pitch 1.

2 29m 5b Follow *Moonraker* to the small cave; then swing right into the chimney of *The Hood*. Break right again and step down to a small ledge, which is followed rightwards until it ends above the abyss. Climb steeply into a large scoop, and take the wall on the right to the cave stance of *Dreadnought*.

3 23m 5b *Dreadnought* pitch 3.

8   Dreadnought   E3   78m   R

FA F E R Cannings, P Littlejohn (VL) 1969

A tremendous climb which combines a difficult and serious traverse above the lip of the great cave with very exposed climbing on the hanging wall above. Prusiks or ascenders are useful as a fall would leave the climber hanging free and with nowhere to lower to.

1 35m 5c Follow *Moonraker* to the chockstone, and step up and right (old peg). Make a slightly rising traverse on a band of very steep rock to a corner which leads more easily to the big overhang. Continue rightwards with difficulty to a good hold; then a further 3 metres of traversing gains a tiny ledge. Hanging stance and multiple cam belays.

2 20m 5b Traverse left and climb the hanging groove to the roof (peg). Step left and move up to a deep slot; then climb up left again to a large scooped ledge. The short wall on the right leads to a deep cave with a huge thread belay through its left side.

3 23m 5b Step left and climb steeply to a shallow groove on the right leading to a ledge (thread). The wall above leads to an overhang, which is taken centrally on good, well-spaced holds. Go easily to the top.

9   Caveman   E6   119m   R

FA A Meyers, M Fowler (VL) 1982

A phenomenal route breaking through the massive overhangs above the great cave. Very strenuous and sustained climbing in amazing positions. Start some 6 metres to the right of the start of *Moonraker*, in a short corner beneath a large roof.

1 24m 5b Traverse right between two bands of overhangs to a niche (often damp) and break up right onto the wall above. Traverse right into a corner, and then rightwards again to an old bolt and foothold stance.

2 9m 6a Climb to the roof (peg) and trend out rightwards on flakes to gain a niche at the inner end of the prominent red flakes which hang down from the flat roof of the cave. Peg belay.

3 14m 6a Move across the first hanging flake to gain an obvious hand-traverse crack leading out around the lip. From a projecting red foothold, move right and slightly down along the lip of the overhang to a stance after 5 metres.

4 27m 6a Traverse back left to the projecting foothold. Continue traversing between the overhangs, past an awkward bush, to join and follow *Dreadnought* to its hanging stance.

5 24m 5b Climb the hanging groove on the left as for *Dreadnought* but move right at the capping overhang to gain a shallow groove. Climb this, and move left at its top to gain a groove leading to the right-hand end of an oblong roof. Climb the short corner to a small stance.

6 21m 5b Move left and surmount the overhang to gain an awkward crack. Climb this and continue straight up to the top.

The hanging black groove above the right-hand side of the Great Cave is taken by **Depth Charge** (E5 6a R), while the awe-inspiring roof crack above the cave platform gives **Cocoon** (E8 6c R). More amenable is **Man O'War** (E6 6a R), which climbs to the roof of *Cocoon*, then traverses right around the arête to join *The Yardarm*.

10 The Yardarm   E2 5b   43m   R

FA P Littlejohn, D Roberts 1977

Wildly exposed but the holds are positive. It basically takes the seaward side of the arête above the cave platform. Care must be taken to minimize rope drag. Belay above the first move of the easy traverse to the cave platform. Pull up into a niche, and then make a gently rising traverse left for 9 metres to some small ledges beneath a slight rib. Climb direct for 5 metres to a thread (optional stance); then move left and down into an exposed bay. Climb diagonally left out of the bay to gain a bottomless groove, which is followed for a short way before breaking left again to a small roof. Pull round and continue to an easier crack which leads to a good belay.

★★★ **11 Magical Mystery Tour** E1 335m R
FA R Baillie, J Cleare 1967

The famous sea-level traverse of the Old Redoubt, linking the cave platform with the rocky promontory 300 metres to the south. Now a superb and popular DWS – traditionalists will find a rope and a few bits of gear useful for the crux pitch and the tyrolean at the end. The best time to start is half an hour or so before low tide, and it should be noted that upward escape is highly problematic beyond the first difficult section.

Traverse around the Great Cave to the start of *Moonraker* and continue easily to an overhanging nose just above the water. Pass this strenuously (4c) to arrive at a small zawn beside an overhanging buttress. This is traversed on a line about 9 metres above the sea, descending gradually on the far side to a stance (5b). Easier climbing, past the Green Grotto, leads to a sea-filled cave which cuts through the headland – the Blue Grotto. Cross this with a swim and tyrolean and climb leftwards out on to the promontory. In reasonably dry conditions it is possible to climb through the Blue Grotto rather than make the swim (5b).

Rainbow Bridge Cliff

Rainbow Bridge Cliff is an extensive wall of superb sculpted limestone. It provides some of the best deep water soloing in the UK. The traverse of *Rainbow Bridge* itself is subject to the seasonal restriction, but the other routes described may well have no restriction if seabirds have not nested. An on-site red disc notice indicates when the crag is closed to climbers.

Approach   Abseil 15 metres from a post at the start of the traverse into the Great Cave. This reaches a thread anchor. Leaving enough hanging rope to be able to pull out of the water can save a long swim.

★ **12 Way Down** S0 F5b 12m
FA Unknown

Climbs the obvious rib of the abseil line. A good warm-up, it also provides the descent and escape route for the cliff during the nesting season.

Right of *Way Down* is a smooth, pocketed wall featuring two fine lines. The left-hand is **Cutlass** (F8a) while the right gives:

★★★ **13 Verdon Dreaming** S1 F7a+ 11m
FA K Palmer 1997

Delightful climbing. Follow a line of pockets up the beautiful cream-coloured wall.

★★★ **14 Rainbow Scoop** S1 F6c+ 11m
FA N Hancock 1997

At the right-hand end of the smooth wall is a wide chimney. After a hard start through the overhang, follow the obvious line of scoops and jugs above – wild climbing on impeccable rock.

15 Puppy Onsight S1 F6b+ 11m
FA K Palmer 1997

The leaning, pocketed wall right of *Rainbow Scoop* features a high crux. Climb up to a wide, inclined break and follow it rightwards for 2 metres. Grope for a big pocket above, pull over, then good holds lead up left to an obvious handrail. Rock up; then exit on the right.

14 *Raimbow Scoop* **(S1 F7a+)**
Adrian Baxter KEITH SHARPLES

To the right, the traverse of *Rainbow Bridge* passes beneath a prominent pink block. The following route climbs a line just right of the block:

★ 16 The Lost Locals XS 5b   S1 F6b+   14m

FA I Parnell (on-sight solo) 1995

An excellent route. Climb up into the niche and exit it to the right onto good holds.

★ 17 The Wizard of Oz   S1 F7b   (overall grade for the complete traverse)   840m   R

FA K Palmer 2010 (linking many previously established climbs)

A contender for the longest and most sustained piece of high-quality rock climbing in Britain. The only 'four-star route' in the guidebook! A magnificent DWS traverse requiring fitness and stamina as well as all the other skills associated with deep water soloing. It is essential to attempt it when the sea is warm enough for swimming, as in several places a fall can result in a lengthy swim to a safe landing spot. For optimum conditions start one hour after high tide. Food, drink, and dry clothing can be pre-stashed at the end of any section.

Section **1** *The Blue Grotto and Magical Mystery Tour Reversed* 420m   S1 F6a+

Leave the car park, walk through the fort and follow the cliff edge to the south side of the Promontory. At 10 metres above sea level and 50 metres to the right (looking out), a grassy gully and wall beneath are descended to sea level. Traverse right (facing in) to enter the Blue Grotto cave and follow its left wall to a bridging manoeuvre across a chasm after 12 metres (F6a+). Continue to the exit and traverse a flat wall to swim the Green Grotto cave. Onwards to an overhanging buttress which is taken at 10 metres height (F5+). Continue and cross the back of the Great Cave via boulders to resting ledges at its entrance.

Section **2** *Rainbow Bridge* (as DWS) 280m   S1 F7a+

Waterline traversing leads to a streaky wall (F6a+), passes beneath a pink block and continues to Crystal Caves. At a height of 2½ metres a crux sequence on slopers (F7a+) ends at the base of a technical groove. Climb this for 8 metres; then break right to vegetated ledges below an open gully. Down-climb 3 metres left of the gully by dangling off a broken jug to locate a crack (thread) that leads to sea level. Sequency moves around a rib lead into a sea cave, The Cauldron, (F7a). Exit via the rope bridge and return to sea level. Continue beneath a big roof, and then climb a rising jug rail to a white pillar. Drop down and press on to the Terminal Zawn where a rising traverse leads to a hands-off rest in a large niche/hole. Descend 2 metres; then climb rightwards to finishing ledges.

Section **3** *Oz Wall to White Rhino Tea* 140m   S0 F7a

Sea-level moves lead to a rib after 18 metres. Gain height before tricky moves lead down across a blank groove (F6b+). Continue hand-traversing beneath roofs, and then on an easy rising line to the end of the wall. Down-climb on calcite/sandstone jugs to enter the triangular cave. Its left wall leads to a rest on a rock bridge. Now ascend the crystal chimney back to daylight. Drop down to ledges and hand-traverse 6 metres to directly beneath the overhanging prow. Climb the prow, moving right to finish up *White Rhino Tea* (F7a). Congratulations!

Red Wall Area and the Coastguard Cliffs

The small south-facing cliffs on Berry Head itself are distinctly lightweight compared to the Old Redoubt but well worth a visit on a sunny day, summer or winter. There is good swimming and diving off the sea-level terraces. Access is most convenient at mid to low tide but there is climbing at all states of the tide.

above: 16 *The Lost Locals* (S1 F6b+)   Adrian Baxter   KEITH SHARPLES

below: 17 *Wizard of Oz: Rainbow Bridge* (S1 7a+) Ken Palmer   PETE SAUNDERS

Third Bench

Bad Step

A

COASTGUARD AREA

RED WALL AREA

18

WHITE RHINO TEA AREA

Tricky traverse

19 20 21 22 23

Approach from the car park Follow the tarmac track into the Northern Fort; then, about 150 metres past the cafe, take a path which descends gently to the right. The path ends at a polished glacis, which is descended to sea-level terraces. Red Wall is now obvious to the west (right facing seawards) while the Coastguard Cliff is still a few minutes of walking and scrambling away to the east.

White Rhino Tea Area

This is the 45-degree overhanging buttress that can be seen beyond the Red Wall Area. A superb DWS crag which can be climbed on at any state of the tide (obviously things are a little higher at low tide!).

Approach From the cliff-top of Red Wall Area (which can be reached directly via a descent path approximately 80 metres west of the path described above), continue towards the Great Cave/Old Redoubt. This leads to large ledges overlooking the buttress. Continue past a 'bad step' to gain the top of the buttress. From here a groove to the left can be down-climbed (S), otherwise descend further down to a ledge on the right and traverse in. This approach is convenient as your spare boots and chalk bags can be left close to hand.

★ **18 White Rhino Tea** S0 F7a 9m R
★★ FA D Henderson (on-sight solo) 1999

This is one of Devon's best deep water solos: deep water at any tide, big holds, and very steep. Climb the crackline in the middle of the buttress until a long reach gains a protruding block. From here move up into a calcite sidepull, and then make a long reach up right to big holds and an easier finish.

Climbing a line about 2 metres to the right reduces the grade – **Watting Yer Ouzel** (S0 6c R)

Red Wall Area

The right side of Red Wall merges with the quarried landward cliffs, while its left side swings round to a sea cliff featuring three prominent corners.

★ **19 Abbot's Way** VS 4c 15m
★★ FA D Bassett 1961

An excellent steep route taking the left-hand corner. Climb the main corner for 9 metres, and then follow the crack up the slightly overhanging left wall to the top.

✪ **20 Binky** HS 4b 18m
FA E Hammond, J Fowler, F Stebbings 1968

Climbs the right edge of the wall to the right of *Abbot's Way*. Start at a thin crack a couple of metres from the edge. Move up, trending slightly right; then go straight up on small holds to a ledge on the rib overlooking *Chastity Corner*. Finish up a short wall.

★ **21 Chastity Corner** HS 4a 15m
★★ FA P Littlejohn, D Rogers, R Crawshaw 1967

The central corner – a nice little pitch. Make a strenuous move to enter the corner and climb it on good holds to a ledge. Block belays well back.

The right-hand corner is **Red Monk** (VS 4b), a poor route, while just to the right is one of the best climbs hereabouts:

22 Blood   E1 5b   15m
FA P Littlejohn, J Fowler, F E R Cannings 1969

Start 2 metres right of the *Red Monk* corner. Climb easily for 3 metres; then step right and climb straight up the wall above, past a thread, to the halfway ledge. Step left and climb pockets to a flat handhold. Mantelshelf onto this and so to the top.

23 Red Crack   HS 4a   21m
FA D Basset 1961

The obvious crack splitting the centre of Red Wall. Climb a thinner crack right of the main fissure to an obvious traverse line at 12 metres. Move left to finish up a shallow corner, or finish direct at VS 4b.

The Red Wall is bounded on the right by **Ruddy Corner** (VD), while the large, blind corner to the right is **Captain's Corner** (VS 4c).

Coastguard Area

Short cliffs of lovely sea-weathered limestone provide many enjoyable deep water solos, and the odd fine route.

Approach   Walk past the cafe and continue to the small rendered construction. Now follow the descent path to the very end of a long low rock wall before descending. This brings you to the top of the corner of *Swashbuckler*.

Swashbuckler Cliff

All routes are approached via *Walking the Plank*.

⭐ 24 Walking the Plank `S0 F5b` 33m
FA Recorded by R Chappell 1995

A traverse of the buttress starting at the chimney on the left side (facing in). A high line across the opening wall to the big white sloper is nicest. Continue past the arêtes of *Broadside* and **Squall** (`S2 F3`) and into the corner of *Swashbuckler*. Harder moves lead to the arête of **Piracy** (`S1 F3`) and an easy traverse of Jim Jam buttress (see next page) to finish.

⭐ 25 Sirocco S 4a `S0 F4a` 18m
FA A Gallagher, B R E Wilkinson 1979

Delightful finger laybacking up the wall above the big white sloper on *Walking the Plank*.

26 Broadside S 4a `S0 F4a` 30m
FA B R E Wilkinson, A Gallagher 1979

Traverse *Walking the Plank* to the arête. Move up onto the prominent ledge and climb the arête to the top.

⭐ 27 Woe-is-uh-me-bop `S1 F6a+` 17m
FA T Rainbow 2000

The smooth groove immediately right of the arête. Either layback the start of the groove (powerful) or climb the wall further right to enter it higher up. Absorbing technical climbing all the way.

⭐ 28 Diddy Wah Diddy `S1 F6a` 17m
FA P Saunders 2013

22 *Blood* (E1)   Robin Mazinke   MARK DAVIES

The line of calcite pockets immediately right of *Woe-is-uh-me-bop*. Watch out for the slight reef to your right.

⭐ 29 Swashbuckler HS 32m
FA J Hammond, P Littlejohn 1968

Start at the right-hand side (facing in) of Swashbuckler Cliff.

1 12m 4b Reverse *Walking the Plank* to the impressive corner; the crux is rounding the arête.

2 20m 4a Romp up the corner.

30 Douglas Fairbanks Jnr HVS 5a `S2 F5c` 30m
FA P O'Sullivan, M Dunning 1983

Climb the deep corner and break out left to join **Gunga Din** (`S1/2 F6a`), the hanging rib right of *Swashbuckler*. From the ledge on the arête, finish by a rising rightward traverse.

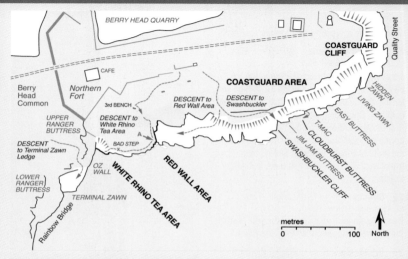

The next wall to the east is Jim Jam buttress, which has some nice routes but with potentially dangerous landings due to a submerged shelf. Immediately east again is an attractive DWS venue dropping straight into deep water:

Cloudburst Buttress

Approach From the right side (facing in), down-climb a short corner to a sea-washed ledge. Traverse left around the arête and move slightly upwards before making a descending traverse across the base of the face to get to the first climb.

31 Hidden Groove VS 4c S1 F4c 34m
FA B R E Wilkinson A Gallagher 1979

Follow the groove to a flat ledge. Make an exciting move right onto the face and finish up leftwards.

32 Earthbound Mystic HVS 5a S1 F5b 33m
FA R Chappell, D Bone 1995

Follow the cracks in the wall right of *Hidden Groove* to the ledge of *Cloudburst* and a scary finish. Avoid pulling too hard on the calcite holds, and exit direct with difficulty or leftwards (slightly easier).

33 Scar Face S1 F5b 17m
FA R Warke 1997

An eliminate squeezed onto the arête left of the groove of *Cloudburst*, and sharing the scary finish of *Earthbound Mystic*.

34 Cloudburst VS 4c S1 F4c 30m
FA A Gallagher, B R E Wilkinson 1979

The obvious bottomless groove in the centre of the wall is exited left to a ledge. Step right and take the pocketed calcite wall to pull over at the right edge of the slab.

⭐ **35 That Riveria Touch**   E2 5b   S1/2 F6a   27m
FA C Alston, S Martin 1997; FDWS M J Crocker 1998
Climb the snake-like cracks left of the perfect open groove to the roof. Alternatively, take the groove until forced to quit left. The calcite wall above the roof is taken by big moves between the better pockets.

⭐ **36 Calcite Diamond**   E3 5c   S2/3 F6b   27m
FA C Nicholson, B R E Wilkinson 1980; FDWS M J Crocker 1998
Bold – whichever style it is climbed in. Climb the independent rib to the right of the face to its top. Swing left to gain a ledge and make your way diagonally right to the arête on poor, fragile holds. Finish more easily.

The Coastguard Cliff
From the glacis at the foot of the descent path, follow the terraces eastwards, going high to pass any obstacles, until they end at a slabby cliff in two tiers. The lower of these is the buttress taken by *Hawkin's Climb*, and the corner bounding it on the left is the somewhat artificial **Crystal Corner** (VD).

⭐⭐ **37 Hawkin's Climb**   HS   30m
FA A Allen, L Message 1961
This joyful little climb is on excellent rock and very photogenic. Mid to low tide is required for the first pitch.

1 12m Make a descending traverse to the base of *Crystal Corner* and continue rightwards on barnacle-encrusted pockets, moving up around the rib to a small stance.

2 18m 4a Climb to the slab proper and follow thin cracks trending right to a large flake. Either traverse right to a crack leading to the terrace or finish more directly at a similar standard. Descend easily or continue up *Flying Fifteen*.

⭐ **38 Flying Fifteen** HVS 41m

FA P Littlejohn, J Hammond 1968

The slab forming the upper tier gives a nice bold pitch (small wire protection). Start 2 metres right of the grassy, vertical fault of 'crystal cake' forming the left edge of the slab.

1 21m 5a Trend slightly right to reach a small shelf at 8 metres, and then move left to reach a comfortable ledge. Climb directly up the slab to a peg belay (good backup wire on the right) on the sloping grass terrace.

2 20m Up to the left is a fairly solid corner in an area of broken ground. Climb this to the top.

39 Quality Street   HS 4a   76m
FA J Taylor, P Littlejohn (VL) 1968

An excellent horizontal adventure on perfect sculpted limestone, linking the Coastguard Cliff to Berry Head Quarry. Take your trainers for the walk back! Stances and belays according to preference. Follow *Hawkin's Climb* to the stance; then traverse rightwards via a narrow ledge. Move up for 3 metres from the end of the ledge and traverse at this level until forced to step down again to continue the traverse to the cave piercing the headland. Climb the outside of the cave to the floor of the quarry. Either walk out via the quarry track or climb the 60-metre rib directly above to the old Coastguard Lookout and walk back to the normal descent path.

Daddyhole Area   OS Ref SX 925 629

A popular, easily accessible area, featuring some high-quality routes taking striking lines on the Main Cliff (the first important climbs to be discovered in Torbay).

Approach   The simplest approach from Torquay is to take the Babbacombe road from the harbour for 100 metres to traffic lights, where Daddyhole Plain is signposted to the right and amply signposted thereafter.

The car park on the Plain is directly above Daddyhole Cove. The Main Cliff forms the western arm of this cove while the descent path winds down on the east side, initially through trees, until above an obvious quarry – Meadfoot Quarry. To reach the flat base of Meadfoot Quarry continue straight on down a little ridge. For the Daddyhole Main Cliff take a path which traverses above slabs into the back of the cove before descending to the boulder beach. The boulder beach can be crossed at any state of the tide to reach the base of the cliff.

40 The Watchtower   E3   180m
FA P H Biven, F E R Cannings, M Springett (with swim) 1969; K Darbyshire, H Clarke 1972

This is a traverse of the cove to the east of a natural rock arch known as London Bridge, which is about midway between Daddyhole Plain and Torquay harbour. It offers good sustained climbing with one outstanding pitch (requiring dry conditions) and is possible at all states of the tide unless a high sea is running.

From Daddyhole Plain, follow Rock End Walk westwards (towards Torquay harbour) for 300 to 400 metres, passing the Watchtower itself, until the path levels after some descending zigzags. Climb over the fence and bear rightwards down the slope to reach a rocky scoop 25 metres east of London Bridge.

Traverse pleasantly for 75 metres (moves of 4b) to a thread belay on the edge of a deep zawn (Thunder Hole). Either swim or proceed as follows: climb to the top of a flake, fix a sling, and use this to tension across the zawn to holds on the opposite wall (which can be done without aid if you're tall enough). Traverse horizontally right for 8 metres; then move up to an overhang (high thread) and continue rightwards with difficulty to good holds on the edge of the wall and a belay slightly lower (5c, a superb pitch). Move right, climb a groove for 3 metres, and bear right across the slabby wall to a break leading to a tree near the cliff-top (5a). Step around the corner and descend a groove to high-tide level. Traverse on good holds to smoother rock and then climb steeply to ledges (4a). Continue to a thread belay at the right-hand end of a long ledge. Step up to a good foothold and climb direct on small holds to easier ground (5c) or, much better, continue traversing to the promontory beyond (6a).

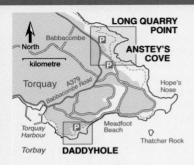

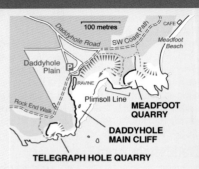

Telegraph Hole Quarry

Situated behind (south-west of) Daddyhole Main Cliff in a small cwm above the sea, this crag offers some excellent slab climbing and is a natural suntrap. It is easily reached after completing a climb on the Main Cliff (see below) and is only a few minutes walk from the car park on Daddyhole Plain. Take the cliff-top path towards Torquay harbour (Rock End Walk) from the Plain until about 30 metres after the first arch; then break left down a faint track which arrives at a stone wall above the cliff. Follow this until a retaining wall is reached, climb over, and descend an easy rib to the flat base of the quarry.

41 Blinding Flash   E4 6a   30m

FA P Littlejohn, T Penning 1983

A sustained route taking the most continuous part of the main slab. Start 5 metres up the slope from the large tree at the base. Climb straight up for 12 metres to a very thin crack running up left towards a protection peg. Make a series of thin moves to the peg, step up, and climb the steep slab above, bearing right, to better holds and the top.

42 Flashdance   E3 5c   27m

FA P Littlejohn, T Penning, P Cresswell 1983

An excellent pitch following the natural line of weakness on the main slab. Start beneath the right-hand side of the slab, 8 metres up from the large tree. Climb to a protection peg at 6 metres and continue up for 3 metres before moving left to gain a sloping ramp and twin pegs. Climb the steep slab above, past a projecting peg, to reach a large handhold above a further peg. Move up to a narrow white ledge and so to the top.

43 Crinoid   E1 5b   27m

FA P Littlejohn, P H Biven 1967

Another open, delicate climb taking the right-hand edge of the main slab. Start as for *Flashdance*. Follow *Flashdance* to the first peg; then move up and right to gain the rib. Climb the rib (peg) to a thin diagonal fault which leads leftwards to a large flat handhold and the top.

44 The Midas Touch   HVS 5a   21m

FA F E R Cannings, P Littlejohn, P H Biven 1967

An attractive and popular route following the shallow scoop right of the rib of *Crinoid*. Start 5 metres up from the higher tree. Climb bearing left for 9 metres; then go straight up to the steeper final wall, which is climbed moving slightly left.

Daddyhole Main Cliff

The crag is dominated by three great corners: the smoother left-hand corner is *Last Exit*, *Triton* climbs the huge leaning corner in the centre, while the smaller one high on the right gives the top pitch of **The Pearl** (VS 4b).

The best way off from the top of the climbs is the thorny path which ascends along the cliff edge before turning left to emerge again beside Daddyhole Plain. It is possible to approach by this path and set up an abseil to the cliff base (useful if you plan to climb several routes on the cliff). Another path runs off at a right angle to the cliff-top (near the finish of *Last Exit*) and leads down into Telegraph Hole Quarry (which is also easily approached from above). The traditional and most interesting way back to the cliff base after a climb is via the **Pinnacle Traverse** (VS 4c). This is reached by descending the broad ridge formed by the cliff-top to ledges beside a short pinnacle, where a traverse-line 5 to 6 metres above high water mark leads back around to the Main Cliff.

main: **44 *The Midas Touch*** (HVS)
James Rich
inset: **43 *Crinoid*** (E1)
Rob Stanfield
MARK DAVIES

45 Tobacco Road VS 4b 24m
FA F E R Cannings, P Littlejohn, P H Biven 1967

Good holds, nice positions, and low in the grade. It takes the tobacco-coloured wall leading up to the large overhang near the left edge of the cliff. Start at a smooth slab running up left. Climb the slab; then move left and up the wall until beneath the roof. Traverse delicately left to the edge and thence to the top.

46 Gargantua E1 42m
FA F E R Cannings, P Littlejohn 1967

Excellent steep climbing up the left arête of *Last Exit* and through the overhangs above. Start at a bank of shale below the arête.

1 27m 5a Scramble up the shale, and then climb rightwards and up a steep flake crack to a ledge. Climb into the open groove above and move up left (peg) to a resting place. Take the bulge above direct and continue up the arête on good holds to the niche of *Gates of Eden*.

2 15m 5a Traverse right using a line of small holds, step up, and then move back left above the bulge on better holds. Climb a short steep groove to easier ground.

47 Gates of Eden VS 40m
FA S Dawson, J Hammond 1967

The route that launched climbing in Torbay. The line breaks leftwards out of the corner of *Last Exit* to a bottomless corner in a fine position. At the foot of the crag is a huge leaning block, the left side of which forms a wide chimney. Start here.

1 18m 4b Climb the chimney for a couple of metres, move left onto the wall, and climb to a ledge. Continue a short way up the crack ahead and fix good protection; then lean left on a sidepull and step onto the lip of the overhang guarding the big corner. (Alternatively, pull steeply over the bulge into the corner – 5a.) Climb the corner for 4 metres to good medium and small nut belays.

2 11m 4a Climb the corner to where it begins to overhang; then traverse left and step up into a niche. Peg and nut belays.

3 11m 4a Step around left into a bottomless corner and climb it to the top.

Pinnacle Traverse

★
★
★
48 Last Exit (to Torquay) E1 36m

FA P H Biven, A Alvarez 1967

A great natural line giving steep and exposed climbing on perfect rock. Start as for *Gates of Eden*.

1 18m 5a *Gates of Eden* pitch 1, taking the direct pull over the bulge into the corner.

2 18m 5b Climb the corner to the first overhanging section and make difficult moves to better holds leading to a second bulge. Pass the bulge using holds on the right wall and continue easily to the top.

above: 48 *Last Exit (to Torquay)* (E1)   Rob Stanfield
right: 47 *Gates of Eden* (VS)   James Rich
MARK DAVIES

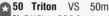

49 Zuma E4 42m
P Littlejohn, C King 1977

An inspiring pitch up the magnificent arête to the right of *Last Exit*.

1 18m 4b *Gates of Eden* pitch 1.

2 24m 6a Climb for a metre or two; then step right into a tiny groove (peg). Climb the face above to reach good jams beside the obvious projecting block; then continue climbing slabby rock on the right for 3 metres to regain the arête where it becomes smooth and overhanging. Move up the arête, and then use pocket holds on the left before trending rightwards towards the arête to finish.

50 Triton VS 50m
FA P H Biven, F E R Cannings 1967

Safe, strenuous climbing up an impressive feature – the open-book corner right of *Last Exit*. Well protected with large nuts or cams. Start as for *Gates of Eden*.

1 27m 4b Climb to the ledge; then move up and rightwards, following the broken edge of a large flake until some steep moves lead to ledges in the corner. Belay beneath an overhang.

2 23m 5a Move over the bulge to a ledge. Continue up the corner-crack until difficult moves gain holds on the left and the top.

Meadfoot Quarry

A very pleasant, relaxing venue, unaffected by tides and having good routes throughout the grades. The main face is bounded on the left by a well-defined rib (*Diamond Rib*) right of which is the clean slab of *Mayday*. The darker, smoother 'coal face' in the centre of the crag is taken by *Median* and *Revolver*. High to the right of this, the smooth, impending wall gives *Pegs' Progress*. Meadfoot Beach, with its ice cream and refreshment kiosks and toilets, is just around the corner to the east.

Recent felling of the trees above the quarry has reduced the choice of belays to the larger remaining stumps and the metal fence. The route lengths have been increased to take account of the extra rope required.

51   Diamond Rib   HS   4b   35m
FA P H Biven, C Fishwick 1967

As its name suggests, a little gem, giving neat and delicate climbing with nicely spaced protection. Follow the rib with increasing interest until forced to step right at 18 metres. Finish directly up the slab on the right.

52   Mayday   VD   35m
FA B Neely, P Littlejohn (AL) 1967

A nice route for the less experienced, starting a whisker to the right of *Diamond Rib*.

1 21m Climb straight up the clean slab for 9 metres to a shallow groove. Climb this and the little corner above and continue to a stance on the left.

2 14m Climb bearing leftwards to the top.

53 Median   HVS 5a   35m
FA P H Biven, E Grindley, A Long, M Owens

The most amenable HVS in the quarry, featuring delicate climbing with reasonable protection. Start at a shallow groove containing a borehole. Climb the groove, passing a good thread placement, to a steepening (peg). Traverse right for a couple of metres before moving up on fragile rock, past twin pegs, to better holds. Finish just right of the overhung groove, passing a final peg.

54 Revolver   E1 5b   35m
S Bell, C Gibson 1976

Fine open climbing with reasonable protection. Start 3 metres left of the overhanging groove. Delicate moves lead past a suspect peg and two small cam placements for the observant. Trend right to meet the top of the groove and a welcome resting ledge. Enter the shallow groove system on the left and follow it to a finish direct up the slabby wall.

55 Nest Egg   HS 4a   40m
FA T Lindop, E Phillips 1967

Interesting climbing on perfect rock, following a series of grooves directly to the big open niche which bounds the *Pegs' Progress* wall on the left. Care is required to protect it (mainly with small wires). Start at a slight rib directly below the niche. Climb, trending slightly left, to a ledge at 9 metres; then follow the grooves above to reach the niche. Climb the corner above to the overhang, and pass it steeply on the right to finish.

The break running diagonally leftwards up to the niche is taken by **Tree Root** (VD). It finishes easily, left of the overhang. The impending wall to the right is split by two cracks: *Pegs' Progress* takes the more central crack, while the equally fine but harder **Clotted Cream** (E4 6a) takes the crack soaring up the right-hand edge of the wall. A pleasant pitch.

56 Fawlty Towers   E3 6a   25m
K Palmer, P Saunders 2014

A fine recent addition to the quarry, taking the rising diagonal crack below the headwall of *Pegs' Progress*. Start as for *Tree Route*. Follow the shallow groove forming the left side of a rock pillar to gain its top (poor peg). Climb up to jugs below the crack of *Pegs' Progress*, and fix a high wire before launching rightwards (peg) to follow the diagonal crack all the way to its end (peg to protect the final crux moves). Finish easily up to the rib.

57 Pegs' Progress   E3 5c   32m
FA B Woodley 1983

Steep, thrilling, and (with care) well-protected climbing. Start 3 metres right of the break of *Tree Root*, below a niche at 6 metres. Climb to the niche, break left, and then climb steeply to the start of the crack, which is followed to better holds on the left before moving back rightwards to finish.

58 Hermeda   VS 4b   18m
E Grindley, R Gibbs, J Hammond 1968

The grooved arête of the wall is short but full of character. Belay at the base of the arête, a few metres below the viewpoint railings. Climb up onto a projecting ledge above the void, and continue up cracks until it is possible to pull out rightwards onto the slab. Climb a crack on the left to finish.

To Daddyhole
Main Cliff

MEADFOOT
QUARRY

59

'Anvil'
Pinnacle

The slabby sea cliff immediately west of Meadfoot Quarry gives a delightful traverse linking the quarry with Daddyhole Main Cliff:

★★ 59 Plimsoll Line S 60m

FA P Littlejohn 1967

Best enjoyed on a sunny day when the limestone gleams and the sea sparkles. Start in the notch beside the 'anvil' pinnacle at the seaward edge of Meadfoot Quarry. At low to mid tide, descend the easy ramp; then step up on to the slabby face and traverse just above high water mark. (At high tide the traverse is begun by traversing left beneath an overhang about 5 metres above the high-tide mark, and then descending some sloping cracks to reach the normal line. This is VS 4c and good climbing.) Continue the traverse, stepping down occasionally and belaying as required, until bigger holds lead to the arête of the cliff. Traverse the slab beyond to the boulder beach leading to Main Cliff. As a continuation from here, *Gates of Eden*, followed by dropping into Telegraph Hole for *The Midas Touch*, is recommended as a winning combination with steadily increasing difficulty.

59 *Plimsoll Line* Pete Saunders PEDRO SILVA

Long Quarry Area

To reach this area from Torquay, take the Babbacombe road from the harbour for just over a mile, passing a sharp right turn signposted to Anstey's Cove. Either park on the roadside 100 metres past the turning, or patronize the garden centre and use its car park. Walk up a metalled track (beside the garden centre) leading up onto an open common (Walls Hill Downs) above the cliffs.

OS Ref SX 934 651

Anstey's Cove

This is the rocky bay to the south of Long Quarry Point, the beach nearest the point being known as Redgate Beach (once very popular with holidaymakers but now closed to the public because of 'rockfall danger'). The crags are a strange mixture of quarried and natural limestone and may be uninspiring at first glance. However, they are a natural suntrap and offer some of the best hard climbing in Torbay.

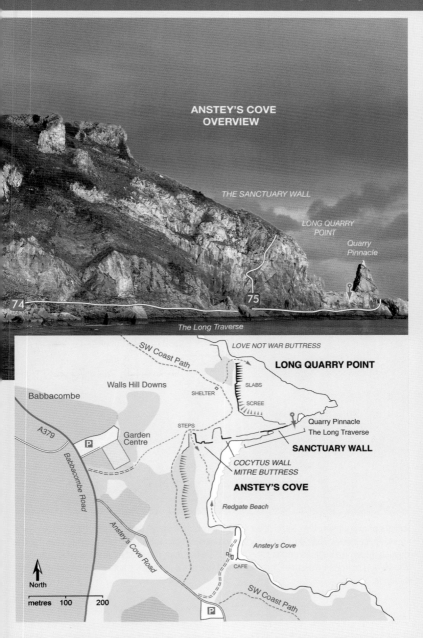

ANSTEY'S COVE
OVERVIEW

THE SANCTUARY WALL

*LONG QUARRY
POINT*

Quarry
Pinnacle

The Long Traverse

74

75

SW Coast Path

LOVE NOT WAR BUTTRESS

LONG QUARRY POINT

Walls Hill Downs

SHELTER

SLABS

SCREE

Babbacombe

STEPS

Garden
Centre

A379

P

Quarry Pinnacle
The Long Traverse

SANCTUARY WALL

*COCYTUS WALL
MITRE BUTTRESS*

ANSTEY'S COVE

Redgate Beach

Anstey's Cove

CAFE

North

metres   100   200

Babbacombe Road

Anstey's Cove Road

P

SW Coast Path

A flight of overgrown steps leads down from the common above Long Quarry Point into Anstey's Cove. These pass initially through a bay formed by a vertical wall on the right (looking down) and a bulging, prow-like buttress on the left. This is Mitre Buttress, the stepped arête of which provides *The Mitre*. The severely overhanging walls either side of the arête of the buttress give powerful sport climbing.

60 Empire of the Sun   F7b   27m
FA N White, P Bull, A Turner 1988

A fully bolted pitch, which 'flows' well with no unduly fierce moves. Start 6 metres left of the arête of Mitre Buttress, at an obvious groove. Follow the groove to its end; then step right to a wide horizontal break. Move up left to a good pocket (crux), swing up left to a jug, and continue past a horizontal crack to a strenuous exit rightwards.

Three to five metres left of the arête is the ferociously steep **Just Revenge** (F7c+).

61 Might and Main   F6c+   22m
FA N White, B Woodley 1989

A popular route, mainly taking the left side of the arête of Mitre Buttress. Start at the true arête and climb it to the niche at 4 metres. Continue up the impending wall just left of the rib till the angle relents near the top and a lower-off is reached.

62 The Mitre   E3 6a   30m
FA F E R Cannings, P H Biven, P Littlejohn (1 pt) 1968. Finish as described: P Littlejohn, J Hammond 1969; FFA S Bell, B Woodley 1979

After some fierce but safe starting moves this gives excellent sustained climbing on the classic line of the buttress. Start 2 metres right of the arête. Climb to a bolt at 3 metres (good nut or cam just before it) and pass this with difficulty, moving left to gain a large recess on the arête. Pull directly over the bulge above and continue to an uncomfortable niche. Step left to a small spike; then swing up on good holds to the start of a sloping ramp. Climb diagonally left across the vertical wall to good footholds round the rib. Step up right and continue more easily to a lower-off.

63 How the Mighty Fall   F7a+   18m
FA N White, M Barnes 1988

Strenuous climbing leads to a taxing finish. Start as for *The Mitre* but move up right to the obvious ledge. Bear left to a small niche; then steep climbing on sloping holds gains a resting ledge. The final wall is climbed using pockets and edges which are tricky to spot.

Starting 3 metres right of *The Mitre*, a bolted line up a shallow, overhanging scoop gives **The Mightier** (F7c), a superb pitch, while the low-angled slab forming the right side of Mitre Buttress is taken by **The Cope** (HS 4b), a pleasant pitch up the extreme left edge. About 30 metres right of Mitre Buttress the cliff splits into two tiers, the lower of which is smooth, overhanging, and adorned with colourful streaks. This is the mighty Ferocity Wall, home to the South West's hardest sport routes.

64 Devonshire Cream/Creaming Dream   E5   36m
FA C Nicholson, N White 1984; N White, P Gardner 1987

A dynamic duo of pitches – the first giving bold climbing up the sharp left arête of Ferocity Wall, the second giving some hard, bolt-protected moves on the tier above.
   1 21m 6a Gain and climb the arête passing two bolts – the first being a nerve-racking clip. (If the initial arête is too bold for you, climb the left side past two bolts, and then move right to gain the original first bolt.) Move down to the right to a bolt belay beneath a wall shrouded by a rightward-slanting roof.
   2 15m 6b Powerful climbing up to the right, past two bolt runners, leads to an even harder move through the roof (peg). Climb leftwards up the wall above to the top.

Immediately right of *Devonshire Cream* is the shallow, bolt-protected groove of **La Crème** (F7c+). The awesome wall to the right of this is now criss-crossed with high-grade sport routes, courtesy of star performer Ken Palmer. They are worth a look even if you have no intention of climbing them!

65 Tuppence F8b 15m
FA K Palmer 1990

Start 6 metres right of *La Crème* at a hairline crack and climb the wall via six bolt runners.

66 A Fisherman's Tale F8b 15m
FA K Palmer 1991

Start 5 metres right of *Tuppence*, climb up to a faint overhanging groove which leads to the slanting fault. Pull past the overhang, move rightwards to an undercut, and then finish direct.

67 The Cider Soak F8a 15m
FA N White 1988

Superb moves and a good introduction to the grade. At the right side of Ferocity Wall is a leftward-facing groove. Climb to a bolt at 4 metres; then trend up and leftwards to gain the diagonal faultline. Pull up rightwards to gain the groove, follow it to the next break, and then attack the airy finishing groove.

Right of *The Cider Soak* is an impressive overhanging crack – **The Lynch** (F7b+), a well-protected but super-strenuous pitch. Beyond Ferocity Wall is a large quarried basin where the cliff becomes much higher. The long white slab forming the left side of the basin gives *St Gregory the Wonder Worker*, while on the right is a smooth wall with a prominent cave in it, marking the line of *Moonshot*.

68 Sunshine F6a 60m
FA K Palmer 2010

Pleasant and nicely positioned, climbing the left side of the *St Gregory...* slab before slinking left on an exposed traverse.
   1 35m F5a Climb the slab past several bolts.
   2 25m F6a Move left across loose ground to a rib, climb this, and traverse left along the lip of the overhangs to exit at a white wall. Belay to the fence.

69 St Gregory the Wonder Worker VS 55m
FA M Springett, P H Biven (VL) 1967

Pleasant climbing but very sparsely protected. It climbs the long white slab and the steeper rib above.
   1 34m 4a Climb the slab fairly easily but cautiously to belay beside an iron spike.
   2 21m 4b Traverse left across the smooth slab for 3 metres, and climb straight up the rib to traverse right round the nose on the obvious line a few metres from the top.

72 *Cocytus* (F6c)
Tom Muller JUSTIN TIMMS

65 *Tuppence* (F8b)
Alexis Perry   CHRIS JONES

70 The Lumpy Universe   E3 5c   27m
FA C Nicholson 1986

The best quality climbing on the *Moonshot* wall, starting as for *Moonshot*. Climb to the cave, and break leftwards following a faint seam to reach a large pocket after 5 metres (thread). Climb straight up, passing a peg in a groove, and continue directly up the final wall.

71 Moonshot   E1 5b   21m
FA P Littlejohn, J Hammond 1968

A good little route especially when taken as a continuation to *Cocytus*. Start by scrambling up to a peg belay below the cave in the right wall of the quarried basin. Follow a line of flakes to the cave, step up on the left, and traverse back right across the top of the cave to good holds at a small bush. Move up and slightly left; then go straight up the slabby face to the top.

Below and to the right of the quarried basin is a very steep, amber-coloured wall having a strikingly smooth groove on its left side.

72 Cocytus   F6c   21m
FA E Grindley, P Littlejohn (VL, 2 pts aid) 1968; FFA P Littlejohn, D Garner 1976

Thin, sustained climbing up the superb groove. Climb the groove to a sloping ledge, then straight up the continuation corner to a lower-off. The start of *Moonshot* can be reached by climbing up to the left from here.

374

The wall to the left of *Cocytus* gives excellent short pitches which can be led or top-roped from the belay of *Cocytus*. The best is **American Express** (F7a+), which takes the first weakness left of the arête, while the arête itself is **Torbay or Not Torbay** (F7b). Right of *Cocytus* a line of bolts marks **More Steam, Bigger Women** (F7b), while the central line of the orange-streaked wall is taken by **Blonde Bombshell** (E5 6b). **The Shroud** (E5 6b) takes the leftward-leaning corner beneath the big overhang. Further right again the ground rises to the foot of an obvious corner-crack:

73 Acheron HVS 42m

FA P Littlejohn, E Grindley, J Taylor 1968

The slanting corner/crack system above and to the right of the overhang which shrouds the amber wall. Start at a short wall beneath the crack.

   1 27m 5a Climb to the corner and follow it to a sloping ledge beneath the overhang. Continue up the awkward leaning corner above; then move up and left across the slab to a good stance and belay station (abseil option).

   2 15m 4a Climb up for 2 metres; then traverse 9 metres right. Continue, keeping left of the bushes to reach the top and iron spike belays.

375

The Sanctuary Wall

This is the dramatically overhanging crag which runs out to Long Quarry Point from Anstey's Cove. It overlooks *The Long Traverse* and takes its name from the halfway zawn – The Sanctuary – which often provides the crux of that traverse. The routes are very steep and with phenomenal exposure for their length. Until mid tide, all the climbs can be approached from either Anstey's Cove or Long Quarry Point via *The Long Traverse*. Around high tide, *Madness* must be approached from Anstey's while *Sacrosanct* and *Call to Arms* can be reached from Long Quarry Point via an 8-metre abseil to *The Long Traverse* from an iron spike on the landward side of Quarry Pinnacle.

74 The Long Traverse VD 107m
FA J Worsley 1962

Used mainly as an approach to routes on the Sanctuary Wall (from either direction) but a worthwhile excursion in its own right, especially if rounded off with a route on Quarry Pinnacle. Start at low to mid tide from the large boulders in Anstey's Cove. (At higher tides the traverse is still possible but the standard goes up with the water level.) Traverse on enormous holds, with one strenuous move, to gain the promontory beside the Sanctuary (a double zawn which is very difficult to cross at high-tide except by an invigorating swim). Continue around the Sanctuary, and then easily again beneath Sanctuary Wall to the base of Quarry Pinnacle, which is rounded to boulders beneath its east face.

The corner dividing the two summits is **Storm Child** (S) while just to its right a cracked slab leads up to an obvious groove and gives **Sea Slip** (VD), a pitch consistent with the rest of *The Long Traverse*.

The Long Traverse

At the left side of the Sanctuary Wall is an obvious groove overlooking the Sanctuary. This is taken by **Call of the Wild** (E6 6b) which gains the groove by fierce climbing up the overhanging wall directly below it.

★ **75 Sacrosanct** HVS 36m
★ FA P Littlejohn, E Grindley, P H Biven 1969
★ The classic of the Sanctuary Wall, giving steep
climbing on positive holds and with terrific exposure
for the grade. Starting up the great central fault
(which begins as an overhanging crack and
becomes a huge broken corner higher up), it veers
right to a sensational crackline. Approach via *The
Long Traverse* and scramble up to belay in a small
corner about 6 metres right of the fault and 9 metres
above the high-water mark.

  1 12m 4c Move up, arrange gear, and then
  swing leftwards along a line of good jugs to gain
  the fault/crack, which is climbed to a large ledge
  and belays.
  2 24m 5a Traverse right across the slab and
  follow its right edge to an airy ledge. Climb the
  overhanging crack above to reach easier ground
  and the top. Belays well back.

From the (*Sacrosanct*) belays, either descend the ridge to Long Quarry Point (Diff climbing or abseil from an iron spike) or ascend it via a prickly path to the prominent tower of rock which caps Quarry Wall. The front face of this gives **The Grey Tower** (VS 4c), a nice way to finish the trip if heading back into Anstey's Cove.

76 Free the Spirit   E6 6a   30m
FA M J Crocker, N A Coe 1988

The 'one-in-three' overhanging wall between *Call to Arms* and *Sacrosanct* provides one of the most dramatic and pumping pitches in the South West. Some small-to-medium-sized wires are required to supplement the *in situ* gear. Start from the uppermost of the ledges some 6 metres left of *Call to Arms*. Pull up to gain a short ramp and a hand ledge above. Reach for a jug, and then trend leftwards on good small flakes to a pockety crack. Climb direct to the centre of the *Madness* ramp; then pull straight over the lip above to a sloping shelf. Continue more easily, first right, then left to the top.

77 Call to Arms   E4   39m
FA S Monks, E Hart 1980; pitch 2 S A Lewis, J Codding 1983

A superb and very strenuous route taking the obvious challenge of the overhanging groove which soars up from sea level to join the upper groove of *Incubus*. Start beneath the groove, which is the first real weakness to the right of the huge central fault taken by *Sacrosanct*.

1 24m 6a Climb the groove to a stance where it joins the larger groove of *Incubus*.
2 15m 5c Climb the groove to the overhang and pass this on the right with difficulty. Trend rightwards above to belay on an iron spike.

78 Incubus   E1   29m
FA P Littlejohn, P H Biven (VL) 1968

With a 'wow factor' out of all proportion to its length, this route sneaks in to the right-hand side of the Sanctuary Wall to enjoy its fantastic positions. Well above the waves but especially exciting at high tide during rough seas. Start from the grass platform of Long Quarry Point, in the notch at the foot of the ridge behind Quarry Pinnacle.

1 8m 5b Step down and traverse left on steep rock to take a stance on the slabby left wall of the groove.
2 21m 5b Climb the groove to the overhang. Pull round its left-hand side and move up the corner for a couple of metres until the wall on the left can be climbed to finish. Belays well back.

79 Madness   E5   76m
FA P Littlejohn, T Penning 1983; pitches 1 and 2 P Littlejohn, H Clarke 1977

The obvious soaring traverse-line across the Sanctuary Wall gives strenuous, intimidating, and wildly exposed climbing. From the promontory forming the outer edge of the Sanctuary, climb a slab to easy ground and continue scrambling to reach a belay spot near the start of the line.

1 18m 5c Traverse into the obvious groove; then continue rightwards along the shelf to a hanging stance at a corner.
2 24m 5c Move round the corner and traverse to where the ledge ends at some suspect incuts. Swing down and continue at a slightly lower level to a long, overhung ledge. Move up from the right end of this to an obvious hold; then pull up and round the rib on the right. Descend until a good crack on the right is reached and climb it to the stance of *Sacrosanct*.
3 34m 6a Move right and up as for *Sacrosanct* to a small ledge. Launch out across the traverse-line, which becomes difficult and strenuous, and follow it to join *Incubus* at the bulge. Either climb leftwards to the top as for *Incubus*, or pass the bulge on the right as for *Call to Arms*.

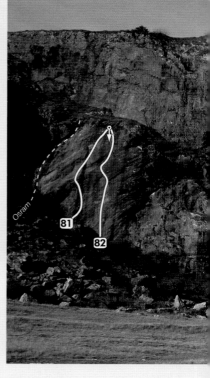

Long Quarry Point

The descent path to the Point begins in front of the large concrete shelter on the seaward fringe of the Downs. The quarried platform which forms the Point is backed by two sharply contrasting cliffs, both 60 metres in height. The right-hand cliff is a mass of smooth, grey slabs which split into two tiers near their left side, the lower tier merging into the left-hand crag – a somewhat featureless and less attractive quarried wall. Left of this is the twin-summited Quarry Pinnacle, which marks the end of *The Long Traverse* (page 376 – the sea-level link between Anstey's Cove and Long Quarry, and the means of reaching routes on the Sanctuary Wall).

Quarry Pinnacle

The most prominent of several around the rim of the point. It can be climbed (or descended) most easily by the landward arête (D) but the best climbing is on the smooth seaward face, which is accessible from low to mid tide by scrambling down from the flat plateau of the Point.

80 Seaward Edge VS 4c 27m

FA Unknown: climbed in various incarnations since 1968

The best way to climb the pinnacle – a good varied route. Start at the bottom left corner of the face and climb diagonally rightwards following a crack into a niche. Climb a short white groove before traversing left past a hole to a small sloping ledge on the arête. After a tricky move, climb steeply on better holds until the slabbier, left side of the arête is followed to the summit block, which is taken direct.

The Slabs

The obvious curving groove at the junction of the slabs with the quarried wall is **Osram** (HVS 5a), a good pitch, and just to the right of this is a smooth black wall which offers harder climbing with unusual character.

81 Up the Styx (without a Paddle)   F7b   30m

FA N White, A Turner 1987

Start below and right of *Osram*, at a shallow ramp running up rightwards into the middle of the black wall. Climb to a bolt; then step up and right before following some small incuts up to the left to gain a ledge. Climb rightwards up a smooth ramp, and then straight up to a ledge where the difficulties ease. Move right, then up to bolt belays (abseil point).

Shadowstyx (F7c) is a good link-up breaking left above a bulge 15 metres up *Shadow Beast* to join the upper part of *Up the Styx…* via a precarious traverse.

★
★ **82 Shadow Beast** F7c+ 30m
★ FA N White 1988

Superlative climbing which is technical rather than brutal, taking the centre of the smooth wall. Now entirely bolt protected. Start 6 metres right of *Up the Styx*, beneath a bolt. Climb up and rightwards to a good hold, and then back left to the bolt. Sustained climbing follows until it is possible to move left and rest. Step back right and make a perplexing series of moves to a good hold. Continue strenuously and climb the wall above to the abseil point.

The easiest route on the slabs – **Ruby in the Dust** (VS 4b) – takes the conspicuous vegetated break which rises across the slabs from left to right. Large cams are useful on the first pitch.

★
★ **83 Renegade** E4 54m
★ FA N White, P Bull 1986

Another superb route taking the steep, clean rock immediately left of *Black Ice*. Rather bold to start and to finish. Start 3 metres left of a small tree.

1 24m 5c Climb straight up on small holds and cross the vegetated break to reach a peg. Follow the line of poor pegs leftwards until it is possible to climb straight up the wall above the last of these to a stance and bolt and peg belay.

2 30m 6a Climb straight up above the belay for 8 metres to gain a large foot ledge and good runners in a horizontal crack. Move up and right to a peg and continue rightwards to a small resting ledge. Climb straight up past two more pegs until steep moves using a flake gain easier ground.

★
★ **84 Black Ice** E3 64m
★ FA P Littlejohn, K Darbyshire 1973

A brilliant sustained route which takes the steep central mass of the slabs. The rock is generally clean and solid. Start at the extreme left end of the quarried wall at the base of the slabs.

1 37m 5c Climb steeply to a peg; then either go straight up to better holds leading to a white scoop, or move right, and then climb leftwards to the scoop (easier). Step up to the break, move a little right, and then climb the wall above for a few feet before traversing left (peg) to reach better holds at some vertical cracks. Follow the thin cracks up and slightly right until difficult moves gain ledges and a peg belay.

2 27m 5c Move right and climb to a narrow ledge (peg). Continue to the obvious horizontal crack which is followed back leftwards onto the final wall. Move up until a crack can be reached high on the left, and then a few steep moves gain easier ground and a fixed belay station/abseil point.

★ **85 Coup de Grâce** VS 63m
FA P Littlejohn, B Housley 1967

The original route of the slabs and the second big cliff to be climbed in Torbay after Daddyhole. Vegetated in the middle but with plenty of good varied climbing. Start beneath the highest point of the quarried wall at the base of the slabs.

1 24m 4a Meander up the wall, with little protection, to a long grass ledge. Peg and thread belays beneath a slab running up to the left.

2 27m 5a Move up to a ledge and continue to a thin grassy crack running across a smoother slab (peg and microwires). Move across lef, climb delicately straight up to a grassy ramp, and follow this to a smoother wall (peg). Step right and up to better holds (peg) before traversing right to a ledge and belays.

3 12m 4b Step back left and move over the bulge into a leftward-leaning corner-crack which is climbed to the top.

★ **86 Safari** E1 125m
★ FA P Littlejohn, P H Biven, E Grindley 1969

An adventurous, rising traverse of the slabs giving pleasant and sustained climbing despite a liberal smattering of vegetation. Some peg runners may be in place but generally protection is provided by small wires and cams. Start about 5 metres in from the right-hand end of the quarried wall at the base of the slabs.

1 23m Climb to a thin crack; then bear left up a ramp to a vague groove which leads to grassy rock, and continue to a grass stance.

2 21m 4c Climb to another grass ledge, and step up and delicately left to good holds. Continue traversing left for 9 metres until steep climbing on good holds gains a stance in a corner.

3 21m 4c Traverse left for 5 metres; then move down and left. Continue the traverse to a large white ledge.

4 18m 5b Move 5 metres left to a sharp flake, step down, and traverse thinly to better holds on a ramp, which is followed to a narrow grass ledge. Move right to belay so that the rope protects the second.

5 24m 4c Pull up into the wide curving crack. Climb this and continue up over grass to a cleaner, grey slab. Traverse left and move diagonally left over more vegetation to a stance.

6 18m 5a Above and to the left is a ramp leading onto the exposed upper wall. Follow the ramp and climb the wall for a short way before stepping right to good holds. Continue direct until a steep move right gains the top.

Ladram Bay

OS Ref SY 097 854

The Old Red Sandstone sea stacks at Ladram Bay in South-East Devon provide a novel climbing experience, the closest thing we have to 'desert rock' in the UK. Great entertainment is guaranteed, usually with an epic element. The bay is situated about half a mile east of Otterton, the turning being up a steepening lane opposite the village garage. Parking, beer, and ice creams are available at the caravan park, from which a lane leads down to the bay.

For an easy introduction, the stack immediately in front of the slipway, Ladram Lady, is climbable by its seaward arête, though hiring a float is advisable as the tide never quite goes out far enough. The classic ascent of the area, however, is the Big Picket Rock, the largest and most easterly of the stacks.

383

88 *Big Picket* (E1)
Dave Talbot   HENRY CASTLE

High Peak

Ladram Lady

CHOCOLATE FINGER

LADRAM BAY

⭐ **87 Chocolate Finger** 24m E1

FA P H Biven, J Fowler 1971

The most westerly of the Ladram stacks is also the least tidal and has better-than-average climbing. It is accessible during neap tides when the traverse to *Big Picket* can be impassable. Start at the seaward arête and climb trending left on a line of ledges (past a couple of old nails); then move up rightwards to gain the large grassy shoulder. Belay here; then continue more easily up the final wall.

Big Picket Rock

Big Picket Rock is roughly half a mile east of Ladram Bay, in an impressive setting in front of the 150-metre cliffs of High Peak. Approach along the foreshore and time the ascent around low tide. Only a very fast party will get back with dry feet and low spring tides are definitely an advantage.

⭐ **88 Big Picket/Razor Fish** E1 42m

FA P H Biven, K Darbyshire (VL), J Fowler 1971; B Woodley, J Pyne 1998

The essential Devonshire pinnacle tick! Unfortunately, the original route up this pinnacle has suffered rockfall and *Razor Fish* now provides the most amenable method of gaining the summit. The timid may be a little disheartened by the sandy nature of the rock (on second thoughts, the timid should avoid it altogether). All gear is *in situ* (bongs, angles, and other oddments) and a bit of cheating is possible if you want to bag the summit at the original grade of HVS. Take several long slings to reduce rope drag and, for reasons which will become clear, it is unwise to attempt this route with a single rope. Start by climbing easily onto the plinth, and belay beneath an obvious cave/chimney in the west face.

    1 15m Follow a stairway of ledges up to the left (rusty nail *in situ*) until a traverse right gains the cave stance.

    2 27m 5b From the cave/chimney the original route swung right. Move out to the left, traverse to a crack which is climbed until a 'grovel' rightwards gains the summit. Don't forget to sign the Big Picket Visitors' Book, which is wrapped in several plastic bags wedged between the summit blocks.

Descent is by a simultaneous (see-saw) abseil via the east and west faces. The climber descending the west face should land on the plinth and retain a firm hold on the rope while his/her partner swings across the east face to reach the platform. At low tide this is unnecessary. Return to Ladram Bay by walking, wading, or swimming!

Jersey

11 *Perihelion* (HVS)
Kevin Davey KEVIN ELOURY

With granite cliffs galore and a host of other attractions, Jersey more than justifies the effort required to get there and is perfect for those who wish to combine climbing with a more relaxed holiday. As the most southerly of the Channel Islands it enjoys weather which is more akin to France than the British mainland, with a daily average of eight hours sunshine during the summer.

The island is accessible by plane from many UK airports, and by ferry from two or three points on the South Coast as well as from St Malo in northern France. Any travel agent, or an Internet search, can supply up-to-date details. Except in the off-season when B&B is relatively cheap and plentiful, accommodation (including campsites – rough camping being strictly forbidden) should be booked in advance and is more expensive than on the mainland. Details of this and general information about the island can be obtained from the Tourism Department, St Helier, Jersey (www.jersey.com). The tourist office also sells the 1:25000 Official Leisure Map from which the map references below are taken.

In spite of the scale of the island (nine miles by five) some means of transport is highly desirable as buses are infrequent and only link the main towns. So most visiting climbers will hire a vehicle or bring their own on the ferry.

The cliffs are granite and strongly reminiscent of Cornwall but, although one or two cliffs are as high as any in West Penwith, many are slightly less steep and offer a superb range of routes in the lower and middle grades. The best and highest cliffs are on the north-west coast, while in bleaker weather the south coast is an attractive alternative and its best area is described here.

Like the Bristol Channel, Jersey has a huge tidal range of up to 12 metres so tide information is useful, although good climbing is available at any state of the tide in moderate seas. The routes are described anticlockwise round the coast, beginning on the north-west-facing stretch of coastline known as Les Landes. All the cliffs in this selection may be reached easily from the car park at Grosnez Point.

Jersey has a small but active climbing fraternity and the website www.jerseyclimbs.com gives useful information such as partner contacts, additional topos, maps, etc.

Le Vyi

OS Ref *Jersey* 551 567

This fine slabby buttress forms the seaward tip of the first headland north-east of Grosnez Point. From the car park, take the coast path north-east for 250 metres, keeping near the cliff edge, until the top of the crag appears as a prominent dome (with two smaller, sharper points either side). A small path down the slope immediately north-east of the dome leads to ledges at the base of the cliff. The face is bounded on the left by a clean corner high up. This gives:

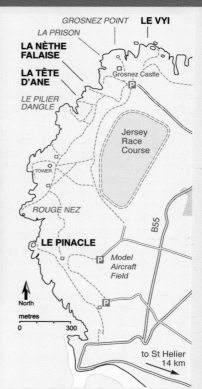

★★ **1 The Sword and the Shield** HS 36m
FA D Beck 1967

Start at a stepped groove directly below the clean corner.

1 18m 4a Follow the groove to belay beneath the corner.

2 18m 4b Climb the offwidth crack and narrow chimney. Continue up onto the wall above; then traverse right at a small ledge to reach rounded cracks which lead awkwardly to better finishing holds.

★★★ **2 Shout About** HVS 42m
FA R Grice, S Morgan 1977

A plum line. Well to the right of the previous route is a small rectangular ledge above sea level.

1 24m 5a Step right and climb into the sentry-box feature. Continue up the corner until it is possible to step right into a shallow groove in the arête. Follow this delicately, past a square-cut roof on the right, to belay beneath the final hanging arête of *Citizen's Edge*.

2 18m 4c Move left under the arête and climb the face cracks to the top.

★★★ **3 Citizen's Edge** E2 42m
FA A Rouse, J Curran, R Hazko 1984; pitch 2: R Valentine, D Cobley 1984

The main arête of the cliff – a superb climb. Belay 2 metres lower and to the right of the rectangular ledge of *Shout About*.

1 22m 5b/c Climb up rightwards to gain the arête and follow it to a small stance below the overhang.

2 20m 5c Move left below the roof, continue to gain a small ledge from the left, and climb the arête.

3 *Citizen's Edge* (E2)
Niick Thorne   KEVIN ELOURY

The Fish
Pond

4 5

La Nèthe Falaise

OS Ref *Jersey* 548 564

This large slabby cliff is perhaps Jersey's most 'traditional' climbing area. It is very accessible, being located immediately south-west of the Castle car-park at Grosnez, and popular despite not receiving much sun. It consists of three main buttresses, the left-hand of which is easy to approach (down the grassy slope from the castle to the large rock pool – the Fish Pond). This part of the cliff is not tidal and offers some of the island's better and longer climbs at an easier standard. It can be climbed almost anywhere, although the following routes are particularly good.

★★ **4   Scimitar**   HS   60m
FA Unknown

Start from the Fish Pond at the base of the slabs.

1 25m Climb the slabs to the chimney formed by the right-hand side of an obvious pinnacle. Climb this and belay on top.

2 35m 4b Move up and left to a red, crescent-shaped slab (the Scimitar Slab). Climb this to an overhang and layback around to cracks which lead to easy ground.

5   The Anvil   S   62m
FA R Haycraft, J Speller, A Perchard 1970s; finish as described: P Clarke, A McKenny 1973

Quite adventurous, and regarded as one of the best of the easier climbs on the island. Start immediately right of the Fish Pond.

1 27m 4a Climb slabs on the left of a deep chimney until level with the top of a pinnacle. Traverse right into the gully on an obvious line.

2 10m 4a Step right from the gully floor onto the face and move right, under the 'Anvil', to an exposed crack which is followed to easy ground.

3 25m 4a Climb up to the right, on slightly vegetated rock, until below a slab split by a crescent-shaped crack. Climb the crack to a small overhang; then step right and climb towards an obvious bigger crack, which is joined at half height and followed to the top.

The right-hand buttress is approached at low tide by scrambling down to the bottom of the seaward face of the promontory, traversing left (facing the cliff) to the edge of the buttress, and moving around to a good ledge at its base. Being the most seaward, it offers good climbing on clean, weathered granite.

6   La Fête de Claire   VS   54m
FA P Clarke, A McKenny 1972

A steep and direct route starting from the left end of the ledge.

1 9m 4b Climb the crack to a stance beneath an overhang split by deep cracks.

2 24m 4c Climb the left-hand crack and continue to a square-cut overhang below two parallel grooves. Pass a detached flake with care, and then steep climbing leads to a stance on a narrow ledge.

3 21m 4c Step left and climb a crack to a ledge. Continue to the final overhang and take this direct.

7   Sunshine Ramp   VS   48m
FA P Clarke, A McKenny (VL) 1972

Start from the centre of the ledge at a left-facing, shallow corner.

1 15m 4c Follow the corner through the bulge and up to a rock pedestal. Climb the short overhanging crack to the right and belay on the top.

2 12m 4b Climb up, and then follow a crack rightwards to a stance on the right of a sloping ledge.

3 21m 4b Climb the wall, moving leftwards; then either follow the wide crack to the top or hand-traverse out right along a distinctive crack to finish.

8   Green Gully   HS   45m
FA Jersey Rock Climbing Club 1965

Start at the right-hand end of the ledges (12 metres right of *La Fête de Claire*) below a gully line.

1 12m 4a Move into the gully, which is followed to a ledge.

2 18m 4b Climb the steep corner above until a move right leads to a second corner. Continue for 5 metres past jammed boulders to a sentry-box belay.

3 15m 4a Follow the crack on the left to the top.

La Tête d'Ane

OS Ref *Jersey* 547 563

This cliff is situated about 400 metres south-west along the coast path from the car park at Grosnez, and is distinguished by a 'donkey's head' (or 'rabbit's ear', depending on your view) rock formation above its north face. The crag is best viewed from the top of Le Pilier Dangle, the next headland south.

The front of the Tête d'Ane promontory consists of an elegant square-cut buttress with a smooth front face, the right edge of which gives *Perihelion* and the left *The Ragged Edge*. An easy path down into the amphitheatre on the north side of the buttress gives access to *L'Oreilles* at most states of the tide. Other routes are approached at low to half tide by scrambling down a ridge some 60 metres south of the buttress to the rock platforms at its base.

12 *Thoughts of Ice* (HVS)
Gregor Menzies   KEVIN ELOURY

9 L'Oreilles HVS 42m

FA A Rouse, I Smith, R Haszko 1984

Just left of the sharp arête between the north and west faces are two smooth black grooves. Start beneath the smaller, left-hand groove.

  1 20m 5b Climb the groove, past an old peg, to a good ledge.

  2 22m 4b Climb the corner above, passing an obvious fin of rock, to the top.

10 The Ragged Edge E5 42m

FA R Valentine, D Cobley 1984

A fine, serious route giving delicate open climbing and requiring good rope management. It takes the left side of the sheer front face of the buttress. Start on the ledges below the buttress.

  1 13m 5a Move up and left into a corner, climb to the roof, and exit left to a ledge.

  2 29m 6a Traverse back right above the roof, and move round the arête onto the face. Climb the face with difficulty until a move can be made to the left edge, which is followed directly to the top.

11 Perihelion HVS 5a 30m

FA A Rouse, R Haszko 1984

An excellent pitch taking an improbable line for the grade. It follows cracks running up the right-hand side of the front face of the buttress. Start on ledges beneath the buttress. Climb up to the right to skirt the first overhang, and then traverse left above it, across a corner, to good holds on the crest of the buttress. Follow the cracks above to a ledge, and continue via cracks just left of the arête to the top.

Bounding the square-cut buttress on the right is **Haycraft's Corner** (VS 4c), which follows the corner to the ledge on the left and then takes the centre of the wall above. Breaking right from this is an obvious crackline:

12 Thoughts of Ice HVS 5a 30m

FA W Dark, M Brown 1984

Climb *Haycraft's Corner* to the top of its chimney strike out right, and follow the obvious curving crack all the way to the top.

13 Senior Citizens HVS 5a 30m

FA R Haszko, J Curran 1984

A sustained but well-protected pitch up the steep, cracked wall to the right of *Haycraft's Corner*. Start below the left-hand crack. Climb the easy chimney; then go directly up the wall, past two small overhangs, to the top.

The next headland south, Le Pilier Dangle, provides a number of fierce, gritstone-like pitches up to 6b standard, taking obvious cracks in the vicinity of the overhanging prow. On the south side of this point the cliff relents in steepness and gives a number of easier climbs in an area known as Dangle Dell. This is more sheltered and gets more sun than other crags on this section of coast – a perfect place for beginners or a more relaxed day. It is virtually non tidal and particularly useful for this reason. There are about a dozen short routes in the Diff to Severe range taking the obvious breaks, and several pitches of a higher standard mainly towards the right.

Le Pinacle

OS Ref *Jersey* 544 554

This is Jersey's finest cliff and a remarkable coastal feature. It consists of a 60-metre monolith which is steep on all sides and connected to the mainland by a flat neck of land, upon which are the remains of some Neolithic buildings. The easiest route to the summit of the pinnacle (D 30m) ascends the buttress just behind the building outlines to gain the north-east ridge, which is followed to the top. This is also the descent route.

To reach the climbs descend easily on the right-hand side (facing seaward) of the pinnacle to terraces which are exposed at all states of the tide, but which shelve and become tidal as they run round beneath the steep main face. The most obvious weakness in the highest part of the cliff is the rightward-trending, scooped groove taken by *Homesick Angel*.

★ 14 Rainmaker HVS 5a 45m
FA R Valentine, R Townsend, D Cobley 1984

This popular climb provides a good first excursion onto Le Pinacle. Below the left side of the face a large boulder leans against the cliff. Start to the left of this on a pointed boulder and trend leftwards from here up into a scoop which leads to a rightward-rising ramp. Follow the ramp past a small rectangular roof; then move up and leftwards to reach a long, ragged crackline which is followed to the top.

★ 15 Forbidden Planet E2 5c 42m
FA K Eloury, P Brown 1989

A big sustained pitch which can be split if required. Start left of the large boulder and move up to reach an overhanging, leftward-rising groove. Climb this, and follow an intermittent crackline until beneath the large overhang (optional stance on the left). Climb leftwards through the overhang to gain the niche above (big cam useful) and then go up to a quartz pocket. Continue to a short diagonal crack leading to a small bulge and an exit onto the shoulder.

★ 16 Richard's Field HVS 50m
FA R Valentine, R Townsend, D Cobley 1984

A quality climb which weaves its way up the main face and is not affected by tides. Start at the large boulder.

1 35m 5a Climb the boulder; then traverse easily rightwards to the base of a steep, cracked groove. Follow the groove, and then continue to the left side of a large slanting roof. Pull through on good holds and follow a crack rightwards to its end. Step right and trend left up a ramp to belay at a small corner.

2 15m 4c Move left and climb to a ledge below a red overhang. Pull through rightwards to a grassy ledge and finish to the left.

★ 17 Tax Exile E5 55m
FA A Rouse, P Burke 1984

One of the 'top routes' of the island, taking the steepest part of the cliff by a series of right-facing layback flakes. To the right of *Richard's Field* the base of the crag impends. Start at an overhanging groove leading to a prominent block, about 18 metres right of the large boulder at the base.

1 12m 5c Climb boldly to the block; then trend right up the wall to an undercut, and exit onto a sloping ledge.

2 22m 6a Climb the wall above via some leftward-trending cracks to a quartz strip below a large overhang. Climb strenuously through the roof and the flake above (large cam) and continue directly through the bulges until the difficulties ease and a stance on the left is reached.

3 21m 5a Move right and climb directly through the black scoops to easier ground and the top.

★★★ **18 Homesick Angel**   HVS   61m

FA M Whitaker, M Birkett 1984

A very fine route taking the central groove line up the impressive main face. Start at low to mid tide by some rock pools approximately 25 metres right of the large boulder, where a line of flakes leads up leftwards to a prominent ledge.

1 18m 4c Follow the flakes to reach a ramp/ledge just left of the long overhang; then move left to a stance below the main groove line.

2 20m 4c Climb the long groove through several bulges to a grassy ledge. Stance just above and good belays (hard to spot) higher still.

3 23m 4c Follow the groove to its end; then move right through the black scoops until an exposed move gains an easy rake leading leftwards to the top.

★★★ **19 Dreamtime**   E3   55m

FA G Gibson, N Prestidge 1987

Sustained and on perfect rock, this follows a black streak towards the right side of the main face. Start as for *Homesick Angel*.

1 31m 5c Climb directly up the slab to a small right-facing flake; then move up left to reach a break and make a hard move to gain a jug. Move right and up to the roof, pull up left on good holds, and go straight up to a crack. Step left and follow the black streak to a large niche.

2 24m 5b Move up right, then back left via a crack, to a bulge and flake. Pull over, move up left, and then back right to a niche. Exit right to finish.

South Coast – La Cotte Point

This is the headland bounding St Brelade's Bay to the east. An obvious feature on the beach side is a very smooth, quarried cliff with more broken ground to its right. The

Point itself forms a natural arch with a hollowed-out cavern beneath. The wall forming the north side of the arch is split by a stunning crackline – **The Right Stuff** (E2 5b) which is gained by traversing in from the right. On the south side of the point is La Cotte Pinnacle, and this forms a steep-sided zawn with the south face of the Point (slightly reminiscent of the Great Zawn at Bosigran). Routes on the Pinnacle can be reached from low to mid tide by walking out from the beach and scrambling around the point. At high tide the routes can be reached by parking above the headland and walking down to the beach on the east side of the pinnacle. The base of the pinnacle can then be traversed (Diff if the best line is taken) to reach the climbs.

La Cotte Pinnacle

20 Paradise Postponed   HVS 5a   36m
FA P Littlejohn, H Clarke 1987

An interesting, well-protected route on the
south-west side of the pinnacle, taking the
black groove with a very prominent crack in
its left wall. At lower tides scramble up to a
large flat ledge with a crack at its back,
below a less attractive groove which is just
left of the black groove. At higher tides
traverse in to the ledge from the beach. Move
up right into the groove and follow it to a
ledge at 9 metres. Step left and climb thin
cracks to reach the main crack and groove.
Climb the crack to its top, step right, and
finish up the obvious corner.

21 The Good Life   HVS 5a   42m
FA P Littlejohn, H Clarke 1987

Good climbing in a fine pure line. Cams
provide protection. Right of *Paradise
Postponed* is a groove with a very clean-cut
crack at its back. Start directly below this at
the cliff base at low tide, or at high tide
traverse in to ledges 9 metres up. Climb the
slab directly to the base of the groove. Follow
the groove on improving jams to large ledges.
Scramble off to the right.

Other Isles

South-western UK has several other islands which offer worthwhile rock climbing. Guernsey is well
developed, having several hundred routes on granite cliffs which don't quite match the height and
rock quality of those on Jersey, but are attractive nevertheless and mainly south-facing. There is a
little recorded climbing on Sark and more scope, but the bigger cliffs here are decidedly loose. The
Isles of Scilly (40 miles off Land's End) have one well-developed area – Peninnis Head on the west
coast of St Mary's (several routes from VS to E2) and there is also an attractive 20-metre cliff with
striking lines at the eastern tip of St Martins. All the islands have good bouldering and coastal
traversing, so climbers visiting for a 'normal' holiday should be sure to take rock shoes!

Locations

An OS grid reference is printed against the heading for most crags in this guidebook (which correspond generally to the locations listed here). Below or beside each is printed a QR code. Scanning any of these codes with a smartphone will reveal a Google Map. The same image can be revealed by clicking the relevant link from the corresponding list on the Climbers' Club website. Go to www.climbers-club.co.uk/shop/books/guidebook-downloads/south-west-crag-locations/, or scan the above QR code.

The image will show a green pin where the target location is deemed to be, and a red teardrop labelled 'A' which usually indicates the nearest road or public footpath. Once you have loaded the Google Maps page you can click on the 'A' to bring up the usual menu to access the various available features ('Get Directions', local amenities, etc.).

Google Maps may not provide the clarity, detail, and accuracy of OS maps or the specially drawn guidebook maps, and any directions or implied approach route information may not be consistent with the guidebook's guidance, or appropriate in potentially hazardous cliff environments. Users may find the information useful, but should anyway interpret it with discretion and with deference to the more traditional information provided in the guidebook. The satellite layer will often be found the most revealing.

The decimalized latitiude and longitude coordinates may be useful for those with GPS devices.

Hurlstone
https://maps.google.com/?q=51.231834,-3.578731
Sir Robert's chair
https://maps.google.com/?q=51.234982,-3.747045
Valley of Rocks
https://maps.google.com/?q=51.232388,-3.852358
Yellow Stone
https://maps.google.com/?q=51.234344,-3.853881
Wringcliff Bay
https://maps.google.com/?q=51.231377,-3.862964
Baggy Point
https://maps.google.com/?q=51.144123,-4.259036
Focal Buttress
https://maps.google.com/?q=51.159740,-4.670895
Wolfman Jack Wall
https://maps.google.com/?q=51.168934,-4.678039
First Buttress South
https://maps.google.com/?q=51.169544,-4.678950
First Buttress North
https://maps.google.com/?q=51.170387,-4.679064
St Patrick's Buttress
https://maps.google.com/?q=51.171177,-4.679561
Flying Buttress
https://maps.google.com/?q=51.172531,-4.680547
Devil's Chimney Cliff
https://maps.google.com/?q=51.179935,-4.673881
Deep Zawn
https://maps.google.com/?q=51.180386,-4.673500
Egyptian Slabs
https://maps.google.com/?q=51.181042,-4.673331

Beaufort Buttress
https://maps.google.com/?q=51.185440,-4.677431
Grand Falls Zawn
https://maps.google.com/?q=51.186157,-4.674839
The Parthenos
https://maps.google.com/?q=51.187042,-4.676097
Three Quarter Buttress
https://maps.google.com/?q=51.187683,-4.675275
The Devil's Slide
https://maps.google.com/?q=51.190430,-4.675517
The Diamond
https://maps.google.com/?q=51.191631,-4.675544
Arch Zawn
https://maps.google.com/?q=51.194965,-4.678983
The Constable
https://maps.google.com/?q=51.201229,-4.674647
Chudleigh
https://maps.google.com/?q=50.597370,-3.603325
Haytor
https://maps.google.com/?q=50.580257,-3.755194
Low Man
https://maps.google.com/?q=50.579826,-3.756797
Hound Tor
https://maps.google.com/?q=50.596928,-3.778228
Bonehill Rocks
https://maps.google.com/?q=50.582993,-3.793003
Combshead/Cuckoo Car Park
https://maps.google.com/?q=50.506134,-4.019800
Combshead Tor
https://maps.google.com/?q=50.501907,-3.994456

Cuckoo Rock
https://maps.google.com/?q=50.500824,-3.997617

Dewerstone
https://maps.google.com/?q=50.454296,-4.062978

Cheesewring
https://maps.google.com/?q=50.524841,-4.457608

Roughtor
https://maps.google.com/?q=50.597046,-4.621361

Hawks Tor
https://maps.google.com/?q=50.560196,-4.467028

Trewortha Tor
https://maps.google.com/?q=50.556267,-4.476703

Kilmar Tor
https://maps.google.com/?q=50.547436,-4.467908

Helman Tor
https://maps.google.com/?q=50.422176,-4.729442

Blackchurch
https://maps.google.com/?q=51.013519,-4.426392

Gull Rock
https://maps.google.com/?q=50.925426,-4.551928

Cornakey Cliff
https://maps.google.com/?q=50.919659,-4.556547

Vicarage Cliff
https://maps.google.com/?q=50.907543,-4.564503

Lower Sharpnose Point
https://maps.google.com/?q=50.886185,-4.566656

Compass Point
https://maps.google.com/?q=50.828495,-4.557130

Lye Rock
https://maps.google.com/?q=50.675682,-4.741422

Tintagel
https://maps.google.com/?q=50.669266,-4.763858

Kellan Head
https://maps.google.com/?q=50.592937,-4.862534

Doyden Point
https://maps.google.com/?q=50.589882,-4.873803

Pentire Head
https://maps.google.com/?q=50.590542,-4.924617

Carn Gowla
https://maps.google.com/?q=50.314957,-5.234528

America Buttress
https://maps.google.com/?q=50.320038,-5.225581

Zennor Cliff
https://maps.google.com/?q=50.197693,-5.577653

Gurnard's Head
https://maps.google.com/?q=50.189610,-5.600114

Carn Gloose
https://maps.google.com/?q=50.186512,-5.603736

Bosigran
https://maps.google.com/?q=50.175674,-5.620680

The Great Zawn
https://maps.google.com/?q=50.172565,-5.622125

Kenidjack
https://maps.google.com/?q=50.131260,-5.703192

Sennen
https://maps.google.com/?q=50.075932,-5.709411

Land's End
https://maps.google.com/?q=50.067562,-5.715872

Pordenack Point
https://maps.google.com/?q=50.057831,-5.710006

Carn Lês Boel
https://maps.google.com/?q=50.050205,-5.694186

Carn Barra
https://maps.google.com/?q=50.044052,-5.690250

Fox Promontory
https://maps.google.com/?q=50.041862,-5.687611

Chair Ladder
https://maps.google.com/?q=50.036396,-5.681239

Lamorna: Tater-du
https://maps.google.com/?q=50.051914,-5.579131

Serpent's Buttress
https://maps.google.com/?q=49.985474,-5.245791

The Horse
https://maps.google.com/?q=49.979568,-5.247859

Lizard Point
https://maps.google.com/?q=49.959442,-5.215378

Pen Olver
https://maps.google.com/?q=49.961403,-5.190503

Bass Point
https://maps.google.com/?q=49.962521,-5.185969

Sharp Tor
https://maps.google.com/?q=50.215977,-3.782908

Berry Head
https://maps.google.com/?q=50.396397,-3.491328

Daddyhole Area
https://maps.google.com/?q=50.455860,-3.513853

Long Quarry Area
https://maps.google.com/?q=50.475510,-3.501842

Ladram Bay
https://maps.google.com/?q=50.660450,-3.277317

Le Vyi
https://maps.google.com/?q=49.258350,-2.243214

La Nèthe Falaise
https://maps.google.com/?q=49.256355,-2.248381

La Tête d'Ane
https://maps.google.com/?q=49.255749,-2.249339

Le Pinacle
https://maps.google.com/?q=49.247627,-2.253520

La Cotte Point
https://maps.google.com/?q=49.175743,-2.188030

OS Map Information

Location	1:25,000 (Explorer)	1:50,000 (Landranger)	page
Exmoor	**OL29**	**180/181**	**20**
Hurlstone Point	OL29	181	22
Sir Robert's Chair	OL29	180	35
Valley of Rocks	OL29	180	38
Baggy Point	**139**	**180**	**54**
Scrattling Zawn	139	180	56
Long Rock Slab	139	180	57
Slab Cove	139	180	61
Promontory Slab	139	180	63
Lundy	**139**	**180**	**66**
Southern Lundy	139	180	69
Jenny's Cove	139	180	81
Devil's Slide Area	139	180	88
Northern Lundy	139	180	96
Inland Devon & Cornwall	**107/109/110/OL28**	**191/201/202**	**100**
Chudleigh Rocks	110	202	102
Haytor	OL28	191	115
Low Man	OL28	191	118
Dartmoor Bouldering	OL28	191/202	122
The Dewerstone	OL28	201	126
Cheesewring Quarry	109	201	139
Bodmin Moor	107/109	200/201	149
The Culm Coast	**111/126**	**190**	**154**
Blackchurch	126	190	156
Gull Rock	126	190	162
Cornakey Cliff	126	190	165
Vicarage Cliff	126	190	169
Lower Sharpnose Point	126	190	174
Compass Point	111	190	184
The Atlantic Coast	**104/106/111**	**200/203**	**188**
Lye Rock	111	200	190
Tintagel Head	111	200	192
Kellan Head	106	200	197
Doyden Point	106	200	203
Pentire Head	106	200	206
Carn Gowla	104	203	209

Location	1:25,000 (Explorer)	1:50,000 (Landranger)	page
West Penwith North	**102**	**203**	**226**
Zennor Cliff	102	203	228
Gurnard's Head	102	203	229
Carn Gloose	102	203	235
Bosigran	102	203	237
The Great Zawn	102	203	253
Kenidjack	102	203	257
The Sennen Cliffs	102	203	261
Land's End	102	203	267
West Penwith South	**102**	**203**	**276**
Pordenack Point	102	203	278
Carn Lês Boel	102	203	283
Carn Barra	102	203	286
Fox Promontory	102	203	292
Chair Ladder	102	203	296
Lamorna: Tater-du	102	203	311
The Lizard	**103**	**203**	**312**
Serpent's Buttress	103	203	315
The Horse	103	203	316
Lizard Point	103	203	317
Pen Olver	103	203	321
Bass Point	102	203	326
South Devon Coast	**110/115/OL20**	**192/202**	**328**
The South Hams	OL20	202	330
Berry Head	OL20	202	335
Daddyhole Area	110	202	353
Long Quarry Area	110	202	366
Ladram Bay	115	192	383
Jersey	**Jersey Official Leisure map**		**386**
Le Vyi	Jersey Official Leisure Map		387
La Nèthe Falaise	Jersey Official Leisure Map		390
La Tête d'Ane	Jersey Official Leisure Map		393
Le Pinacle	Jersey Official Leisure Map		396
La Cotte Point	Jersey Official Leisure Map		398

Index of Crags

Index of Climbs

Index of Climbs

Accident Procedure

Rescue

In the event of an accident where further assistance is required, **dial 999**.

- For incidents on inland crags, ask the operator to connect you to the **Police**. The Police are responsible for coordinating all land-based rescues and will contact other services as necessary.

- For incidents on the sea cliffs, ask the operator to connect you to the the **Coastguard**. The Coastguard and Maritime Agency is responsible for coordinating rescue operations on the sea cliffs and shorelines and will contact other services as necessary.

- Even if you do not have a signal on a mobile phone, you may still be able to call 999, but be aware that the emergency services may not be able to call you back in this situation.

- State that you require cliff rescue, and report the exact location and details of the accident. You will find a grid reference for each crag in this guidebook against its heading. Try to give as much information as possible, including the number of casualties, nature of injuries, weather on scene (cloud level, wind strength, sea conditions, etc.). The colours of the clothing of the casualty and party are very useful to aid spotting the incident, especially from a helicopter.

- Be prepared to give your own name and home address if asked. Also give a second mobile phone number at the location if possible.

- Follow any further instructions or requests issued.

First Aid

In the first instance, take care to protect yourself.

- If spinal or head injuries are suspected, do not move the patient without skilled help, except to open the airway and to maintain breathing, or if this is essential for further protection.

- If breathing has stopped, clear the airways and start artificial respiration. Do not stop until the patient recovers or expert opinion has diagnosed death.

- Summon help as quickly as is compatible with safety. Do not hesitate or delay.

Helicopter

In the event of a helicopter evacuation, all climbers on or off the cliff should take heed. A helicopter flying close to the cliff will make verbal communication very difficult and small stones will be dislodged by the rotor downdraught. All loose equipment should be secured and climbers in precarious positions should try to make themselves safe.

The people with the injured person should try to identify their location by standing up and holding both arms vertically in a Y-shape. **No** attempt should be made to throw a rope at the helicopter, but assistance should be given to the helicopter crew if requested. Do not approach until directions are given by the crew. In particular, keep well clear of the main rotor, the tail rotor, and the engine exhaust.

At night, use torches or similar to identify yourselves, but do not shine torches directly at the helicopter as the pilots may be using night vision goggles.

410

Follow-up

After an accident, a report has to be compiled. Normally the details will be collated at the scene by the Police or rescue team, who will then pass the information to the Mountain Rescue Council Statistics Officer.

If unreasonable equipment failure is suspected then the British Mountaineering Council's technical committee may wish to investigate: contact the BMC at 177-179 Burton Road, West Didsbury, Manchester, M20 2BB. In the event of a serious accident, any equipment used by the casualty may be impounded.

Local Hospitals

A & E Units (24-hour)

Barnstaple   North Devon District Hospital, Raleigh Park, Barnstaple, EX31 4JB

Taunton   Musgrove Park Hospital, Musgrove Park, Parkfield Drive, Taunton, TA1 5DA

Exeter   Royal Devon and Exeter Hospital, Barrack Road, Exeter, EX2 5DW

Plymouth   Derriford Hospital, Derriford Road, Crownhill, Plymouth, PL6 8DH

Penzance   West Cornwall Hospital, St Clare Street, Penzance, TR18 2PF

Truro   Royal Cornwall Hospital, Treliske, Truro, TR1 3LJ

Torquay   Torbay Hospital, Newton Road, Torquay, TQ2 7AA

Walk-In Centres and Minor Injuries Units

Bridgwater   Bridgwater Hospital, Salmon Parade, Bridgwater, TA6 5AH

Minehead   Minehead Community Hospital, Luttrell Way, Minehead, TA24 6DF

Ilfracombe   Ilfracombe Tyrrell Hospital, St Brannocks Park Road, Ilfracombe, EX34 8JF

Newton Abbot   Newton Abbot Community Hospital, West Golds Road, Jetty Marsh, Newton Abbot, TQ12 2SL

Launceston   Launceston General Hospital, Link Road, Launceston, PL15 9JD

Bideford   Bideford Hospital, Abbotsham Road, Bideford, EX39 3AG

Bude   Stratton Hospital, Hospital Road, Stratton, Bude, EX23 9BP

Bodmin   Bodmin Community Hospital, Boundary Road, Bodmin, PL31 2QT

Tavistock   Tavistock Community Hospital, Spring Hill, Tavistock, PL19 8LD

Liskeard   Liskeard Community Hospital, Clemo Road, Liskeard, PL14 3XD

Newquay   Newquay Hospital, St Thomas Road, Newquay, TR7 1RQ

St Austell   St Austell Community Hospital, Porthpean Road, St Austell, PL26 6AD

Helston   Helston Community Hospital Meneage Road, Helston, TR13 8DR

Climbers' Club Guides
Edited by Paul Robertson

South West Climbs
Volume Two

Selected Climbs in
Devon, Cornwall, & the Granite Isles

Pat Littlejohn
Martin Crocker

Artwork
Mark Davies   Don Sargeant

The Climbers' Club

South-West Climbs (Diadem Books 1979) by Pat Littlejohn

South West Climbs (Diadem Books 1991) by Pat Littlejohn

South West Climbs Volume 2 (The Climbers' Club 2014) by Pat Littlejohn

© The Climbers' Club 2014

Littlejohn, Pat   South West Climbs Volume 2   Climbers' Club Guides

British Library Cataloguing in Publication data

A catalogue record for this book is available from the British Library

796.522

ISBN 978-0-901601-98-8

Front Cover: *Immaculate Arête* (Pordenack Point, E4) Paul Harrison   DAVID SIMMONITE
Title page: *Atlantic Ocean Wall* (Land's End, E4) Benno Wagner & Wojciech Szymanowicz   TOM LAST
Frontispiece: Bishop Buttress   PETE O'SULLIVAN
Rear Flap: *Darkinbad the Brightdayler* (Pentire Head, E5)   Andi Turner   MIKE HUTTON

Typesetting and layout by John Willson
Original design and cover design by Ian Smith
Produced by Vertebrate Graphics   www.v-graphics.co.uk
Printed by Latitude Press Ltd
Distributed by Cordee   www.cordee.co.uk

Contents

THE CLIMBERS' CLUB

www.climbers-club.co.uk

The publisher of this guidebook is the Climbers' Club, founded in 1898 from origins in Snowdonia and one of the foremost mountaineering clubs in Great Britain. The club has been continually publishing guidebooks since 1909. The club was a founder-member of, and is affiliated to, the British Mountaineering Council. Its objectives are to encourage mountaineering and rock climbing, and to promote the general interests of mountaineers and the mountain environment.

It is a national club with widespread membership, and currently has eight huts: in Cornwall, Pembrokeshire, Derbyshire, Snowdonia (three), The Lake District, and Lochaber. Club members may also use the huts of other clubs through reciprocal arrangements. The Climbers' Club produces an annual Journal and runs a full programme of climbing meets, dinners, and social events. The club membership fluctuates around 1,700, and at present there are no limits on growth. Members of two years' standing may propose a competent candidate for membership and, provided that adequate support is obtained from other members, the Committee may elect him or her to full membership; there is no probationary period. Membership details are on the club's website; click on About » How to Apply.

Climbing Style

The following policy statement on climbing style was agreed in principle at the Climbers' Club Annual General Meeting on 25 February 1990:

The Climbers' Club supports the tradition of using natural protection and is opposed to actions which are against the best interest of climbers and users of the crags. This applies particularly to irreversible acts which could affect the crags and their environs.

Such acts could include: the placing of bolts on mountain and natural crags; retrospective placing of bolts; chiselling, hammering, or altering the rock appearance or structure; excessive removal of vegetation and interference with trees, flowers, and fauna.

The Climbers' Club policy is that guidebooks are written to reflect the best style matched to the ethos and traditions of British climbing.

New Routes and Comments

To submit new-route information for any Climbers' Club guidebook area (or to provide comment on information in the guides) in order to ensure that it is available to the editor of the next guide, please visit the Climbers' Club website, click on Information » New Routes » Submit New Route, and follow the simple instructions.

The Count House, Bosigran   SIMON CARDY

Supporting Climbing

The Climbers' Club Colin Kirkus Guidebook Fund was established in 1999 as a means of distributing a portion of the profits earned from guidebooks to assist climbing-related projects in keeping with the aims of the club, though not nrcessarily confined to the club's guidebook areas.

The Fund has made significant annual contributions to the BMC's Access and Conservation Trust as well as donations to volunteer cliff and mountain rescue organizations, and the club supports a variety of local events.

Guidebook Disclaimer

This guide attempts to provide a selection of the best climbs in the areas covered, and is compiled from a consensus of opinion from a wide range of climbers and with information from a variety of sources. The inclusion of any route does not imply that it remains in the condition described. Climbs can change unpredictably: rock can deteriorate and the existence and condition of *in situ* protection can alter. All climbers must rely on their own ability and experience to gauge the difficulty and seriousness of any climb. Climbing is an inherently dangerous activity.

Neither the Climbers' Club nor the authors and editor of this guidebook accept any liability whatsoever for any injury or damage caused to climbers, third parties, or property arising from the use of it. While the content of the guide is believed to be accurate, no responsibility is accepted for any error, omission, or misstatement. Users must rely on their own judgement and are recommended to insure against injury to person and property and third-party risks.

The inclusion in this guidebook of a crag or routes upon it does not mean that any member of the public has a right of access to the crag or the right to climb upon it. Before climbing on any crag in this guidebook, please read the access and conservation notes in the general and crag introductions.

The Climbers' Club endorses the BMC participation statement that:
Rock climbing, hill walking, and mountaineering are activities with a danger of personal injury or death. Participants in these activities should be aware of and accept these risks and be responsible for their own activities and involvement.

Foreword by Dave Turnbull

Welcome to South West Climbs Volume 2, your gateway to one of the most adventurous and exciting climbing areas in the UK. If sea cliffs, cream teas, and a holiday atmosphere are your idea of fun then this is the guidebook for you. From Torquay to The Lizard, and from Land's End to the obscure delights of the Exmoor coast, it offers up a wealth of climbing opportunities on rock types as diverse as anywhere in the UK. The best of Lundy and Jersey are also featured alongside the Dartmoor Tors and the assorted esoterica of inland Devon and Cornwall.

As a student at Plymouth Polytechnic in the late 80s I was lucky to have many of these crags on my doorstep. My first ever climbing experience was a club meet at a wave-swept Berry Head one windy October day. Someone had got the tide times wrong and the traverse in to *Moonraker* was under water. Two of the more experienced members of the club decided to abseil in, and spent the rest of the day struggling up the sheer walls of the Old Redoubt as I peered down from a cliff-top vantage point, freezing cold but captivated by the spectacle. I didn't make it back to Berry Head until the February of my second year, when a late start on the classic E3 *Dreadnought* resulted in fourteen hours benighted on an uncomfortable belay stance 20 metres from the top. It took a while to live that down but still I'd thoroughly recommend Berry Head (though maybe not to a beginner) – it's a gobsmacking crag and a visit will last long in the memory.

But the South West isn't all about big scary cliffs – far from it. Land's End and Lundy offer some of the most enjoyable granite sea-cliff climbing you'll find anywhere. The Culm too has its moments of greatness and is home to the unique Lower Sharpness Point, whose jutting fins of vertical sandstone are a geological wonder. The Lizard has an 'away from it all' feel, while Baggy Point – home to *Scrattling Crack* (VD), one of the earliest recorded sea-cliff climbs in the UK and still a classic at the grade – is a great place for the sea-cliff newcomer with its solid rock, friendly feel, and sunny aspect.

Enjoy this guidebook, check your tide timetables, and take care out there.

1979-1991

Preface by Ian Smith

The Climbers' Club produced the first ever 'pocket' guidebook with the publication of *The Climbs on Lliwedd* by Thomson and Andrews in 1909. This book contained all the features of guidebooks since, with route descriptions, photodiagrams, topos, and action photos. The Club has gone on to produce 'definitive' guidebooks, usually containing all known and reported climbs in the areas covered in Wales and the south-west and south-east regions of England. About sixty years later the first successful 'selected climbs' guidebook appeared in the form of Ron James's *Rock Climbing in Wales* published by Constable in 1970. This has been followed by numerous selected climbs guides from a variety of publishers, except The Climbers' Club, and these two books are the first such publications from the Club.

Originally, *South West Climbs*, published in 1979 by Diadem, was a single-volume publication and was a collaboration between one of the South West's most prolific and important activists, Pat Littlejohn, and one of the most influential of British publishers, Ken Wilson. This rapidly became very popular and introduced many climbers to the joys and pleasures of the sometimes mysterious and occasionally remote south-west peninsula of England. A further edition in 1991 expanded the coverage adding, for example, the climbing on the Channel Island of Jersey and the Lizard in Cornwall, amongst others.

For this edition, the climbs of the South West have been split into two volumes; the first, covering areas close to centres of population such as the Avon Gorge, Wye Valley, and Dorset, was written by a talented team of local activists and published in 2012. Volume 2 has been written by Pat Littlejohn (with some sections by Martin Crocker) and covers Devon, Cornwall, Lundy, and Jersey. This has been an exciting and, at times, rocky road for the Club's guidebook team but their first selected climbs project is now complete and ready for use. We hope it provides you with many happy hours in one of our most exciting and spectacular of climbing areas.

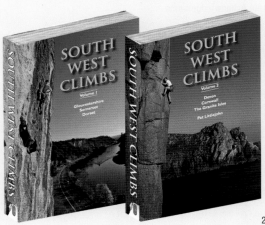

2012 & 2014

Acknowledgements

The authors would particularly like to thank the following for providing local information, comments on the draft script, and various support and assistance: the family of the late Terry Cheek, Simon Cardy, Barnaby Carver, Jonathan Crocker, Paul Harrison, John Harwood, Dave Henderson, David Hope, Ken Palmer, Ian Parsons, Carl Ryan, Pete Saunders.

Thanks also to the proofreaders Andy March, Helen Barry, Nigel Coe, and Bob Mott (with special thanks to Andy for also checking out the storm damage after February 2014).

We should also like to thank everyone who submitted photos, even if we weren't able to use them.

The CC guidebook team headed up by John Willson were superb to work with – thanks John, Don, Mark, and Paul.

Finally we owe a debt of gratitude to all the pioneers, named in each route description, who by climbing in the best adventurous traditions have helped build the South West into the world-class adventure climbing area it is today.

Pat Littlejohn
Martin Crocker
March 2014

Map and Diagram Acknowledgements

Maps redrawn by Don Sargeant

Reproduced by permission of Ordnance Survey on behalf of HMSO

© Crown copyright 2014. All rights reserved

Ordnance Survey Licence number 100047354

Photodiagrams by Mark Davies. Photoplans and overviews by Don Sargeant.

Photos for diagrams:

Mark Davies pp 30, 31, 32, 33, 39, 42, 43, 45, 65, 162, 166, 167, 169, 171, 173, 175, 177, 179, 181, 183, 184, 185, 186, 337, 338, 346, 355, 362, 364, 368.

Simon Cardy pp 70, 72, 74, 77, 80, 83, 85, 87, 88, 91, 92, 95, 98, 99, 228, 229, 235, 238, 240, 249, 257, 259, 262, 263, 265, 267, 270, 272, 273, 279, 281, 282, 287, 290, 293, 298, 302, 307, 309.

Don Sargeant pp 24, 29, 37, 46, 51, 59, 62, 104, 106, 107, 109, 111, 116, 128, 131, 132, 135, 136, 141, 142, 147, 149, 150, 151, 157, 158, 160, 199, 200, 204, 207, 211, 213, 215, 218, 223, 224, 233, 236, 250, 255, 286, 292, 295, 296, 311, 315, 317, 319, 323, 325, 326, 331, 332, 333, 385.

Deryck Ball p 195. Nigel Barry p 91. Simon Caldwell p 79. James Clapham pp 118,119. Kevin Eloury pp 388, 390, 393, 395, 396, 399. Hans Groenendijk pp 81, 93. Chris Jones pp 366, 372, 374, 375. Tom Last pp 153, 285.

Pat Littlejohn pp 352, 359, 377, 380, 381. James Mann p 163. Pete Saunders pp 348, 351.

Tim Martindale (aerial photos) pp 165, 174, 177, 191, 196, 197.

Introduction

Welcome to the South West with its promise of a lifetime of climbing pleasure. After nearly fifty years of climbing here the area remains endlessly inspiring for me, whether on classic routes done time and time again or when seeking out the new. When I joined the Exeter Climbing Club in 1965 the established climbing venues of the region could be counted on the fingers of two hands. Now they number hundreds, and new discoveries continue to be made each year. With 600 miles of convoluted coastline and its high moorlands of granite tors, the region has cliffs of all rock types and climbing to suit every mood and taste. The best routes stand comparison with any in England and Wales in terms of length and quality. This is a guidebook to the finest routes, and to many other climbs whose special qualities (such as setting, interest, character, and strength of line) make them well worth doing.

In the best traditions of *South West Climbs*, many routes here are currently not covered by any other guidebook (most notably on the Exmoor Coast). Hopefully, even long-term devotees of the area will find something new here to inspire future trips.

Climbing Style

The South West is the epitome of an 'adventure' climbing area. Very few cliffs are littered with bolts and other fixed gear, so the climber can still retain the sense of being in an unspoilt, often majestic, natural environment. Adventure is not synonymous with danger – most of the great adventure climbs in this guidebook may be well protected by competent trad climbers. There are sport climbs in the area too and the best of these are covered by this guide – however, the emphasis is unashamedly on adventurous climbing. Great adventures can be had at any climbing grade, and wild, even awe-inspiring settings can enhance the experience immeasurably. The South West has a wealth of such settings.

Stormy Sea at Pentire Head   HANS GROENENDIJK

Climbing on the Coast

Although there are many delightful inland crags, the South West is justly famous for its sea-cliff climbing. Sea cliffs are more serious because of the extra hazard of the sea itself (especially when it cuts off retreat). Even a small swell can cause lively wave action around the base of an exposed headland, and periodically there will be waves which are far bigger than the average. In all but the calmest seas, climbers should rope up on approach traverses and belay securely at the foot of climbs. Another point to remember is that it is extremely difficult (or even impossible) to swim carrying a rack of gear and a climbing rope. **Therefore, when traversing above the sea, carry your gear bandolier style so that it can be jettisoned in an emergency.**

Weather

As the most southerly of Britain's major climbing areas the South West often gets the kindest weather – rock climbing here is a year-round pursuit rather than one which has to retreat indoors through the winter. Once you get to know the region and its climbing, you very rarely waste a climbing day, thanks to the variety of cliffs on both north and south coasts (some of them very sheltered) and the superb sea-level traverses of Torbay, which can be fun in any weather. Aside from the climbing, the region itself has a unique character, particularly the narrow peninsula of western Cornwall with its clear bright light, strong colours, and fresh sea air.

Tides and Conditions

Tidal knowledge is vital for many climbs and can be a safety factor as well as saving time and frustration. Tide tables are on sale in most newsagents in coastal towns, local newspapers usually publish tide times, and the Internet is very effective for advance planning. Go to the Climbers' Club website (see page 8) and click on Information » Tidal Information; or use the Admiralty EasyTide website: www.ukho.gov.uk/easytide). Other factors to be considered are sea conditions, the prevailing wind, and the orientation of the cliff. This is particularly true in West Penwith where crags face all points of the compass and conditions often vary greatly between the north and south coasts. *Astral Stroll*, for example, climbed at high tide in the morning, when the sea could be threatening, the rock cold and damp, and the crag gloomy and menacing, is a completely different experience to an afternoon ascent at low tide when the cliff may be basking in the sun, bone-dry, and welcoming. By making the right choice of location, the South West can offer perfect climbing conditions even in the depths of winter and again the Internet is invaluable for obtaining weather forecasts and using webcams (especially 'Surfcams') to look at sea conditions around the coast.

Special Skills

Competence in abseiling and prusiking/jumaring is crucial for many of the more inaccessible climbs and cliffs. One may be called upon to perform such feats as passing the knot of joined abseil ropes while spinning in mid-air, controlling the line of an abseil by placing gear in descent, and making well-aimed swings on the end of a rope to reach an overhung ledge or the only dry boulder in the vicinity. Such techniques require common sense, ingenuity, and experience (usually gained by making an awful mess of things on the first try). Some of the more serious cliffs have great epic potential, but epics are only fun when they have happy endings. Make sure that your experience matches your ambitions.

Attractions of the Region

Devon and Cornwall are Britain's most popular holiday areas, and this probably has more benefits than drawbacks for the visiting climber. Accommodation need never be a problem – there are campsites, caravan sites, self-catering chalets and cottages, bed and breakfast establishments and all manner of guest houses and hotels scattered liberally throughout the region, plus a comprehensive network of Tourist Information Centres to tell you about them. It is never far to retire to a cafe or pub after a climb; every other farmhouse offers cream teas in season and some impressive ascents have been fuelled by the ubiquitous Cornish pasty.

Other seaside pursuits should not be ignored. Devon and Cornwall have the best beaches and opportunities for every kind of water sport. The surf is often great when climbing conditions are poor. Most of the bigger resorts have a throbbing night life, particularly in summer, so the

Sue Hazel   PETE SAUNDERS   *Astral Stoll* (Carn Gloose, E1)   Pete Saunders   SUE HAZEL

young-at-heart might like to pack their clubbing gear. For those wanting a more relaxed evening, good pubs abound and the natives are usually friendly.

Using the Guide

The guide is designed to function with no additional maps beyond the most general road map, although the whole region is covered by the OS 1:50,000 Landranger and 1:25,000 Explorer series, and each cliff is given a grid reference. Possession of these maps can give a great deal of useful information to the newcomer (see page 402 for complete list). For climbers with smartphones, Ggogle Maps web references are provided for each crag in the form of QR codes (see page 400). With one or two (it is hoped, logical) exceptions, the climbing areas are presented moving anticlockwise around the coast, with routes being described from left to right on most cliffs.

As well as the routes fully described, passing mention has been made of many other adjacent climbs, particularly when these take prominent features. More details can of course be found in the definitive guides, but it should be possible to climb many of these lines from the details given. Routes described do not always correspond exactly to those in the definitive guides as occasionally pitches or sections of climbs have been juxtaposed to give the best combinations. The hard to define concept of 'quality' has always been the main consideration.

It has been assumed that visitors will expect at least a day's climbing within a reasonable grade range on each of the important cliffs, although in most areas it is simple to move from crag to crag by car. Every effort has been made to obtain an even distribution throughout the grades. The granite areas in particular lend themselves very well to the novice, offering superb easy climbs on completely reliable rock. However, the bulk of the routes are in the VS to E3 range, and therefore within the capabilities of most active climbers, as either leader or second. The harder climbs included are those having an obvious classic quality.

For trad climbs the normal British grading system has been used, and it assumes that people will be tackling routes on sight and making a free ascent. Few, if any, of the routes selected for this guidebook have received extensive practice before their first ascent, hence few of E7 and above. Sport climbs are given a French grade, as are routes normally done as deep water solos (DWS).

	Crag Selector	#	<VD	S	HS	VS	HVS	E1	E2	E3	E4	E5>	Spo
Exmoor	1 Hurlstone Point	28	4	3	5	7	0	5	0	1	2	1	0
Exmoor	2 Sir Robert's Chair	5	0	0	0	0	0	1	1	2	1	0	0
Exmoor	3 Valley of Rocks	16	0	3	2	2	2	1	1	1	1	3	0
Baggy Point	4 Scrattling Zawn	3	1	0	0	0	1	1	0	0	0	0	0
Baggy Point	5 Long Rock Slab	11	0	0	1	4	0	3	0	2	1	0	0
Baggy Point	6 Slab Cove	2	0	0	0	1	0	0	1	0	0	0	0
Baggy Point	7 Promontory Slab	7	0	1	1	2	2	1	0	0	0	0	0
Lundy	8 Southern Lundy	21	1	0	0	3	3	2	4	3	1	3	0
Lundy	9 Jenny's Cove	19	0	1	1	5	2	3	3	2	0	2	0
Lundy	10 Devil's Slide Area	16	0	1	1	4	1	4	1	0	2	2	0
Lundy	11 Northern Lundy	6	0	0	1	1	0	3	1	0	0	0	0
Inland Devon & Cornwall	12 Chudleigh Rocks	29	4	1	4	5	3	3	3	1	4	1	0
Inland Devon & Cornwall	13 Haytor	11	1	1	2	1	2	0	1	0	1	2	0
Inland Devon & Cornwall	14 Low Man	8	0	2	0	1	1	1	0	2	1	0	0
Inland Devon & Cornwall	15 Dartmoor Bouldering	-	-	-	-	-	-	-	-	-	-	-	-
Inland Devon & Cornwall	16 The Dewerstone	13	5	1	2	1	3	1	0	0	0	0	0
Inland Devon & Cornwall	17 Cheesewring Quarry	22	0	0	2	4	2	0	2	2	2	1	7
Inland Devon & Cornwall	18 Bodmin Moor	7	0	0	0	0	1	0	2	1	1	2	0
The Culm Coast	19 Blackchurch	10	0	0	0	2	0	3	1	2	1	1	0
The Culm Coast	20 Gull Rock	12	0	2	2	3	2	1	1	0	0	1	0
The Culm Coast	21 Cornakey Cliff	4	0	1	0	1	1	0	1	0	0	0	0
The Culm Coast	22 Vicarage Cliff	10	1	3	2	2	1	0	1	0	0	0	0
The Culm Coast	23 Lower Sharpnose Point	18	0	0	0	1	5	3	0	2	3	4	0
The Culm Coast	24 Compass Point	9	2	1	0	1	3	0	1	0	1	0	0
The Atlantic Coast	25 Lye Rock	1	0	0	0	0	0	0	0	0	1	0	0
The Atlantic Coast	26 Tintagel Head	12	0	0	0	0	0	0	3	2	3	4	0
The Atlantic Coast	27 Kellan Head	11	0	0	0	0	0	4	1	3	1	2	0
The Atlantic Coast	28 Doyden Point	6	0	0	0	1	0	2	1	1	1	0	0
The Atlantic Coast	29 Pentire Head	3	0	0	0	0	0	0	0	1	0	2	0
The Atlantic Coast	30 Carn Gowla	35	1	2	3	3	6	5	5	5	1	4	0

WS	Aspect	Minutes walk in	Notes	Page	
0	N & W	15	all-season venue with good slab climbs in lower grades	20	Exmoor
0	NNW	30	wild and 'away from it all'; two-pitch sandstone slab	35	Exmoor
0	S & N	5 to 15	sun and fun mix with serious slate; stunning landscape; access conditions apply	38	Exmoor
0	S	25	historic climbs	56	Baggy Point
0	S	20	bird restriction 15 March to 30 June	57	Baggy Point
0	S	20	mutli-pitch slab	61	Baggy Point
0	S	20	superb gritty sandstone	63	Baggy Point
1	S & SW	15	quick access to brilliant Focal Buttress	69	Lundy
0	SW & W	25	home of Deep Zawn	81	Lundy
0	SW & W	35	the famous granite slab, & superb face climbing on the Diamond	88	Lundy
0	W & NW	60	meet the Constable	96	Lundy
0	S	10	classic routes, all grades	102	Inland Devon & Cornwall
0	SW & NW	6	friendly climbs; tourist trap	115	Inland Devon & Cornwall
0	W	7	best climbing on Tors	118	Inland Devon & Cornwall
-	all	1 to 20	take plenty of tape	122	Inland Devon & Cornwall
0	SE & S	10	classic granite	126	Inland Devon & Cornwall
0	SSE & all	10	key regional site; great mix of trad and bolted routes vis à vis	139	Inland Devon & Cornwall
0	all	5 to 15	fine granite problems	149	Inland Devon & Cornwall
0	NW	30	serious multi-pitch & an immaculate slab	156	The Culm Coast
0	S	25	friendly & sunny; tidal	162	The Culm Coast
0	S	25	*Wreckers' Slab* a must	165	The Culm Coast
0	S	25	short solid pitches; popular	169	The Culm Coast
0	S & N	30	some of the UK's best wall climbing	174	The Culm Coast
0	S	10	accessible, friendly venue	184	The Culm Coast
0	W	20	committing adventure	190	The Atlantic Coast
0	SW	15	top sea cliff; sensitive access – conditions apply	192	The Atlantic Coast
0	NW & N	10	black; best when cool and bright; summer sun p.m.	197	The Atlantic Coast
0	SW	10	the most cuddly crag in North Cornwall	203	The Atlantic Coast
0	NNW	20	magnificent 'towering cliffs'	205	The Atlantic Coast
0	W & NW	5 to 10	extensive cliffs, famous climbs	209	The Atlantic Coast

	#	<VD	S	HS	VS	HVS	E1	E2	E3	E4	E5>	Spo
Crag Selector												
31 Zennor Head	3	1	0	0	2	0	0	0	0	0	0	0
32 Gurnard's Head	5	0	0	2	0	0	1	1	1	0	0	0
33 Carn Gloose	1	0	0	0	0	0	1	0	0	0	0	0
34 Bosigran	29	6	2	2	4	5	2	3	4	0	1	0
35 The Great Zawn	13	0	0	1	0	2	1	5	1	1	2	0
36 Kenidjack	7	0	0	1	1	1	3	0	1	0	0	0
37 The Sennen Cliffs	21	3	0	3	3	3	1	2	2	1	3	0
38 Land's End	23	1	2	0	0	4	3	2	3	4	4	0
39 Pordenack Point	12	2	0	2	2	2	1	1	1	1	0	0
40 Carn Lês Boel	5	0	0	0	0	2	0	0	0	1	2	0
41 Carn Barra	15	0	1	1	1	2	3	1	2	4	0	0
42 Fox Promontory	6	0	0	1	3	2	0	0	0	0	0	0
43 Chair Ladder	26	1	2	3	7	5	3	1	2	0	2	0
44 Lamorna: Tater-du	2	0	0	0	1	1	0	0	0	0	0	0
45 Serpent's Buttress	2	1	0	0	0	1	0	0	0	0	0	0
46 The Horse	5	0	0	0	2	1	0	0	1	1	0	0
47 Lizard Point	8	0	1	1	1	2	0	1	2	0	0	0
48 Pen Olver	11	5	1	1	1	0	0	0	1	2	0	0
49 Bass Point	3	0	0	0	0	0	0	0	1	1	1	0
50 The South Hams	5	2	3	0	0	0	0	0	0	0	0	0
51 Berry Head	50	2	0	6	3	2	4	1	2	0	5	1
52 Daddyhole Area	22	2	1	2	6	2	3	1	2	3	0	0
53 Long Quarry Area	42	2	1	0	5	3	3	0	3	2	6	17
54 Ladram Bay	2	0	0	0	0	0	2	0	0	0	0	0
55 Le Vyi	3	0	0	1	0	1	0	1	0	0	0	0
56 La Nèthe Falaise	5	0	1	2	2	0	0	0	0	0	0	0
57 La Tête d'Ane	5	0	0	0	0	4	0	0	0	0	1	0
58 Le Pinacle	6	0	0	0	0	3	0	1	1	0	1	0
59 La Cotte Point	3	0	0	0	0	2	0	1	0	0	0	0

Region labels (left margin): West Penwith North (31–38), West Penwith South (39–44), The Lizard (45–49), South Devon Coast (50–54), Jersey (55–59)

VS	Aspect	Miinutes walk in	Notes	Page	
)	SW	15	evening fun	228	
)	SW & NW	20	top greenstone crag	229	West Penwith North
)	W	30	afternoon venue	235	
)	SW	15	Cornwall's most popular crag	237	
)	W	20	packed with high-standard classics	253	
)	SW	15	natural suntrap	257	
)	W	15	marvellous granite	261	
)	S & W	5 to 10	majestic scenery below clifftop	267	
)	S	15	compact, attractive	278	West Penwith South
)	S	30	take great care in nesting eason	283	
)	S	20	suffered some storm damage 2014	286	
)	W	12	best in the late afternoon sun	292	
)	SW	10	Cornwall's greatest granite sea cliff; suffered some storm damage 2014	296	
)	S	30	refreshingly different	311	
)	S	25	one route only!	315	
)	W	30 to 40	visit late in day	316	The Lizard
)	SW	15	big handsome cliff	317	
)	SW & NW	20	family friendly	321	
)	S	25	Lizard's best	326	
)	SE	10	secluded easy climbs	330	South Devon Coast
5	S & W	5 to 15	bird restrictions on Old Redoubt; some premier DWS	335	
0	SE & S	10	powerful lines on the Main Cliff, & a sunny slab	353	
0	SE & S	10 to 15	hard sport routes in Anstey's Cove	366	
0	S	20	esoteric classic	383	
0	W	10	fine sweeping lines	387	
0	NE	5	earliest Jersey climbs	390	
0	SW	10	island classics	393	Jersey
0	NW	15	Jersey's best and biggest	396	
0	S	10	sheltered and sunny	398	

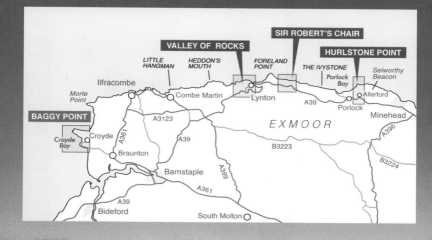

The Exmoor Coast

The twenty miles of coastline forming the northern edge of Exmoor have until now been the preserve of a small group of dedicated local climbers. The massive cliffs of banded sandstone and steep vegetation are among the highest on the British mainland, with Countisbury Cliff attaining a height of over 300 metres. Scattered throughout this impressive landscape are several good climbing areas where the rock is more compact and conventional. The best climbs are on relatively serious, north-facing cliffs but there are friendly areas too, such as Hurlstone Point and the Valley of Rocks. Though perhaps not the most obvious choice of climbing venue for a first trip to the South West, those with a taste for adventurous sea-cliff climbs will find a visit to this majestic stretch of coast most rewarding.

Hurlstone Point

OS Ref SS 898 493

Wild and windswept, Hurlstone Point is the complex headland four miles west of the bustling resort of Minehead. It is a melange of brooding north-facing slabs, walls, and caves – all made up of bands of folded sandstone. At its best in the summer months, Hurlstone is the Exmoor Coast's most 'popular' climbing site and the crag excels in the lower grades. The selection here includes some of Hurlstone's best climbs; not all are well protected, however, and access to those in the Fledgling Slab area is limited by the tide.

Approach   From Allerford on the A39, take a right turn to Bossington where there is a pay car park. Take the path and footbridge over a stream and follow the main track seawards, parallel with the stream, to a gate where the track rises across open hillside. Continue for a further 500 metres to an old coastguard station on top of Hurlstone Point. Coastguard Wall is below and right (facing out) of the building. A faint zigzag path descends the grass slope directly from here to the tip of the Point and the Gull Hole area. For the

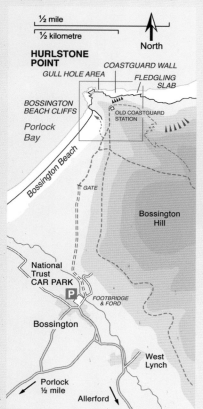

Fledgling Slab and Coastguard Wall routes descend about halfway down the zigzags until a track leads leftwards (facing in) into the stony gully right of Coastguard Wall. Scramble down the gully to beach level. Fledgling Slab is 150 metres further left (east) and is accessible low to mid tide. Gull Hole can be reached low to mid tide by following the cliff base rightwards (west) from the base of the gully or by continuing down the zigzags and scrambling down the eastern arête of the slab at the tip of the point. For the Bossington Beach crags, take the path down to the beach which commences 150 metres before the coastguard station. At low spring tide it is possible to walk all along the base of the cliffs. The promontory visible 1½ kilometres east of the Point is Minehead Bluff, a 25-metre wall of fine sandstone packed with hard routes and surrounded by top-class bouldering.

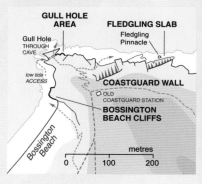

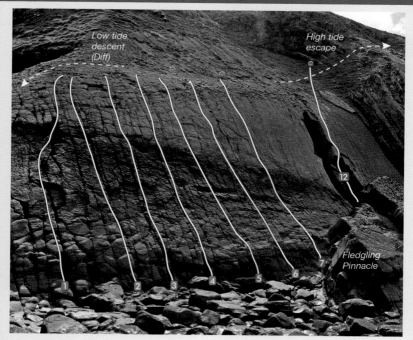

Fledgling Slab

A gem of a slab, very solid, which would be permanently strung with climbers were it located at Baggy Point. All the climbs left of the cave follow strong cracklines and, with the exception of their smooth and wave-washed starts, are well protected. A sloping ramp which rises above the slab from the left provides a *careful* means of descent to a climb down below its base (Diff standard). Currently, belays on the ramp are restricted to two metal stakes serving the first five climbs (which should be backed up) and various nut placements. A nut tool should be taken in case it proves necessary to re-excavate nut belays on the ramp.

In the event of being cut off by the tide here, it is possible to escape to the cliff-top by scrambling diagonally rightwards from the top of the climbs along exposed grassy ramps – various stakes are *in situ*.

The stout pinnacle in front of the slab (Fledgling Pinnacle) offers a clutch of short routes and bouldering on perfect, wave-washed sandstone.

1   Good Breeding   D   15m
FA D E Hope 1992
Start below the first well-defined crack, 9 metres from the left edge of the slab. Climb the crack to a ledge at half height. Take a rightward-rising ramp, and finish up a crack.

12 *Total Quality Creamery* (HVS) Rob Stanfield MARK DAVIES

2 Ill Bred D 15m
FA D E Hope 1992
The left-hand of a pair of cracks, 4 metres right.

3 Tidal Race S 4a 18m
FA D E Hope 1992
The right-hand of the pair of cracks, past a narrow pedestal ledge at 15 metres.

⭐**4 Losing Dreams** S 4b 21m
FA D E Hope 1992
A prominent crack rises just to the right of a narrow pedestal ledge at 15 metres. A hard start up the initially wide crack leads to the main crack, which is followed easily to the stake belays on the ramp.

⭐**5 Family Business** VS 5b 21m
FA D E Hope 1992
Four metres right of *Losing Dreams* is a blind crack which becomes better defined higher up. An even harder start on near frictionless rock leads to the main crack. Saunter up without incident to the stakes on the ramp.

⭐ 6   Pop Up   HS 5a   21m
FA D E Hope 1992

The characteristically slippery start leads to better holds below a fine finger crack. Climb the crack, eventually using its twin on the right to reach the stakes on the ramp.

⭐ 7   Pippin Direct   VS 5a   28m
FA D E Hope 1991

Start below a short blind slot in a small overhang 4 metres up. Climb to the slot with difficulty. Gain the crack above at a shallow rectangular recess. Follow the crack to the ramp.

⭐ 8   Blue Raisin   VS 5a   28m
FA D E Hope 1992

The better-defined crack next right; started to its right.

9   Parallelogram   VS 4c   28m
FA M J Crocker (solo) 2002

The next crack is interrupted by an obvious shallow parallelogram-shaped scoop at two-thirds height. Climb to the scoop and follow the crack which curves slightly rightwards.

⭐ 10   Jailbird   VS 4c   28m
FA D E Hope 1992

Climb the final crack before the right-hand arête of the slab.

9 *Parallelogram* (VS)
Rob Stanfield MARK DAVIES

★ **11 Touch Our Lives** E1 5c 28m

FA M J Crocker (roped solo) 2002

Elegant and well positioned, this climb takes the very thin, right-facing corner in the right-hand arête of the slab. From a huge block, behind the pinnacle, climb easily to a sloping, jutting ledge below the corner in the arête. Make a hard move into the corner, and continue with interest to incut holds. Trend leftwards onto the ramp.

11 *Touch Our Lives* (E1)
Rob Stanfield MARK DAVIES

A narrowing chimney rises from a cave, **Shatter Cave** (E1 5a), and slices into the centre of the bank of slabs containing Fledgling Slab. The slab right of the cave hosts the next three climbs. Stake belays above it can be supplemented with cams.

⭐**12 Total Quality Creamery**   HVS 5a   30m
FA D E Hope 1992

An excellent route, reminiscent of Long Rock (Baggy Point) climbing. Start below the steepening corner right of the chimney. Scramble up the corner to an overhang (old peg). Stretch round for jugs, and pull over awkwardly. Step left onto an exposed arête overlooking the chimney and follow it to the top.

⭐**13 Hobby Horse**   VS 4b   30m
FA S Mooney, N Burton 1996

A good line up the most obvious crack in the slab. Follow the crack, passing just to the left of a narrow overlap near the top of the slab.

⭐**14 Mojo**   E1 5a   30m
⭐
FA S Mooney, N Burton 1996

Enjoyable and steady, notwithstanding a bold section high up. Climb the centre of the slab right of the chimney to a crack which slants right before ending 5 metres beneath the left end of a narrow overlap near the top of the slab. Follow the crack to its close; then step right. Delicately move up to where the crack restarts just below the overlap (good wire). Pull over the overlap and continue direct.

The slabs to the right have been climbed all over; one of the better lines is **Jam Dingo** (E1 5a), which takes the obvious topless crack.

Old Coastguard Station

Coastguard Wall

This is the 60-metre high, concave slab under the old coastguard station. It is probably the most impressive sweep of rock at Hurlstone Point which, considering its looks, is remarkably well supplied with holds – if not protection. There is a range of belay stakes above the slab. The two (non-tidal) routes described here start in the descent chute at the right edge of the slab, at the level of a round, vegetated clump on the slab.

⭐ 15 Severance E1 5a 50m
FA M J Crocker, T Cheek 2003

An engaging lead up the bare centre of the slab; the protection is very spaced, though technical difficulty is low. Climb easily, diagonally leftwards, into the centre of the slab and continue up to a small niche with a ledge formed by three spikes, 5 metres beneath a flake with a narrow overlap beneath it (possible stance). Move up and climb slightly rightwards up the slab, right of the flake, and then direct to some good protection in a slight leftward-trending crack. Continue straight above, past a flake with a crozzly undercut, to the top.

⭐ 16 Coastguard Slab VS 4b 45m
FA S Mooney, T Cheek 1996

This is the right-hand and deeper of the twin cracks in the right-hand side of the slab. It provides a mammoth and quite popular pitch with reasonable protection for the most part. The left-hand crack is **Complicated Simon** (VS 4c), which starts just left of the vegetated clump and deepens above two-thirds height.

Gull Hole Area

Gull Hole is the through-cave on the tip of the headland, which is actually the sea-blasted core of an anticline. There is no shortage of hard routes either side of the cave but, unlike many of the rest, the following are based on superb-quality sandstone. They occupy the leaning wall right of a shallow cave 25 metres east of Gull Hole (eastern entrance). They can be climbed at most tidal states, though at high tide access is by abseil down the corner-crack that rises from the cave, climbed by **Lazarus** (E1 5a). There are two routes left of the corner: **Anthropoid** (E3 6a) up the overhanging crack; and **Gorilla** (E4 6a/b) up the centre of the grey wall.

17 Hashish E4 6b 15m

FA M J Crocker 1997

A powerful climb up the dog-legged crack right of the cave. Stainless steel pegs. Grasp the obvious hand shelf (peg); fling yourself right to a developing crack (peg) and move up to finger locks and a semi-rest up to the right. Swing left to a short corner and make out-of-balance moves up it to exit via a sloping ledge on the left.

31

18 Feel the Full Effect   E6 6b   15m

FA M J Crocker, L Holm 1997

'Immaculate'. Start under a narrow right-facing corner right of *Hashish*. Take the initial corner to a small roof. Arc into the main corner and progress up it and the thin crack on the right to the top. Arm-burning but very protectable.

Finally on this wall, the hanging pillar overlooking the cave to the right is **Bhang** (E4 6b/c).

Bossington Beach Cliffs

The west side of the Point is made up of a weird mix of banded sandstone crags that overlook the vast pebble beach of Porlock Bay. Though receiving the sun most of the day, they are steep and often serious and tend to lack the quality and appeal of the slabs nearby. However, the routes described here are amongst the exceptions, and their rock and protection are mostly good.

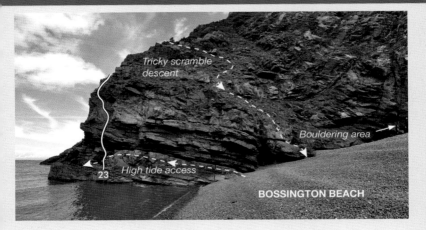

Tricky scramble descent

Bouldering area

High tide access

23

BOSSINGTON BEACH

The first crags encountered when approached from the path down to the bay offer some hard bouldering above a pebble landing.

From the beach, a narrow ledge runs leftwards above a smooth 5-metre wall onto a triangular promontory, and gives access at most states of the tide to the following four climbs. To descend from them, either walk left to the zigzag path on the Point, or scramble carefully down a steep gritty path on the right to the beach (the inexperienced should remain roped up). The first two start from a large sloping green ledge left of the promontory.

⭐**19 Nameless** HS 4b 15m
FA D Massey 1978
Climb a blunt rib to a short corner right of a projecting roof (just left of *One Way Street*). Take the corner and easier ground above to the top.

⭐**20 One Way Street** VD 15m
FA R Miles, R Hayns 1971
A good climb up the broken groove and crack. Climb the groove to an overhang. Move left and back right to pass the overhang. Follow a groove to ledges.

21 Evening Orl' VD 12m
FA R Hayns, R Miles 1971
Starting from the promontory, climb a steep crack and groove to the top.

⭐**22 Evening Crack** S 12m
FA R Hayns, R Miles 1971
Take the crack in the wall immediately right of *Evening Orl'*.

⭐**23 Munchkin** VS 4c 12m
FA T Cheek, M Sleight 1981
The steep groove and left-trending crack on the wall facing the beach.

23 *Munchkin* (VS)
Rob Stanfield   MARK DAVIES

Sir Robert's Chair

OS Ref SS 780 499

This compact 60-metre sandstone face is one of Exmoor's best-kept secrets, or at least it was until now. Situated on a remote part of the coast, yet with reasonable (for Exmoor) access, its main face offers some very fine steep slab climbs of mainstream appeal. A foreshore stack (Sir Robert's Chair) immediately in front of the face holds some shorter pitches. The site is haunted.

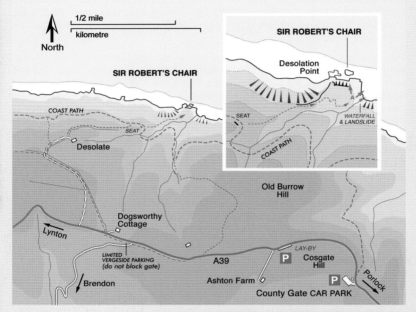

Approach Sir Robert's Chair is located midway along the coast between Porlock and Lynmouth, a kilometre from the A39. There is limited parking at the road junction (signposted Brendon) at OS Ref 777 489. Walk westwards along the A39 for 200 metres to the public footpath past Dogsworthy Cottage. Follow this for 600 metres and then take the right of way on the right, past the farmhouse of Desolate, going downhill and heading eastwards

to intersect the coast path. Follow the coast path eastwards until it turns sharp right around a ridge (wooden seat here). Sir Robert's Chair is located out of sight at the far (eastern) end of the ridge below. So, leaving the coast path, descend the ridge (hopping over a small wall initially) and follow it through woods for several hundred metres to a point close to the stream on the right.

35

There is a vegetated abseil to the beach from good trees immediately west of the waterfall. The main face and stack are 200 metres to the west around a subsidiary slab. For the direct abseil approach, go slightly leftwards (facing out) through the trees, aiming for the indistinct cliff edge and eventually descending steeply to a tree which marks the end of an exposed ramp that runs across the top of the slab (the 'exit ramp'). A 60-metre abseil from the ramp gains the base of the cliff. Please check that there is no one else on the slab before abseiling in, as the abseil route corresponds with some of the climbs.

Characteristically, the main face faces north, but it is not that exposed to the prevailing wind. The base of the cliff is tidal, but is clear mid to low tide. If the abseil approach is used the period of operation can normally be extended an hour either side of high tide, since the walk-in approach becomes cut off first.

The main face is a 50-metre by 50-metre slabby face, which is split centrally by the line of cracks and grooves of *Desolate*. All but one of the routes described here take the more amenably angled and solid slabs to its left. The diminishing overlap running from bottom left to top right is taken by *Strange Days*, which commences from a cave at the left edge of the slab. Twenty metres right of the cave is the prominent vertical crackline of *Lamina Flow*. Apart from *Ghost Job*, the routes right of *Desolate* tend to be friable and peg-runner dependent.

24 Strange Days   E2 60m
FA N Barnes, S Mooney (AL) 1995
A sustained route of great character that follows the rightward-trending overlap across the slab. Start at the left end of the slab where the overlap begins as a corner.
  1 35m 5b Climb the corner via a short slick chimney to ledges. Continue up the corner, following it as it curves rightwards, and traverse right to multiple peg belays.
  2 25m 5b Climb up and rightwards (peg) to a bulge under the upper slab. Step right and follow the rising overlap to a good nut slot where it ends. Move right on good footholds; then pull up to the stake belay on the exit ramp.

25 The Moonies   E4 50m
FA M J Crocker (pitch 1 roped solo) / M J Crocker, T Cheek 1998/1999
A technical and protectable pitch 1 is complemented by a run-out pitch 2 (E3). Start 3 metres left of the vertical crack of *Lamina Flow*, below a left-trending ramp/crack.
  1 25m 6a Move straight up to 'stuck-on' fingerholds under an overlap. Reach a vertical slot over a slight bulge (good wires) and proceed with difficulty to better holds. An easier crack leads to the common peg belay.
  2 25m 5a/b Climb up and rightwards (peg) to a bulge under the upper slab. Climb up 2 metres to fix gear in a slot in the slab, step back down, and traverse right along the lip of the overlap for 2 metres. Follow positive crystal nubbins and edges near the right edge of the slab to the exit ramp – only some lightweight spike runners interrupt the sweep of the ropes.

26 Lamina Flow   E3 50m
FA S Mooney, N Barnes 1995
Probably the route of the crag: superb and enjoyable all the way, though the start is tough.
  1 25m 5c Work through bulging rock to reach the prominent vertical crack. Take the crack and its little grove to an easing in the angle where feet come into play. Climb the crack to the common peg belay.

2 25m 5a/b Climb up and rightwards (peg) to a point beneath a thin crystalline crack in the upper slab. Ease up on pockets to meet the crack and follow it to a move right onto the exit ramp.

⭐ **27 The Phantom** E1 50m

FA T Cheek, S Pryce 1995; S Mooney, N Barnes 1995

An entertaining and generously protected pitch 1. Start under a groove/crackline (with overhangs to the right), 25 metres from the left edge of the slab.

1 25m 5a/b Climb the groove to a bulge and gain the sloping ledge above from the left. Continue up a juggy corner, and pull into a crack that leads leftwards without incident to the common peg belay.

2 25m 5b Step left and make a stiff pull over a bulge onto the easier (but somewhat vegetated) upper slab. Climb to a little overlap and trend rightwards up a line of weakness to the top.

The commanding line of cracks and grooves in the centre of the face is taken by **Desolate** (E5 6a), a magnificent though scary lead with begrudging protection. Right of this in the convex slab is a striking crack – the objective of the next route.

⭐ **28 Ghost Job** E3 47m

FA M J Crocker, J Harwood 1997

A major line, especially demanding with its direct start. Start near the right edge of the face under an overhanging shelf.

1 12m 4c Climb a short groove to pass to the right of the overhanging shelf. Traverse left above the shelf to a good small ledge with wire belays.

1a Direct Start 10m E4 6a Make committing moves through a break in the overhanging shelf, directly gaining the stance.

2 35m 5c Move into a scoop above the belay. Make bold moves over a bulge – some wobbly holds – to the crack. Now better protected, take the crack and continuation flakes to stake belays on the exit ramp.

An interesting walk a kilometre eastwards leads to the Amphitheatre, a hotchpotch of bizarre folded sandstones and shales. There are about fifty climbs here.

Valley of Rocks

OS Ref SS 707 498

One of Exmoor's renowned geomorphological wonders, this tourist hot-spot nestles just a mile west of Lynton, from which it is well signposted. Famous for its jagged inland rocks and characters from *Lorna Doone*, the valley is mere window dressing for acres of hidden and often untouched and inaccessible sea cliff that make up some of the grandest coastal scenery in the South West. A number of contrasting cliffs are sampled here; all

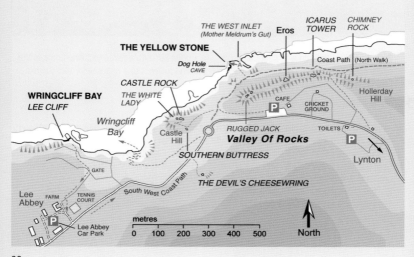

comprise the finely banded slates and sandstones of the Lynton Beds – very much an acquired taste.

There are two large 'pay and display' car parks in the valley. Park in the westerly of the car parks next to a cafe – Mother Meldrums Tea Garden & Restaurant. A hundred metres further west along the road is a roundabout/turning-circle from which the approaches to the cliffs are described.

The Outcrops

A peppering of rock outcrops and tors make the valley well named. Most are around 10 metres high and provide relatively light-hearted and sunny climbing. The conical hill above the roundabout (Castle Hill) is topped by two block-like outcrops: Castle Rock and the White Lady.

The largest outcrops hereabouts – including the Icarus Tower – are located mostly out of sight of the car parks on the seaward, north-facing side of the rocky ridge east of Castle Hill, while on the opposite side of the valley is:

The Devil's Cheesewring

The lichen and ivy decorated pinnacle.

29 4000 Metre Pursuit HS 4b 16m
FA A Evans, F West 1992
The prominent crack on the east side of the pinnacle.

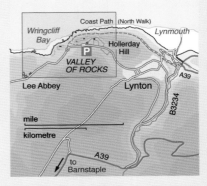

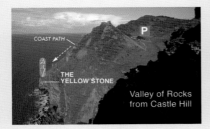

Valley of Rocks from Castle Hill

★ **30 Crack of Doone** HS 4b 16m
★ FA J Fowler, C Gibson 1976

A popular climb up the leftward-leaning crack in the north face. Climb the crack past a large jammed flake to a ledge. Step right and finish up the steep wall on superb holds.

★ **31 Olympic Wall** HVS 4c 16m
FA A Evans, F West 1992

Climb straight up the centre of the north face, finishing as for *Crack of Doone*. Bold, green, and furry – but deceptively good.

31 *Olympic Wall* (HVS)
Jack Bradbrook MARK DAVIES

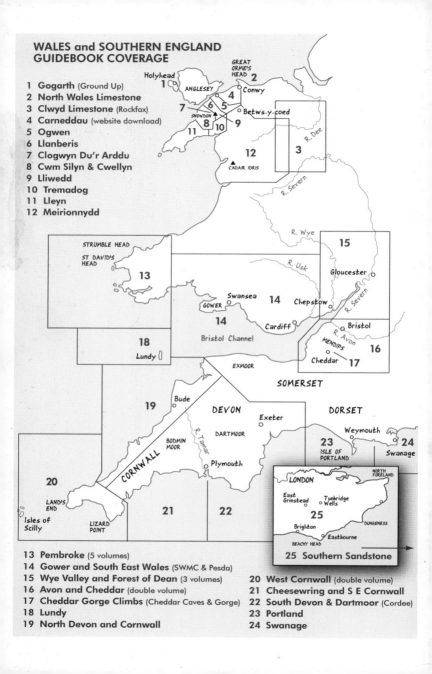

WALES and SOUTHERN ENGLAND GUIDEBOOK COVERAGE

1 **Gogarth** (Ground Up)
2 **North Wales Limestone**
3 **Clwyd Limestone** (Rockfax)
4 **Carneddau** (website download)
5 **Ogwen**
6 **Llanberis**
7 **Clogwyn Du'r Arddu**
8 **Cwm Silyn & Cwellyn**
9 **Lliwedd**
10 **Tremadog**
11 **Lleyn**
12 **Meirionnydd**

13 **Pembroke** (5 volumes)
14 **Gower and South East Wales** (SWMC & Pesda)
15 **Wye Valley and Forest of Dean** (3 volumes)
16 **Avon and Cheddar** (double volume)
17 **Cheddar Gorge Climbs** (Cheddar Caves & Gorge)
18 **Lundy**
19 **North Devon and Cornwall**
20 **West Cornwall** (double volume)
21 **Cheesewring and S E Cornwall**
22 **South Devon & Dartmoor** (Cordee)
23 **Portland**
24 **Swanage**
25 **Southern Sandstone**